D0493251

NOV 2013

WITHDRAWN FROM STOCK
LIBRARIES IN

Microsoft® Office for Mac® 2011

PORTABLE GENIUS

Microsoft® Office for Mac® 2011

PORTABLE GENIUS

by Dwight Spivey

Wiley Publishing, Inc.

Microsoft® Office for Mac® 2011 Portable Genius

Published by
Wiley Publishing, Inc.
10475 Crosspoint Blvd.
Indianapolis, IN 46256
www.wiley.com

Copyright © 2011 by Wiley Publishing, Inc., Indianapolis, Indiana

Published simultaneously in Canada

ISBN: 978-0-470-61019-0

Manufactured in the United States of America

10 9 8 7 6 5 4 3 2 1

No part of this publication may be reproduced, stored in a retrieval system or transmitted in any form or by any means, electronic, mechanical, photocopying, recording, scanning or otherwise, except as permitted under Sections 107 or 108 of the 1976 United States Copyright Act, without either the prior written permission of the Publisher, or authorization through payment of the appropriate per-copy fee to the Copyright Clearance Center, 222 Rosewood Drive, Danvers, MA 01923, (978) 750-8400, fax (978) 646-8600. Requests to the Publisher f   s Department, John Wiley & Sons, Inc., 111 River Street,   )8, or online at http://www. wiley.com/go/permissions.

LIBRARIES NI	
C700522384	
RONDO	07/01/2011
005.6	£ 20.99
OMAOMA	

Limit of Liability/Disclaimer   presentations or warranties with respect to the accur   and specifically disclaim all warranties, including witho   rpose. No warranty may be created or extended by sal   s contained herein may not be suitable for every situat   publisher is not engaged in rendering legal, accountin   nce is required, the services of a competent profession   the author shall be liable for damages arising herefrom   to in this work as a citation and/or a potential source o.   r the publisher endorses the information the organization of Web site may provide or recommendations it may make. Further, readers should be aware that Internet Web sites listed in this work may have changed or disappeared between when this work was written and when it is read.

For general information on our other products and services or to obtain technical support, please contact our Customer Care Department within the U.S. at (877) 762-2974, outside the U.S. at (317) 572-3993 or fax (317) 572-4002.

Wiley also publishes its books in a variety of electronic formats. Some content that appears in print may not be available in electronic books.

Library of Congress Control Number: 2010938833

Trademarks: Wiley and the Wiley Publishing logo are trademarks or registered trademarks of John Wiley and Sons, Inc. and/or its affiliates in the United States and/or other countries, and may not be used without written permission. All other trademarks are the property of their respective owners. Wiley Publishing, Inc. is not associated with any product or vendor mentioned in this book.

WILEY

About the Author

Dwight Spivey is the author of several Mac books, including *Mac OS X Leopard Portable Genius* and *Mac OS X Snow Leopard Portable Genius*. He is also a software and support engineer for Konica Minolta, where he specializes in working with Mac operating systems, applications, and hardware, as well as color and monochrome laser printers. He teaches classes on Mac usage, writes training and support materials for Konica Minolta, and is a Mac OS X beta tester for Apple. Dwight lives on the Gulf Coast of Alabama with his wife Cindy and their four beautiful children, Victoria, Devyn, Emi, and Reid. He studies theology, draws comic strips, and roots for the Auburn Tigers in his ever-decreasing spare time.

Credits

Senior Acquisitions Editor
Aaron Black

Project Editor
Christina Wolfgang

Technical Editor
Julian Dolce

Senior Copy Editor
Kim Heusel

Editorial Director
Robyn Siesky

Vice President and Executive Group Publisher
Richard Swadley

Vice President and Executive Publisher
Barry Pruett

Business Manager
Amy Knies

Senior Marketing Manager
Sandy Smith

Project Coordinator
Sheree Montgomery

Graphics and Production Specialists
Ana Carrillo
Joyce Haughey
Jennifer Henry
Andrea Hornberger

Quality Control Technician
Lindsay Littrell

Proofreading
Melissa D. Buddendeck

Indexing
Joan Griffitts

To the newest member of our family, Johnathan Reid.

God bless your every step, my sweet boy.

Love, Daddy

Acknowledgments

 First, I must thank my family and friends for putting up with my many absences during the writing of this book. I love you all!

Many thanks to my agent, Carole Jelen McClendon. Couldn't do this without you, Carole!

Sincere appreciation goes to my project editors for this book, Jama Carter and Chris Wolfgang, and to my acquisitions editor, Aaron Black. Thank you all for being so good to me from start to finish of this book. Jama and Chris, you have both been a joy to work with, and my work is so much better because of you. Aaron, thanks so much for bringing me into such a great project.

Special thanks and salutations to my technical editor, Julian Dolce, for his determination to keep my work accurate and honest.

To everyone else who has had a hand in getting this book from raw manuscript to the beautiful publication that it is, I cannot thank you enough. You make my work so much better than I deserve. I sincerely thank you for all of your hard work and dedication to this book.

Contents

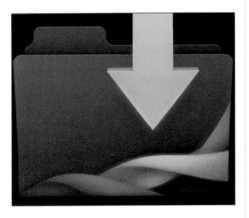

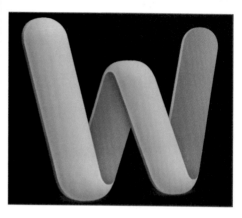

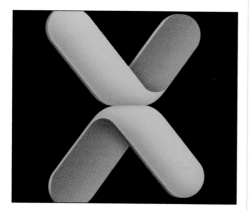
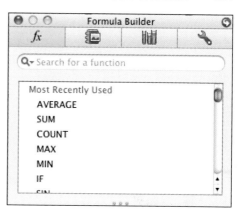

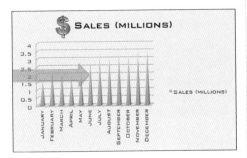
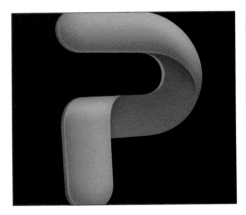
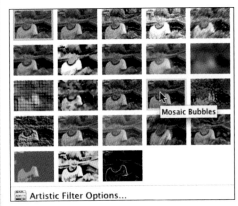

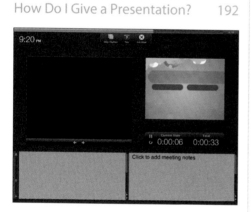

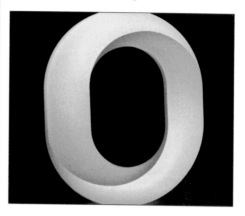

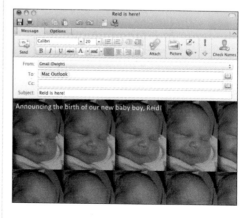

chapter 14

How Can I Organize Contacts and Tasks? 246

chapter 15

How Can I Work More Efficiently? 274

Introduction

Every few years we Mac users are treated to something very special. While the excitement doesn't quite reach the level of a new Mac OS X release, it is surprisingly close for some. The special something I speak of is the release of the latest version of Microsoft's Office suite of productivity applications for the Mac.

Excitement of this level for software releases is something that is typically found only in the Mac world; most PC users simply don't get it. "What's all the fuss? It's just a piece of software, for goodness sake!"

Mac users have always taken dedication to their favorite computing platform very seriously, as anyone who's ever been in an Apple Store when a new version of Mac OS X is about to be released will attest (not to mention the mile-long lines for iPhones). Granted, sometimes this dedication has been taken to the extreme (come on, people; shaving an Apple logo into your hairdo is a bit much), but for the most part is simply due to customers being loyal to a company that has been loyal to them by consistently providing the best computing experience on the planet.

Okay, so what does this loyalty and new software release fever have to do with Microsoft?

Think about it: Mac users don't just use their operating system; many other applications factor into their user experience. Take a guess as to which software is one of the most popular for people who work with Macs (beside the operating system): that's right, Microsoft Office for Mac. I would venture to say that most people who own a version of Office for Mac spend the majority of their time working in one of the Office applications. It stands to reason that when these fiercely loyal Mac users hear about a new release of the third-party software they use more than any other, their interest in the matter is slightly more than mild.

And Mac users have every reason to be excited about the latest release of this iconic suite, Microsoft Office for Mac 2011! This version is easily the best in quite some time (for some, Office 2008 was a bitter disappointment), incorporating the ribbon, feature parity with the latest versions of Office for Windows (even surpassing its Windows counterparts in some features), and the long-awaited return of Outlook. Office for Mac 2011 is going to bring smiles to the faces of many Mac users.

Want another reason to jump on board the Office for Mac 2011 train? Microsoft's Macintosh Business Unit gets it. It gets what it means to be a Mac fan, because the people in the unit are Mac fans.

This book was written for you in the same vein: by a Mac fan for Mac fans. It's my hope that it quickly gets you on your feet and running with the newest version of Office for Mac, and that you have a little fun along the way, too.

What Are the First Things I Need to Know?

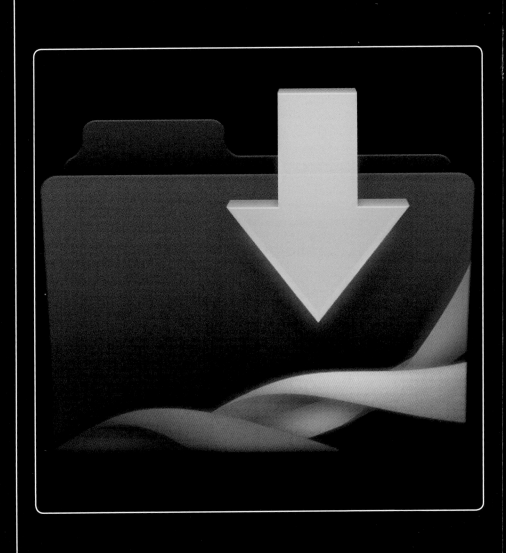

There's something in the air. It's that time again. Time for the next release of Microsoft Office for Mac! This version offers plenty to be excited about, and that's part of what this chapter discusses. Along with new features, I also explain how to install the latest incarnation of Office for Mac, and how to get started from the ground floor in case you're new to Office.

Installing Office for Mac 2011

It's time to get moving with your new copy of Office 2011 for Mac! First things first, however; you need to get those legendary Office applications installed on your trusty Mac before you can go too far into anything else. So, insert the Microsoft Office 2011 Installation DVD and get this party started.

Installing using the Office Installer

Microsoft has automated almost the entire installation process for you, so this will be a breeze. Follow these steps:

1. **Insert the Microsoft Office 2011 Installation DVD into your Mac's disc drive.**

2. **In the Microsoft Office 2011 window, double-click the Office Installer program.**

3. **Click Continue in the Welcome to the Microsoft Office for Mac 2011 Installer window.**

4. **Read the license agreement, click Continue, and then click Agree.** If you don't click Agree then you are at an impasse.

5. **Select the destination on your Mac for your Office installation.**

6. **At the next window, you have to decide whether to install the entire Office suite of applications or perform a custom installation.**

   - To install the entire Office suite, skip to step 9.

   - To install only portions of the Office suite, continue with the next step.

7. **Click the Customize button at the bottom of the window.**

8. **In the Custom Install window, seen in Figure 1.1, determine which items you want to install:**

   - To install an item, select the check box to its left.

   - To find out more about an item, click it once to highlight it, and a description will appear in the window below.

Note

If you see the word Upgrade next to the name of some of the items in the custom installation list, this just means that those items are already installed on your Mac.

9. **Click Install.**

10. **When prompted, type the username and password you use to log in to your account on the Mac, and click OK.**

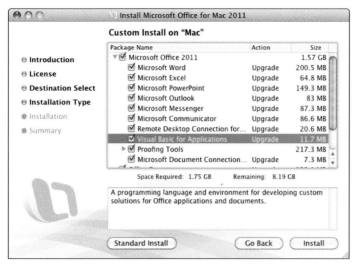

1.1 The Custom Install window lets you decide what components of Office to install.

11. **The installer application flies through the installation process and alerts you when it's complete.** If your installation doesn't "fly through" don't blame me or Microsoft, but your Mac; the installation speed is directly related to your Mac's processing power and memory capacity.

12. **Once finished, the Microsoft Office Setup Assistant launches and asks you to type the product key that came with your copy of Office 2011.** Enter the product key or your trip through Officeland will be a short one.

How do I access my applications?

The Microsoft Office Installer knows exactly where it wants to put your applications, but it never tells you where that is. If you allowed Office to perform a standard installation, you will see icons for your Office applications patiently waiting for you in the Dock, as you can see in Figure 1.2.

1.2 The Office application icons are placed in your Dock by the Installer.

Simply click one of the application icons in the Dock to launch it.

If you're one of those folks (like me) with a curious fascination when an Installer puts something on your Mac but doesn't say where, you might still like to know just what went where.

The Office Installer dumps everything you need into the default Applications directory on your Mac. To find your applications, follow these steps:

1. **Open a Finder window.**

2. **Press ⌘+Shift+A to jump straight to the Applications folder (which is located at the root of your hard drive).**

3. **Scroll through the list of applications and you will find a few new Microsoft guys waiting on you: Microsoft Communicator, Microsoft Messenger, and a folder called Microsoft Office 2011.** The Microsoft Office 2011 folder is where Word, Excel, PowerPoint, and Outlook are hiding, along with Microsoft Document Connection and Remote Desktop Connection.

Genius

I don't care for having all the Office application icons lurking in my Dock. While I enjoy the fast access, they take up too much real estate. However, I've found a way to have my cake and eat it, too: Add Microsoft Office 2011 folder to the Dock instead of each individual application. Just open a Finder window to the Applications folder, and drag and drop the Microsoft Office 2011 folder into the right side of the Dock. To access your Office applications simply click the folder and click the application you want from the pop-up menu.

How do I install additional templates?

You may be an Office power user who has been a whiz at Office applications for years. If that's the case, you may have saved years' worth of templates to help you perform your work more efficiently. Well, now you've got the latest Office for Mac and want to use those tried-and-true templates in it, too.

Office 2011 stores its own templates in the /Applications/Microsoft Office 2011/Office/Media/ Templates directory, but that's not where you should put your personal or additional ones. The Office Installer has created a nice, new home for your templates. To see it, follow these steps:

1. **Open a new Finder window.**

2. **Click the hard drive icon in the upper-left corner of the sidebar.**

3. **Browse to the following directory: /Users/username/Library/Application Support/ Microsoft/Office/User Templates/My Templates.** Figure 1.3 gives you a bird's-eye

view of just how deep this directory is (I hope you brought a miner's helmet with fresh batteries for the light).

4. **Drag and drop your templates into the My Templates folder.** This is also where the Office applications will save new templates you create while working within them.

1.3 You've got to dig pretty deep to store your old templates into Office 2011's new My Templates folder.

Note Technically, Office 2011 doesn't really care where you store your templates, but for the sake of organization I think it's a good idea to stick with the plan as originally intended. If you keep templates in a nonstandard location, and then they get moved for whatever reason, you may have some big issues with documents down the road that require those templates.

The Latest and Greatest: Cool New Features in Office 2011

There are lots of new goodies for us all to play with in Office 2011 for Mac, so let's jump right in and learn the tantalizing details of new functionality that awaits.

What's new in Office?

There are lots of new features in Office 2011, and the most important one in my eyes is *feature parity* with Office for Windows. That covers a very broad base, but let it suffice to say that the new version of Office for Mac is ready to stand toe to toe with its Windows cousin, and even has some features that Windows versions don't have yet.

There's a new e-mail client in town this go around: Outlook! (More on that later in this chapter.)

Ever heard of a little thing called the *ribbon*? If you've used Microsoft Office on a Windows-based PC and it was version 2007 or newer, you've definitely heard of it and interacted with it. If you are a Mac user who has strictly used Mac versions of Office, you may have heard of it at some point, but you've certainly never used it. Well, get ready, because the ribbon has arrived for the Mac with the advent of Office 2011.

I hear an odd mix of sounds ranging from rapturous joy to muffled groans of disgust. Some of you who have used the ribbon before may have had a less-than-stellar experience with it, but I'm sure that many others (myself included) have been quite happy with the ribbon.

But I digress; I should explain just what the ribbon is for the uninitiated. The ribbon is a new set of tabs that are visible just underneath the toolbar. These tabs are organized in a very intuitive fashion, and each tab includes easy-to-access buttons that correspond to the functions that people use the most. Of course, the ribbon has somewhat different functionality depending on which of the four main Office applications (Word, Excel, PowerPoint, or Outlook) you are running.

As I mentioned earlier, some love the ribbon and others not so much. I think it's a very valuable addition to Office 2011, so buck up, kick in, and I urge you to give it a fair shake.

As with anything new, there will be detractors, and I'll be honest when I say that the Office button in the Windows versions of Office isn't my favorite item in the world, but here's some news that may alleviate the moans and groans: There is no Office button in Office 2011 for Mac. That's right.

The Office button took many of the familiar menu items that one would normally find under File, Edit, View, and so on, and placed them all in one button, which caused no small amount of confusion. It seems as though Microsoft wanted to wisely avoid such confusion with this latest Mac version of Office.

What's new in Word?

Word 2011 is a great update from Word 2008 and earlier versions. For example, features new to Word 2011 include

- **The ribbon.** The ribbon makes it easier than ever to work with the most common tools for building new documents.

- **Publishing layout.** As seen in Figure 1.4, this essentially turns Word into a desktop-publishing application.

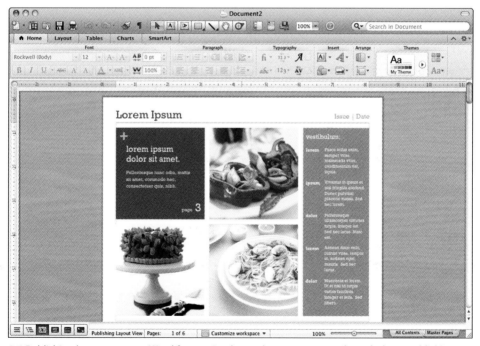

1.4 Publishing layout converts Word from a simple word processor to a robust desktop-publishing app.

- **Full screen view.** This allows you to work with a document in full-screen mode.

- **Dynamic reordering.** This allows you to reorder contents of a document by dragging them in front of or behind one another in a three-dimensional layout that looks like something out of *Star Trek*.

- **Visual style guides.** These make building the perfect document that much simpler.

- **Templates.** Even more have been created to help you build documents, and you can access tons more via the Internet.

What's new in Excel?

There are many new features that await the spreadsheet aficionados in the crowd. As a matter of fact, Microsoft deserves added kudos for getting this update to Excel right. The new features are worth getting:

- **Templates.** A great new array makes putting together budgets and invoices that much easier.

- **VBA.** Visual Basic is back after it went into never-never land with Office 2008 for Mac, one of the most unpopular omissions I can ever remember in a software upgrade. There were lots of technical reasons at play behind the omission, so let's just let bygones be bygones. All those Office 2004 documents that you created using macros? Dust them off, because you can use them again in Excel 2011.

- **PivotTables.** These are included in Excel for Mac for the first time. They allow you to analyze related totals and compare large chunks of information in several ways. They are interactive, so you can manipulate data to see relationships in multiple ways.

- **Sparklines.** Another new addition, *sparklines* are basically tiny charts that can fit into a single cell of a spreadsheet. These sparklines (see Figure 1.5) show trends for large amounts of data in a single cell that can reside right next to the other cells in the spreadsheet, giving the person analyzing the spreadsheet instant information on said trends.

	A	B
10		
11	Year	Sales (millions)
12	January	1.7
13	February	2.3
14	March	2.2
15	April	1.9
16	May	2.1
17	June	2.9
18	July	3.1
19	August	3.1
20	September	3.3
21	October	3.2
22	November	3.5
23	December	3.6
24		

1.5 Sparklines give a visual representation of a trend right in the spreadsheet.

What's new in PowerPoint?

PowerPoint is the iconic presentation tool that you all know and love. There are a couple of new features in PowerPoint 2011 that are really cool:

- **Using Presenter Tools, Excel can now help you rehearse your presentation before you give it, and even keep up with how long each slide should take to present.**
- **You can record audio directly into your presentations.**
- **PowerPoint 2011 now has the capability to broadcast your slide show to anyone in the world, assuming that person has an Internet connection.** This feature alone is pretty awesome.

What's new in Outlook?

What's new in Outlook? Well, the whole thing! This is the first appearance on the Mac for Outlook in quite some time (about ten years, as a matter of fact), and this is the first time it's ever made it in a native Mac OS X format.

Outlook replaces the pretty good, but not quite good enough, Entourage. Entourage was a decent e-mail and scheduling client, but lacked the functionality of a full-blown Outlook. Now Outlook is capable of operating side by side with its Windows counterpart and provides you full, unfettered access to your company's Exchange Server.

Using Office for Mac 2011 Programs

While each of the applications in the Office 2011 suite performs its own unique tasks, it is precisely the things they have in common that make using them such a great experience. Even though each application has its own role, there are still many tasks that are performed in a similar fashion; if you are familiar with one application, you are never truly a novice at the others.

Get to know the ribbon

Let's take a moment to get a quick rundown of the ribbon so that it's not entirely foreign (there's more on the ribbon in upcoming chapters throughout the book).

Go ahead and open one of the Office applications by clicking its icon in the Dock. If you moved the icon, you can click the Apple menu, hold your mouse over recent items, and see if an Office application is listed there. If not, you need to browse through the Finder to /Applications/Microsoft Office 2011 to find one to launch.

Figure 1.6 gives you a quick look at the ribbon and helps you to get a handle on its layout.

1.6 Anatomy of the ribbon.

If the ribbon isn't your cup of tea, you can always hide it by clicking the Hide button in the far right-hand side of the ribbon (the button looks like an upward-pointing arrow).

Do you think the ribbon is cool, but some of the tabs aren't in line with where you'd like? To change it, follow these steps:

1. **Click the Action button in the upper right of the ribbon (looks like a gear).**

2. **Choose Customize Ribbon Tab Order and the tabs undergo an interesting transformation, which you can see in Figure 1.7.**

   ○ Notice that all the tabs in the ribbon now have handles on them (they look like three little lines just to the right of each tab's name). Click and drag a tab's handles to move it anywhere in the ribbon you want.

   ○ Is there a tab that you don't have a particular fondness for? Delete it by clicking the X to the left of the tab's name.

1.7 Move tabs to a different position in the ribbon or get rid of them completely.

3. **Click the Done button when you finish editing the ribbon's tabs.**

The amazing Gallery

Wouldn't it be great to open an application and have it offer all manner of preformatted documents that you could use to create your own? With these preformatted documents you would only need to input your data and information into the preformatted fields and it would appear exactly as you intend. Sounds like a dream, right? Not with Office 2011's Gallery.

Each application — Word, PowerPoint, and Excel — has its own Gallery, which is aptly named (Excel Workbook Gallery, to name one). These Galleries are set to open by default when you launch one of the aforementioned applications. Figure 1.8 shows the Word Document Gallery and the Excel Workbook Gallery side by side so you can get a quick glimpse of the kinds of preformatted documents that are available and how they are tailored to suit the capabilities of each application.

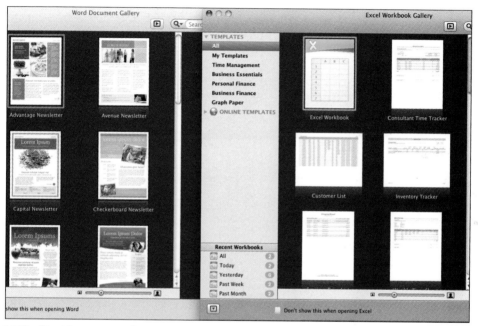

1.8 The Word Document Gallery and the Excel Workbook Gallery side by side.

Starting from scratch: creating a new document

The first item on the left side of the Standard toolbar is the New button. If you are in Word, it's a Create New Word Document button, if you're in Excel it's called New Workbook, PowerPoint calls it a New Presentation button, and Outlook refers to it as a New Message button.

Of course, within each application you can simply press ⌘+N and a new item, depending on the application, springs into being.

Saving your work within Office applications

You're finished working with a document, workbook, or presentation, and now it's time to go home and kick your feet up, right? Not so fast, my friend! You need to save your work first.

13

To save your work from within any application press ⌘+S. If you haven't saved this document before, you are prompted to give the document a name and tell the application where on your beloved Mac to store your new creation, as you can see in Figure 1.9.

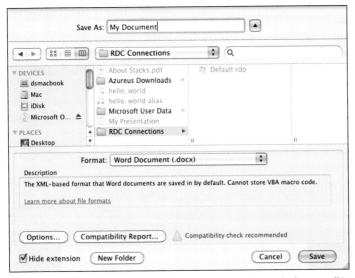

1.9 Tell the application where to save your new creation and what to call it.

Note

I discuss saving documents in much greater detail in the upcoming chapters. There is much more to it than just simply saving, especially if you want to share your files with other people who may not have the same version of Office that you do (aren't you the lucky one?).

Open existing documents

As long as we're sticking to the basics, let's take a look at how to open existing documents within each of the Office apps. Follow these steps:

1. **Open the application of your choice.**

2. **Choose File ⇨ Open.**

3. **Browse your Mac for the file you want to open.**

Done!

There's still another way you can open a document, this time without being in the application. Follow these steps:

1. **Right-click the document to open a contextual menu.**

2. **Hold your mouse pointer over the Open With menu.**

3. **Choose the application you want to use to open your document from the suggestions in the submenu, as shown in Figure 1.10.**

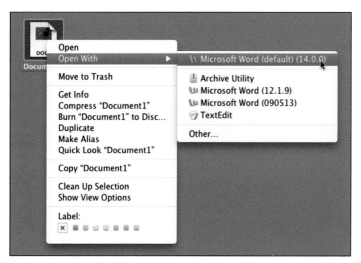

1.10 Choose an application to open your document from the Open With submenu.

Genius

You can always open a document by dragging and dropping it onto the appropriate application's icon in the Dock, or if the icon isn't in the Dock you can find the application in a Finder window and drag and drop the document onto its icon.

Sharing with other Office users

I want to take a moment to answer the question that I hear most often from those who are switching from Office for Windows to Office for Mac: Will the documents, workbooks, and presentations I create in Word, Excel, and PowerPoint for Mac work with Word, Excel, and PowerPoint for Windows? The short and sweet answer is yes.

In some instances you may need to be careful about what format you are saving documents in. For example, if you send your Word document to someone who has an older version of Word (whether on a Mac or PC), you will probably want to save the document in .doc format, which is compatible with all versions of Office. Word 2011 for Mac and newer versions of Word for Windows save documents in the .docx format by default, and older versions of Word are unable to open this format.

What Can I Do with the Toolbox, Media Browser, and the Ribbon?

Office for Mac 2011 is designed for your ease of use. If something isn't relatively easy to use, most people will simply cease to use it and move on to something else. This isn't because we're lazy, but rather that we need to squeeze every last drop of productivity possible from our workday. Naturally, the easier an application is to use, the more productive we will be. Each application in the Office suite offers the Toolbox and the Media Browser, which give you quick access to tools such as formatting options, dictionaries, a thesaurus, your photos and music, and more. The Office for Mac ribbon affords a simple way to do common tasks and to discover more in-depth features of the Office suite, in one central location near the top of every window. In this chapter you explore the Toolbox, Media Browser, and the ribbon to help you understand how each can benefit you in your work.

Understanding Elements in the Toolbox

Toolbox button

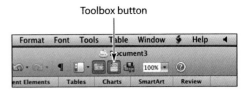

2.1 Click the Toolbox button to display or hide the Toolbox.

I personally find the Toolbox an indispensable part of my daily work within the Office suite of applications. The Toolbox sits neatly in the right-hand corner of my screen and is there to help me quickly format elements on the pages of my documents, build a fast formula for use in a spreadsheet, and myriad other tasks you are about to discover.

The Toolbox may be open by default, and it can easily be found in the upper-right corner of your screen. If the Toolbox isn't open, click the Toolbox button in the toolbar, as shown in Figure 2.1.

Styles

Styles offers a convenient way to apply customized formatting to your text. Utilizing the Styles tool is easy:

1. **Click the Styles button in the Toolbox, as shown in Figure 2.2.**

2. **Highlight the text you want to format.**

3. **Choose a style from the list provided and it is instantly applied to your text.**

2.2 The Styles tool lets you easily format text.

Note The Styles tool is only available in Word.

Genius You can get a bird's-eye view of the styles you apply to a document by selecting the Show Styles Guides check box. A box appears to the left of each line where a style has been applied, and the box is colored and numbered to the corresponding style in the styles list. Pretty handy, if you ask me.

You've perused the list of available styles but didn't quite find what you needed, so what now? That's an easy answer: Just create your own style!

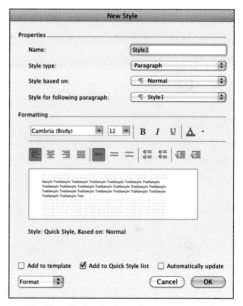

2.3 The New Style window allows you to make a style to your own specifications.

1. **Click the New Style button in the Styles toolbox to open the New Style window, as shown in Figure 2.3.**

2. **Assign a descriptive name to your style, select the type of style you want to create, or base the style on an existing style.**

3. **Use the formatting options to config- ure font settings and text placement.**

4. **Click OK to complete your new style.**

Note The Citations tool is only available in Word.

Citations

The Citations tool helps you quickly and easily insert citations for third-party information sources you're using in your document. Follow these steps:

2.4 Give proper credit to your sources using the Citations tool.

1. **Click the Styles button in the Toolbox, as shown in Figure 2.4.**

2. **Select a style from the Citation Style pop-up menu.** Normally you will choose a citation from the list, but because this is probably your first time using Citations you need to add one or more citations to the list manually by clicking the Add (+) button under the lower-left corner of the list.

3. **In the Create New Source window (shown in Figure 2.5), make a selection from the Type of Source pop-up menu and type the appropriate information for your source.**

4. **Click OK to add the source to your citations list.**

5. **To use a source, position your cursor in the location of your document that you want to place the citation, and then double-click the citation in the list.**

Formula Builder

I'll say it: I like the Formula Builder. If you've created spreadsheets before, you know that creating a formula in a cell can be supereasy or superdifficult depending on the kinds of calculations you need to make. Formula Builder helps you create a formula from scratch using predefined functions. Follow these steps:

Note The Formula Builder tool is only available in Excel.

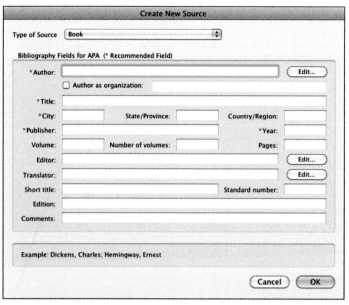

2.5 Create a new citation by typing the proper information for the source.

1. **Click the Formula Builder button in the Toolbox, as shown in Figure 2.6.**

2. **Search for a function by typing its name in the search field, or scroll through the list of functions.**

3. **Click the cell where you want to apply the formula, and then double-click the function you want to use.**

4. **Add or remove arguments for the function using the + and – buttons at the bottom of the Toolbox window.**

5. **Continue to add functions until you are satisfied with the formula you have just created.**

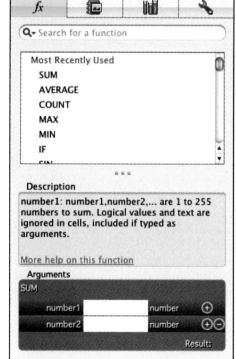

2.6 Calculating data in a cell is simpler, thanks to the Formula Builder.

Custom Animation

The Custom Animation tool helps you to add special effects to your slides to give them a little extra pizzazz. Effects include fades, fly-ins, shimmers, waves, and zooms, just to name a few.

Note The Custom Animation tool is only available in PowerPoint.

Scrapbook

The Scrapbook lets you collect and save items, or *clips*, that can be used across all the programs in the Office suite. These clips remain in the Scrapbook even after you close your Office applications, which makes it kind of like cut-and-paste on steroids.

To add and use Scrapbook clips, follow these steps:

1. **Click the Scrapbook button in the Toolbox, as shown in Figure 2.7.** The Scrapbook window must be open to add items to the Scrapbook.

2. **Add a clip to the Scrapbook in one of three ways:**

   - Highlight an item in a document and click the Add (+) button under the clips list in the Scrapbook window.

   - Add a file to the clips list by clicking the arrow next to the Add (+) button and select Add File. Browse your Mac within the resulting window and choose the file you want to add.

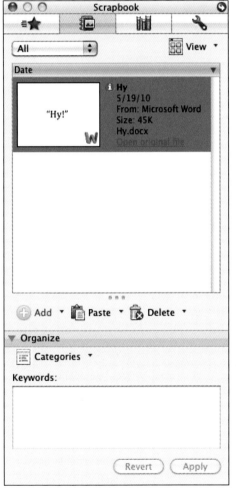

2.7 Scrapbook is the ultimate cut-and-paste replacement for frequently used items.

● Add items in the Mac OS Clipboard to Scrapbook by clicking the arrow next to the Add (+) button and selecting Add from Clipboard.

3. **Paste clips into your document from the Scrapbook in one of three ways:**

    ● Place your cursor in the location you want to paste the clip into your document and click the Paste button (looks like a clipboard with paper attached).

    ● Paste the clip as plain text by positioning your cursor in your document, click the arrow next to the Paste button, and then choose Paste as Plain Text.

    ● Insert the clip as a picture by positioning your cursor in your document, click the arrow next to the Paste button, and then choose Paste as Picture.

Genius

By default, whenever you cut or copy an item in Mac OS X, the item is placed on the Mac OS Clipboard. So if you cut or copy an item while working in an Office application, the item isn't automatically placed in the Scrapbook. If you want items you cut or copy within your Office applications to instantly be placed in the Scrapbook instead of the Mac OS Clipboard, click the arrow next to the Add (+) button under the clip list and select Always Add Copy. Items are only added to Scrapbook when the Scrapbook tool is open, so don't worry about this option hijacking your Mac OS Clipboard systemwide.

Reference Tools

Have you ever found yourself looking for that elusive word that you know will convey exactly what you want to say, only to have your thoughts trip all over themselves the instant before the word comes to mind? Of course, we've all been there, but thanks to the Reference Tools in Office 2011, those hard-to-find words and mysterious definitions are within easy reach.

Thesaurus

As you know, a thesaurus is quite handy when you need alternate words that deliver the same basic meaning. To use the Thesaurus, follow these steps:

1. **Click the Reference Tools button in the Toolbox.**

2. **Type a word or phrase in the appropriately named Word or Phrase text box.**

3. **Click the Thesaurus heading to see the Thesaurus panel, which displays a list of synonyms for the word or phrase you typed (see Figure 2.8).**

Dictionary

I'm a writer. I must have a dictionary, plain and simple. Office 2011 has a dictionary built right in, so there's no need to lug around a printed one (your arms and back will thank you).

1. **Click the Reference Tools button in the Toolbox.**

2. **Type a word or phrase in the Word or Phrase text box.**

3. **Click the Dictionary heading to open its panel and discover the definition of that great new word you discovered (see Figure 2.9).**

Bilingual Dictionary

This is a new addition to the Office Reference Tools. Its specialty is to help you find a word in another language.

1. **Click the Reference Tools button in the Toolbox.**

2. **Type a word or phrase into the Word or Phrase text box.**

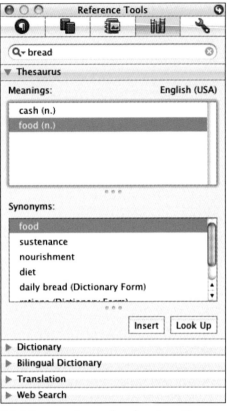

2.8 A thesaurus is one of my favorite writing tools.

3. **Click the Bilingual Dictionary heading to open the Bilingual Dictionary panel.**

4. **Choose the language of the word you want translated on the From pop-up menu.**

5. **Choose the language you want the word translated into on the To pop-up menu.**
    The Bilingual Dictionary does the translation for you, as shown in Figure 2.10.

Translation

The Translation tool is very similar to the Bilingual Dictionary, with the difference being that you can translate entire strings of text instead of single words.

1. **Click the Reference Tools button in the Toolbox.**

2. **Type a word or phrase in the Word or Phrase text box.**

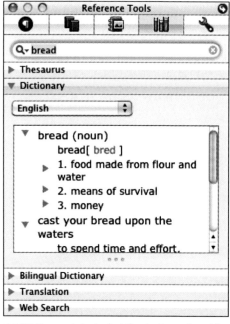

2.9 Dictionary is just what the doctor ordered for finding the meaning of words quickly and easily.

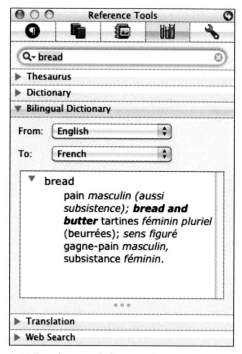

2.10 Translate words from one language to another with Bilingual Dictionary.

3. **Click the Translation heading to open the Translation panel.**

4. **Choose the language of the text you want translated on the From pop-up menu.**

5. **Choose the language you want the text translated into on the To pop-up menu.** The text is instantly translated, as shown in Figure 2.11.

Web Search

Web Search helps you look up a word quickly on the Internet without the need to exit your Office application and open a Web browser.

1. **Click the Reference Tools button in the Toolbox.**

2. **Type a word or phrase in the Word or Phrase text box.**

3. **Click the Web Search heading to open its panel and find your word on the Internet (see Figure 2.12).**

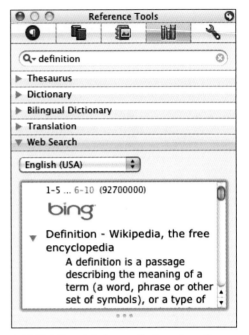

2.11 Language translation is a snap with the Translation tool.

2.12 Web Search helps you find words on the Internet without need of a Web browser.

Compatibility Report

Compatibility Report helps make sure that documents you create in Office 2011 display and print correctly in other versions of the Microsoft Office suite. Compatibility Report ensures compatibility with several versions of Office, which are listed in Table 2.1.

Table 2.1 Office Versions Checked by Compatibility Report

Mac	Windows
Office 98	Office 97
Office 2001	Office 2000
Office X	Office 2002 (Office XP)
Office 2004	Office 2003
Office 2008	Office 2007
Office 2011	Office 2010

To check your document's compatibility with other versions of Office, follow these steps:

1. **Click the Compatibility Report button (looks like a wrench) in the toolbox.**

2. **Select the version of Office you want to make sure your document is compatible with from the Check compatibility with pop-up menu.**

3. **Click Check Document to begin the compatibility check.** If any issues arise they are listed in the Results box, as shown in Figure 2.13.

4. **Click an issue in the Results box to see a detailed explanation in the Explanation box below it.** You may also be given tips on dealing with the issue, as shown in Figure 2.14.

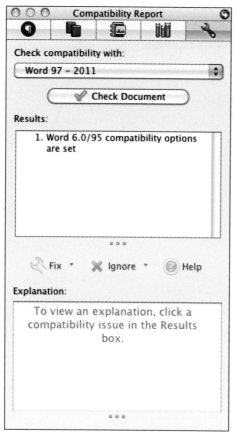

2.13 Compatibility issues are listed in the Results box of the Compatibility Report window.

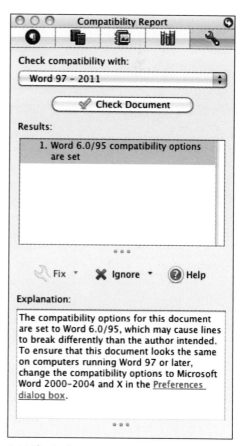

2.14 The Explanation box helps you better understand the issue and how to resolve it.

Adding Objects with Media Browser

Media Browser is a great way to add objects such as pictures and shapes to your documents. Media Browser gives you access to photos, music, movies, clip art, symbols, and shapes, all in one convenient window.

To open Media Browser, simply click the Media Browser button in the toolbar (as shown in Figure 2.15), or select the View menu and choose Media Browser.

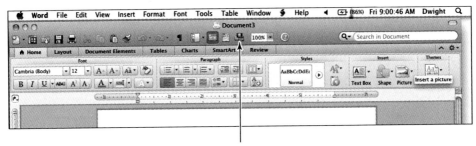

Media Browser button

2.15 Click the Media Browser button to open a doorway to object-placement bliss!

Photos

Nothing spices up a brochure or invitation to a family gathering like a great photo, and Media Browser makes it simple to quickly browse through the photos on your Mac and insert them into your documents.

Note The images used by Media Browser must be located in your iPhoto or Photo Booth libraries. iPhoto is part of Apple's iLife suite of applications, and Photo Booth is a standard application that comes with Mac OS X.

1. Click the Photos button in the Media Browser window.

2. Select the location of the pictures you want to choose from using the pop-up menu at the top of the Media Browser window.

3. Scroll through the list of pictures until you find the one you want to insert into your document.

Genius

If you find it difficult to make out the tiny pictures in the Media Browser window, drag the size slider at the bottom of the window to the right to increase the picture sizes.

4. **Drag the picture you want to insert from the Media Browser window directly into your document (see Figure 2.16).** It doesn't get any easier than that!

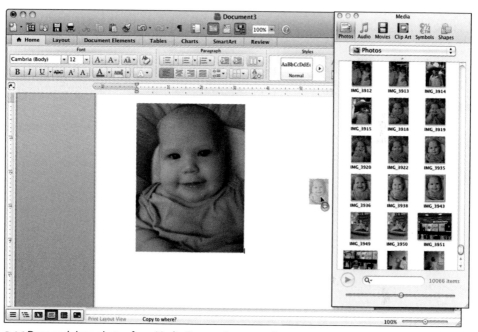

2.16 Drag and drop photos from Media Browser into your documents.

Music

Yes, Virginia, you really can insert music (or any other type of audio file) into your Office documents. And quite easily, I might add, with the astounding Media Browser coupled with your iTunes library. Follow these steps:

1. **Click the Audio button in the Media Browser window.**

2. **Choose the location of the music you want to use by clicking the pop-up menu at the top of the Media Browser window.**

3. **Scroll through the list of audio files until you find the one you're looking for.**

4. **Drag the audio into your document, dropping it on the place you want to insert it, as shown in Figure 2.17.** A speaker icon appears in the document where you placed the audio file. You can play the audio file by double-clicking the speaker icon.

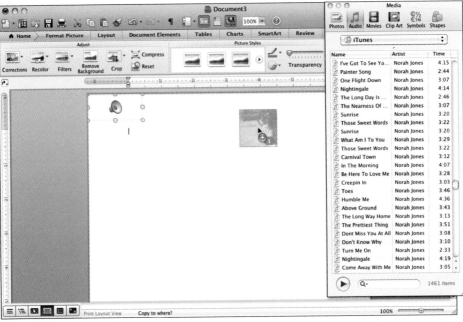

2.17 Add audio to your documents by dragging them from the Media Browser window.

Movies

Movies stored in your iPhoto, Photo Booth, or iTunes libraries can be inserted into your Office documents, too. As usual, Media Browser is the place to go for this cool functionality and ease of use.

1. **Click the Movies button in the Media Browser window.**

2. **Choose the location of the movie you want to add to your document by clicking the pop-up menu at the top of the Media Browser window.**

3. **Scroll through the list of movies until you find the one that suits your needs.**

4. **Drag and drop the movie file anywhere you like in your document, as shown in Figure 2.18.** The movie appears in your document right where you placed it. Play the movie by double-clicking its image.

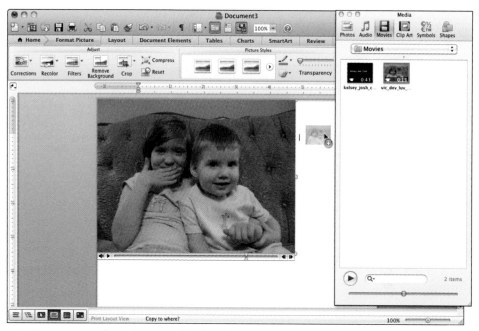

2.18 Movies are a really cool way to add information to your document that mere text may not adequately convey.

Clip art

Microsoft Office 2011 comes generously stocked with clip art that you can freely use in your documents. Of course, trusty Media Browser is there to help you get that clip art into your documents. Follow these steps:

1. **Click the Clip Art button in the Media Browser window.**

2. **Select a category for the clip art you want to insert in your document by clicking the pop-up menu at the top of the Media Browser window.**

3. **Drag and drop the clip art file into your document, as shown in Figure 2.19.**

Symbols and shapes

By now I'm sure you've got the hang of Media Browser, but there's still more you can do with the handy, dandy object-placement tool: Add symbols and shapes.

1. **Click either the Symbols or the Shapes button in the Media Browser window.**

2. **Select a category for the symbols or shapes you want to add to your document by clicking the pop-up menu at the top of the Media Browser window.**

3. **Drag and drop the symbol or shape into your document, as shown in Figure 2.20.**

31

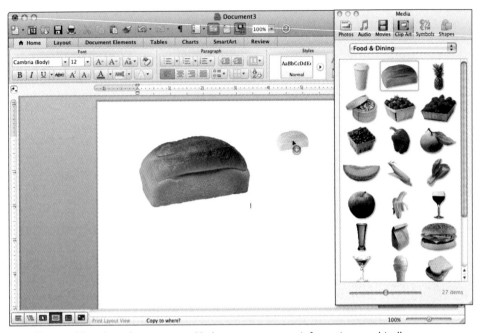

2.19 Clip art adds style to documents and helps to present your information graphically.

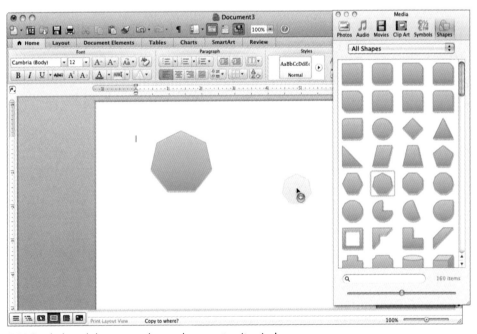

2.20 Symbols and shapes punch up a document quite nicely.

Genius

You can easily change the location of an object you place into your document. Simply click the object, drag it to the new location, and drop it by letting go of the mouse or trackpad button.

Using the Ribbon

The ribbon is a new addition to Microsoft Office for Mac, having made earlier appearances in the Windows versions of the suite. The ribbon is basically a one-stop shop for finding commonly used commands and tasks, which are logically grouped and organized under tabs. The ribbon resides above your document, as shown in Figure 2.21, which makes it instantly accessible.

Ribbon

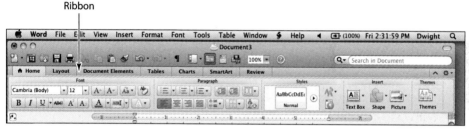

2.21 The ribbon is instantly accessible above your document.

Simply click a tab on the ribbon to see the options available under each, and then make selections as needed under each tab. You can quickly format your documents moving from one tab to the next to set your options, as opposed to going into multiple menus to format text, graphics, and so on.

Table 2.2 gives you a quick guide to the options available under each of the ribbon's tabs.

Table 2.2 Options Available Under Each of the Ribbon's Tabs

Home	Layout	Document Elements	Tables	Charts	SmartArt	Review
Font	Page Setup	Insert Pages	Table Options	Insert Chart	Insert SmartArt Graphic	Comments
Para-graph	Margins	Table of Contents	Table Styles	Data	Edit SmartArt	Tracking
Styles	Text Layout	Header and Footer	Draw Borders	Chart Quick Layouts	SmartArt Graphic Styles	Changes

continued

33

Table 2.2 continued

Home	Layout	Document Elements	Tables	Charts	SmartArt	Review
Insert	Page Back-ground	Citations		Chart Styles	Reset	Share
Themes	Grid	References				Protection
		Text Elements				
		Math				

Hide, show, or disable the ribbon

The ribbon is visible by default, but if you need more screen real estate you can hide it by clicking the Expand or Minimize the ribbon button on the Standard toolbar (see Figure 2.22).

Expand or minimize ribbon button

2.22 Minimize or expand the ribbon to see more or less of your document.

I know some folks who just can't stand to give up so much screen space to the ribbon, and they opt to simply turn off the ribbon and work the old-fashioned way. I advise you to work with the ribbon and give it a fair try before forsaking it; but if you find you can't bear the ribbon, simply turn it off by doing the following:

1. **Click the Word, PowerPoint, Excel, or Outlook menu (depending on which application you're using) and select Preferences.**

2. **Choose Ribbon under the Personal Settings area.**

3. **Deselect the Turn on the ribbon check box, as shown in Figure 2.23.**

Using the format tabs

The Format tab is initially hidden from view. This tab only becomes available when you highlight an element of your document, such as a text box or a graphic. Clicking the Format tab allows you to make quick adjustments to the highlighted element only. Let's look at a quick example using a shape.

1. **Click the Home tab and go to the Insert heading.**

2. **Click Shape and select a shape from the pop-up menu.**

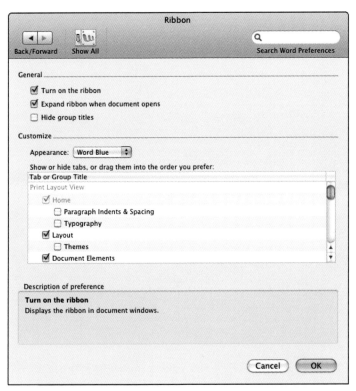

2.23 Turn off the ribbon if you want to save some space on your screen or if you simply like working the old-fashioned way.

3. **Point to the location in your document that you want to insert the shape (the cursor looks like a cross hair), and click and hold the mouse or trackpad button while dragging the pointer until the shape is the size you need.**

4. **Select the shape in your document.** The Format tab now appears to the immediate right of the Home tab.

5. **Click the Format tab.** From this point you can make any adjustments you want to the newly added shape, as shown in Figure 2.24.

Format tab

2.24 The Format tab is a practical way to adjust elements and objects on the fly.

How Can I Set Up My New Documents in Word?

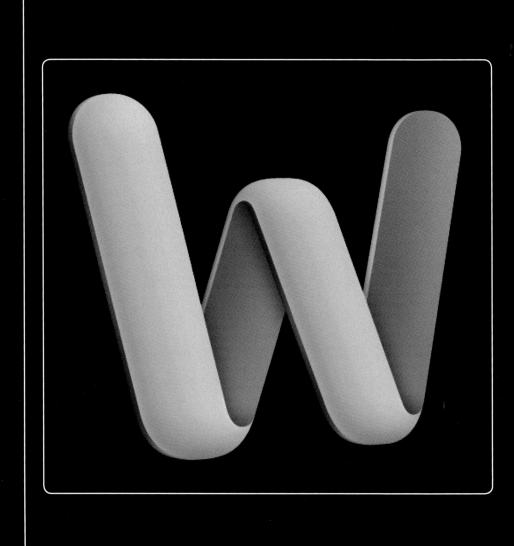

Few applications are as iconic as Microsoft Word. Not only is Word stable and familiar to most computer users needing a word processor, it's also available for Mac OS X and Microsoft Windows. This allows for document compatibility between the Mac and Windows versions of Office; it also offers comforting familiarity to those who may be used to Office on one platform but are switching to another. This chapter acquaints you with the newest version of Word for Mac and gets you quickly started with creating your next textual masterpiece.

Getting Around in Word

It's tough getting around in an unfamiliar town without a good map, and it's just as tough to navigate software applications unless you have a good guide to all the brightly colored buttons and options available to you. Before you get there, though, go ahead and launch Word, if you haven't already, by double-clicking its icon (which looks like a big blue W).

When Word launches, the Word Document Gallery is displayed, as shown in Figure 3.1.

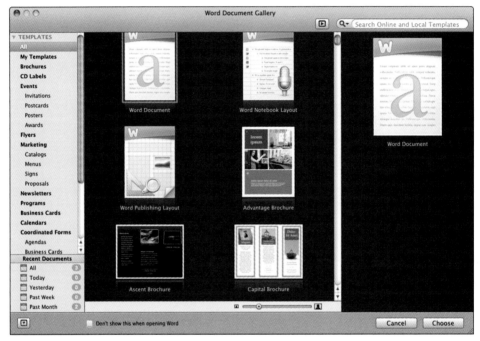

3.1 Click Word Document to create a new blank document window.

You learn a bit more about the Word Document Gallery later, but for now click Word Document from the available options and click Choose to open a new blank document.

Now that you have a new document open you can see what I meant by all the brightly colored buttons and options. There's a ton of them! Thankfully, Tables 3.1 and 3.2, along with Figures 3.2 and 3.3, point out the landscape elements and give you a brief description of them.

Create new Word document

New from template

Open a document

Save this document

Print one copy

Cut   Expand/minimize ribbon

Show/hide Media Browser

Reduce/enlarge display of document

Help   Search field

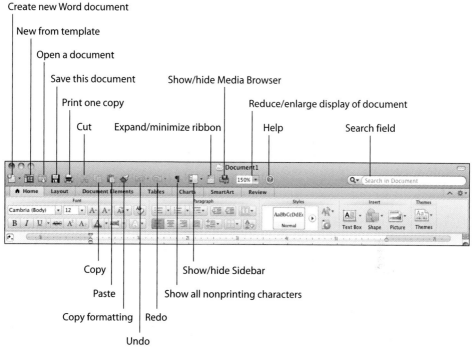

Copy

Paste

Copy formatting   Redo

Undo

Show/hide Sidebar

Show all nonprinting characters

3.2 Options available from the Standard toolbar.

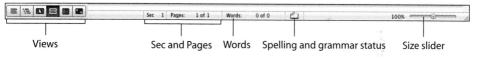

Views   Sec and Pages   Words   Spelling and grammar status   Size slider

3.3 Tools found within the status bar.

Table 3.1 Options Available from the Standard Toolbar

Button/Option	Description
Create New Word Document	Create a new blank document. Click the Action button next to the button to create new documents using the Notebook or Publishing layouts.
New from template	Opens the Word Document Gallery so you can select a template to begin a new document.
Open a document	Allows you to browse your Mac for Word documents you want to read or edit.
Save this document	Opens the Save dialog, where you can select where and how to save your current document.

continued

39

Table 3.1 continued

Button/Option	Description
Print one copy	Prints one copy of the document you are currently working in to your Mac's default printer.
Cut, Copy, and Paste	These are your standard Mac functions that allow you to copy, cut, and paste text you have selected in your document (everybody knows these, right?).
Copy formatting	Helps you quickly copy formatting, such as font size and color, from one block of text to another.
Undo and Redo	Use these buttons to undo and redo tasks you've performed in your document. The Action buttons next to the Undo and Redo buttons give you the option to make multiple undos or redos at once.
Show all nonprinting characters	Makes nonprinting characters, such as paragraph breaks, visible within the document, but they will not print.
Show/hide the sidebar	Opens or closes the sidebar.
Show/hide the Toolbox	Opens or closes the Toolbox window.
Show/hide Media Browser	Opens or closes the Media Browser window.
Reduce/enlarge display of document	Decreases or increases the size of the document on your screen.
Help	Opens the Help window.
Search field	Quickly find text within your document by typing it in this field. Use the arrows on the right side of the search field to move from one instance of your desired text to the next, assuming you find what you're looking for.

Table 3.2 Tools Found Within the Status Bar

Button/Option	Description
Views	Quickly view your document in one of several layouts: Draft, Outline, Publishing, Print, Notebook, and Full Screen.
Sec	Easily see which section of your document that you are currently viewing. Click to specify a section to move to.
Pages	Informs you what page of the document you are currently working in. Click to specify a page to move to.
Words	Gives you a running count of the number of words in your document.
Spelling and Grammar status	Shows the status when Word is checking spelling and grammar in your document. While checking for errors, an animated pen shows over the book. If no spelling or grammatical errors are found, a check mark shows on the book, but if an error is found, a red X appears. If the X appears, click the book to resolve the issue.
Size slider	Drag the slider to the right or left to increase or decrease the size of the document on your screen.

Setting Word Preferences

Word is pretty good right out of the box, but you may want to customize the way you work to make it an even better fit for you. Word allows you to change several preferences so you can do things the way you want, not the way the engineers at Microsoft want (and nice engineers they are, indeed).

To open the Word Preferences dialog, choose Word ⇨ Preferences from the list (or simultaneously press the ⌘+, [comma]). Word displays its preferences in a window very similar to Mac OS X's System Preferences (see Figure 3.4), which makes it that much easier to acclimate to them.

To open a preference pane, simply click an item under one of the three main headings:

- Authoring and Proofing Tools
- Output and Sharing
- Personal Settings

There is such a vast amount of information to cover in these preference panes that I must keep their explanations brief. Thankfully, Microsoft adds a Description of preference window at the bottom of each pane to help you understand what the individual preferences affect. Simply hold your mouse cursor over the preference in question to display its description. There's a bunch to cover here, so I take it one heading at a time.

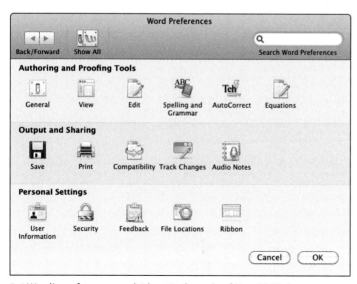

3.4 Word's preferences are laid out in the style of Mac OS X's System Preferences.

Note To immediately get back to the main Word Preferences window, click the Show All button in the toolbar. You can also use the right and left arrow buttons in the upper-left corner of the Word Preferences window to quickly jump between panes you've already visited.

Authoring and Proofing Tools

The options in the Authoring and Proofing Tools section of the Word Preferences window let you determine how your document looks on-screen and how Word should behave when you edit your masterpiece.

Even the best writers need a helping hand every now and then, and Word lends that hand when necessary with spelling and grammar checkers, and can even make corrections automatically if you want. Tell Word exactly how you want it to lend that helping hand by modifying the following settings as needed:

- **General.** The General dialog lets you change some of the more basic settings in Word, such as tracking recently opened documents, automatically opening the Word Document Gallery when Word launches, whether to use WYSIWYG font menus, and quite a bit more. Click the Web Options button to adjust how your documents will look and behave if viewed from within a Web browser, such as Safari or Firefox.

- **View.** The View dialog, as seen in Figure 3.5, lets you choose which objects to display in your document, select nonprintable characters you want to see, and decide what window tools (such as the scroll bars) to make available when working within your document.

- **Edit.** The Edit dialog allows you to modify how Word behaves while you are editing your document.

  - **Grid Options.** Click this button to use grids within your document. Grids help guide you in placing objects and text into your document.

  - **Settings.** Click this button to determine how Word behaves when you paste items into your document.

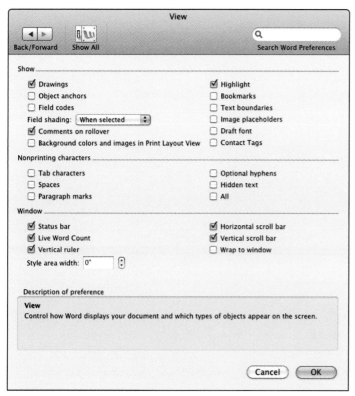

3.5 Determine which objects and tools to display in your document window with the View dialog.

- **Spelling and Grammar.** The Spelling and Grammar dialog (see Figure 3.6) puts you in control of how the spelling and grammar checkers in Word work with your text. You can utilize certain modes that apply to different languages, such as French or Spanish, create custom dictionaries, check your grammar, and more.

- **AutoCorrect.** AutoCorrect is a cool feature of Word that you can use to check the text and format of your document on the fly. The AutoCorrect dialog is where you enable AutoCorrect or make adjustments to how it behaves. The Exceptions button lets you control how AutoCorrect handles automatic capitalization.

- **Equations.** With Office 2011 you can insert and edit mathematical equations directly within Word, as opposed to using the Equation Editor as you did in earlier versions (the Equation Editor is still available, but is only necessary when creating equations that must be compatible with earlier versions of Word). The Equations dialog is where you tell Word how to work with mathematical equations within this particular document.

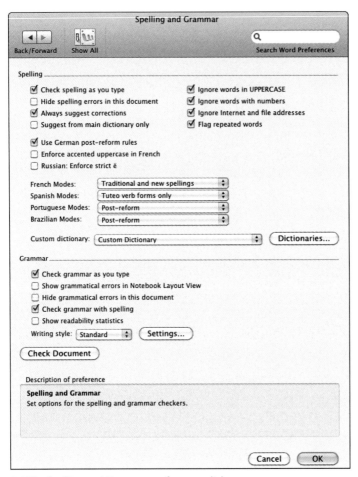

3.6 The Spelling and Grammar preferences dialog.

Output and Sharing

You most likely need to share your documents, and you'll probably want to print them at some point, too. These options let you tell Word how you want to save your documents, how you want them to print, make sure your documents are compatible with other versions of Word, and more.

- **Save.** The Save dialog (see Figure 3.7) is fairly straightforward. It gives you the ability to change how Word saves documents, what format to use by default when saving documents, and adjusts how often AutoRecover information is saved.

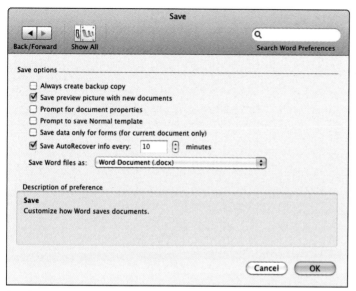

3.7 The Save dialog.

● **Print.** The Print dialog is your one-stop shop for telling Word what elements of your document that you want it to print.

● **Compatibility.** Document compatibility is a big deal for folks who share their documents with others who may be running earlier versions of Word or who may use Word for Windows. The Compatibility dialog is the place to go for making sure that your document is compatible with your friends and co-workers.

● **Track Changes.** When multiple people work on a single document it helps to be able to tell what comments or changes belong to each individual. The Track Changes dialog (see Figure 3.8) is where you tell Word how to display changes that are made to your document.

● **Audio Notes.** Did you know you could add audio notes to a document? Pretty cool! Microsoft provides the Audio Notes dialog to let you specify the quality and audio format of your recorded notes.

Note The higher the quality of your recordings, the more hard drive space will be required for your document. Keep this in mind, too, if you need to e-mail your document to other individuals as there may be file-size limitations to watch for.

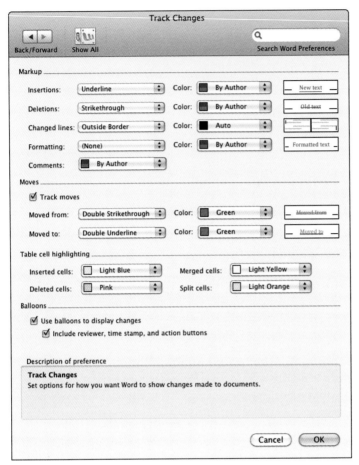

3.8 Track changes your way by modifying these preferences.

Personal Settings

Customize how various elements appear in your documents, add your personal contact information to documents and templates, give Microsoft a helping hand, and secure your documents
from prying eyes or destructive input devices, all with the help of the preferences under the
Personal Settings heading.

- **User Information.** Add your personal information, such as your name, address, and
  phone number, to your document using the User Information dialog (see Figure 3.9).
  Word uses this information to automatically populate fields in certain templates and
  adds this information to the properties of your document.

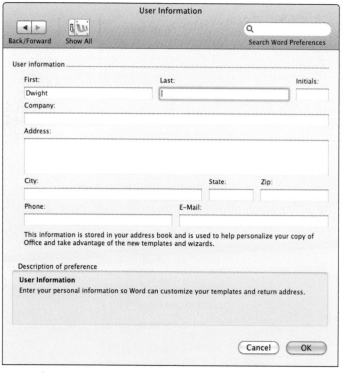

3.9 Word uses your personal information for many purposes.

● **Security.** Sometimes you may need to keep prying eyes from seeing a document that's not meant for them, or to keep the contents of your document from being changed without your consent. The Security dialog allows you to lock down your document. You can allow people to only read the document (preventing them from making unauthorized changes) or set a password that must be typed by the reader to open the document or modify it.

● **Feedback.** Microsoft is requesting your help! The Feedback dialog lets you enable or disable the Customer Experience Improvement Program. If you enable this program, Microsoft can anonymously collect information about your Mac's hardware and how you use your software. Please read the information in this pane carefully before enabling or disabling this program.

● **File Locations.** The File Locations dialog lets you change the default location of where Word stores certain types of files, such as templates and clip art. Select the file type you want to change from the list and click Modify to select a different location.

● **Ribbon.** Customize the appearance of the ribbon, or turn it off altogether, using the Ribbon dialog (see Figure 3.10). You can even hide or display tabs using the options in the Tab or Group Title window.

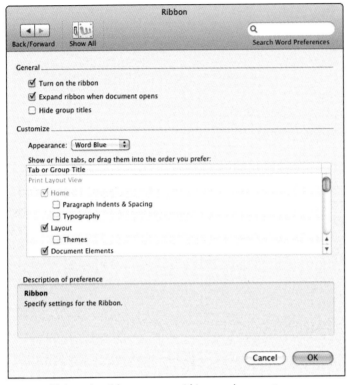

3.10 Modify how the ribbon appears within your document.

Creating New Documents

You're probably pretty familiar with how to create new documents in Word, but if not I'm more than happy to show you how simple it is.

If you're just launching Word, you are greeted with the Word Document Gallery, which you saw earlier in this chapter. From within the Word Document Gallery, you can choose to create a new document with a blank slate, or you can choose from one of myriad templates Microsoft has been kind enough to put together for you. After you find the type of document you want to create, select it and then click Choose in the lower-right corner of the Word Document Gallery window.

If you're already working in a document and want to create a new one, simply click the Create New Word Document button in the upper-left corner of the Standard toolbar.

If Word is open but you aren't currently working in a document, you can create a new document by choosing File ⇨ New Blank Document. You can do it even faster by pressing ⌘+N.

Understanding Document Viewing Choices

A feature that I commonly use in Word is the capability to change the way I view my documents. Word allows you to change document views to accommodate the type of document you are creating or reading. Create a new document and play with the viewing options so you can get a feel for how each view affects your document's content. As you switch from one view to another, notice that the toolbar and ribbon options change to suit the type of view you're using. With your new document at hand, take a look at the six viewing choices available in Word 2011.

- **Draft.** Draft view is the simplest and most basic way to type and edit text. When fancy things like pictures and charts aren't necessary, and all you want is the bare-bones basics of text editing, Draft view is the view for you.

- **Outline.** Outline view helps you align items on your page when creating an outline document. This view and the tools are perfect for creating outlines with multiple levels.

- **Publishing layout.** While Word isn't intended to be a replacement for those needing professional desktop-publishing software, the Publishing layout view in Word offers a simple way to quickly create newsletters and brochures for the casual graphic designer. Publishing layout view, seen in Figure 3.11, gives you fast access to the tools necessary to create slick graphic-intensive documents in a flash, such as buttons to easily insert text boxes, pictures, and shapes.

- **Print layout.** Print layout is Word's default view. Because it is the default view it is the one you work with in this chapter, unless otherwise specified. To me it's the perfect mix between the Draft and Publishing layouts, allowing easy text manipulation while providing basic design tools.

3.11 Publishing layout transforms Word from a word processor into a basic desktop-publishing application.

- **Notebook layout.** Have you ever wanted a digital notebook? Well, with Word 2011's Notebook layout, you now have one! The Notebook layout view is intended to let you take notes and make outlines exactly as you would with a standard notebook, with the added bonus of allowing you to make recorded notes, add section tabs for better organization, and customize the appearance of your notebook.

- **Full Screen.** Sometimes you just need a little more room to work. Just a little bit more elbow room can help you relax and avoid distractions. Word can help give you a little more room, at least on your screen, with the advent of Full Screen layout. Full Screen layout can be used in two modes: writing (see Figure 3.12), for writing and editing your document; and reading, for when you simply want to kick back and check out what the document says.

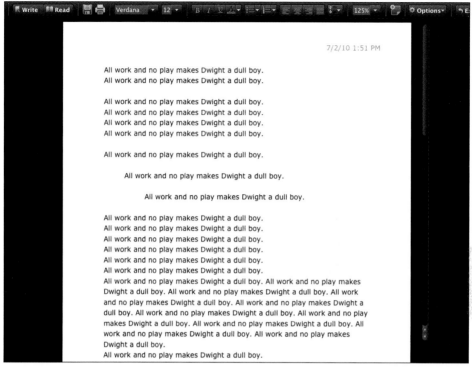

3.12 Writing mode in the Full Screen layout view.

Manipulating Text

What a boring world it would be if the contents of every document consisted only of black text in the Courier font. As any word processor worth its salt would do, Word allows simple methods of formatting your text to give it that extra pop to grab your reader's attention.

Selecting text

I know that it doesn't get any more basic than when it comes to selecting text, but the following is a super-quick peek at it.

The short-and-sweet of it: To select text, simply place your cursor next to the letter or word you want to select, click and hold the mouse button, and drag the cursor over the text. The text will highlight to let you know it's selected. Pretty simple, wouldn't you say? If you need to select all the text in your document, simply press ⌘+A.

Genius

You can speed up the selection process with the use of your mouse or trackpad's buttons. Double-click a word to select the entire word, or triple-click within a paragraph to select the entire paragraph.

Moving, copying, and cutting text

Now, what to do with our selected text? Well, let's see now. Here are some options:

- **Format the text (see the following section for more details).**
- **Delete the text by pressing Delete or the spacebar.**
- **Begin typing to delete and replace the text.**
- **Cut the text by pressing ⌘+X, which deletes the text but preserves it in your clipboard.**
- **Paste the text by placing your cursor at the location in the document that you want to insert it and pressing ⌘+V.**
- **Copy the text by pressing ⌘+C, which leaves the text in the document, but also copies it to your clipboard so you can paste it somewhere in the document or into another document entirely.** You can even paste it into other applications if you so desire.

Choosing and formatting fonts

Fonts are the glue that holds any good document together, visually speaking (if the text is gibberish it won't matter how good the fonts look). Pictures, objects, and tables are nice, but a good font that suits the mood of your document goes a long way in pulling your reader in. Word gives you a couple of really good options for selecting and formatting your fonts.

You can always go the old-fashioned route and simply choose a good font from the Font menu. Follow these steps:

1. **Choose Font and a list of WYSIWYG fonts installed on your Mac appears, as shown in Figure 3.13.**
2. **Scroll through the list of fonts until you see the one you want, and simply click it to begin using it in your document.**

The ribbon is another convenient place for selecting your fonts. Follow these steps:

1. **Click the Home tab in the ribbon.**

2. **Click the pop-up menu (looks like a small gray arrow) next to the font selector to see a WYSIWYG list of your available fonts.**

3. **When you find the font you want, click to select it and begin typing to use the font in your document.**

When using the ribbon method to select a font you might notice all the other options surrounding the font selector. Those options allow you to further format the fonts to your liking.

There is another option for formatting your fonts, too. Choose Format ➪ Font, or press ⌘+D, to open the Font dialog, as shown in Figure 3.14. From here you can perform a bounty of tasks to personalize the fonts to your taste. Be sure to click the Advanced tab for even more formatting options. One thing I like about the Font dialog is the Preview field; from there you can see the effect your changes will have on the text before you actually apply them.

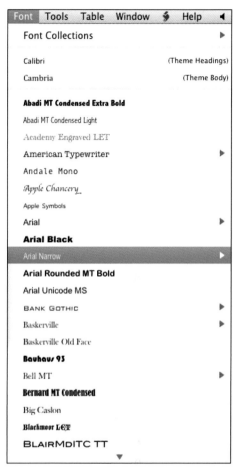

3.13 Word displays your font in a WYSIWYG fashion, making it easier to pick and choose the right font for your document.

Note Notice that some fonts have gray arrows to the right of their names. This indicates that there is more than one option for these fonts.

3.14 The Font dialog provides lots of options and a Preview pane to boot.

Slow Display of Fonts

Does your Mac slow to a crawl when you open your list of fonts? If so, you can quicken the pace a bit by turning off the WYSIWYG font menu and display your fonts as plain text. Here's how to change your font views:

1. **Choose View ⇨ Print Layout, or simply click the Print Layout button in the lower left of your document window.**

2. **Choose View again, then choose Toolbars ⇨ Customize Toolbars and Menus.**

3. **Click the Toolbars and Menus tab, and deselect Show typefaces in font menus check box.**

Finding text in a document

Finding a word among the other 20,000 words in your document can be daunting, to say the least, if not for the nifty little Find tool.

In previous versions of Word, you could press ⌘+F to open the Find dialog, but Word 2011 has eliminated the need for the keyboard shortcut by supplying a search field in the upper-right corner of your document's window. In fact, if you press ⌘+F, the search field is highlighted momentarily, as opposed to a separate Find dialog opening. Simply type the word you are looking for into the search field and it will be highlighted for you in the document, as shown in Figure 3.15.

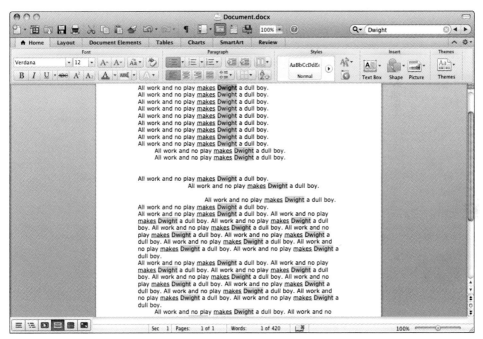

3.15 Finding a word in a document is as simple as typing it into the search field.

If there are multiple instances of the word in your document, press ⌘+G (Find Next) to find the next instance of the word, or press ⌘+Shift+G (Find Previous) to find a previous instance.

Finding and replacing text

I've found myself in the precarious position of needing to replace multiple instances of a word in a document for various reasons. Word's capability to find and replace text has been a lifesaver for me in those times. If you're familiar with previous versions of Word you may want to still follow along, as this function has changed slightly.

To find and replace text, follow these steps:

1. **Press ⌘+Shift+H to open the Find and Replace sidebar.** The main difference with previous versions of Office was that a Find and Replace dialog would open. I like the sidebar as it prevents the Find and Replace dialog from obscuring my vision of the document.

2. **Type the word you want to find into the Search Document field and click the Find button.** Word highlights all instances of the word, as shown in Figure 3.16. The number of matches also displays in the sidebar.

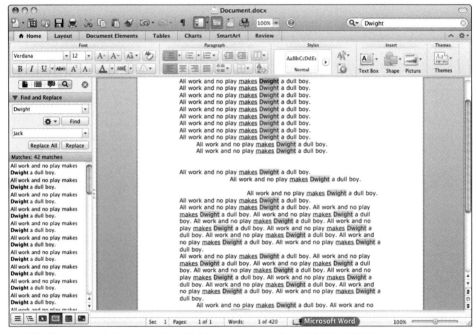

3.16 Finding and replacing a word couldn't be any simpler than with Word 2011.

3. **Type the word you want to use in place of the previous word in the Replace With field.**

4. **Click the Replace button to replace single instances of the offending word, or click Replace All to replace all instances.**

Simple Page Formatting

The layout of your text within a document is vital to how readers disseminate the information you provide them. Proper formatting keeps your text organized and accessible; a page of jumbled words has just the opposite effect. Word comes armed with many tools for getting the layout of your text just so.

Setting margins

For many documents, Word's default margins will be right up your alley, but if not it's a simple task to adjust them. Follow these steps:

1. **Make sure you're in Print Layout view.** If not, click the Print Layout button in the lower left of your document's window.

2. **Click the Layout tab in the ribbon.**

3. **Under Margins, adjust the top, bottom, left, and right margins to meet your needs.**

Setting tab stops

Tab stops are great for quickly zipping to a point in a line (such as a paragraph indentation), as opposed to pressing the spacebar for the number of times you need. You can set tabs using the horizontal ruler in your document window. Follow these steps:

1. **If you cannot see the horizontal ruler in your document window, choose View ⇨ Ruler.**

2. **Click the Tabs button in the upper left of your document window (to the left of the horizontal ruler) and select the type of tab stop you want to set (see Figure 3.17).**

3. **Click the point in the horizontal ruler that you want to set the tab stop to.**

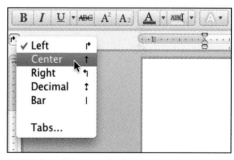

3.17 Select the type of tab stop you want to set using the Tabs button.

You can reset the position of any tab stop by dragging its marker within the horizontal ruler from one location to another.

If you want more accurate control of your tab stops you can do so in the Tabs dialog, as shown in Figure 3.18. To access the Tabs dialog, click the Tabs button (left of the horizontal ruler) and select Tabs.

Adding headers and footers

Headers and footers allow you to add helpful information, such as page numbers and dates and times (you can even add graphics), to the top or bottom margins of your document. Follow these steps:

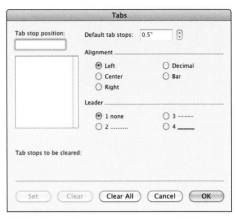

3.18 Indicate the precise placement of tab stops in the Tabs dialog.

1. **Click the Document Elements tab in the ribbon.**

2. **Under the Header and Footer section, click either Header or Footer and select one of the predefined styles, as shown in Figure 3.19.**

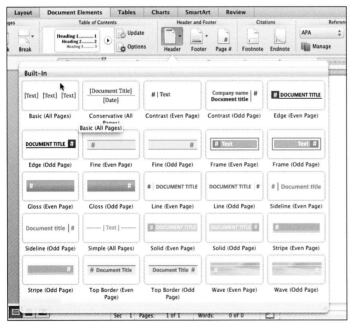

3.19 Choose a style for your header or footer.

Note

You must be in Print layout view or Publishing layout view to set up headers and footers.

3. **Type or insert any information in your header or footer, and then click Close when you finish.**

4. **To edit a header or footer, double-click it, type or remove any information, and click Close again.**

Genius

When you work in a header or footer you might notice that a Header and Footer tab appears in the ribbon. Click this tab to make changes and modifications to your header or footer, such as changing its placement on the page, using different headers and footers for odd or even pages, or preventing headers and footers from appearing on the first page of your document. You can also click the Date or Time buttons to insert one or both into your header or footer.

You can also insert graphics, such as a picture or company logo, into your headers or footers. While in the header or footer, choose Insert ➪ Photo ➪ Picture from File. Browse the Mac for the graphic file you want to insert and select it. You can resize the graphic by selecting it and then dragging the sizing handles.

Using Proper Spelling and Grammar

A great-looking document that's chock-full of spelling and grammatical errors is not a good reflection on the person who created it. Because very few of us have doctorates in English, we all need help in the areas of spelling and grammar from time to time. Word offers the ability to check your spelling and grammar on the fly, which makes life a little easier if spelling and grammar aren't your cup of tea.

Word automatically checks your spelling and grammar as you type. When you misspell a word or the structure of your sentence isn't proper, Word flags spelling errors by placing a squiggly red line under the text and shows problems with grammar using a green squiggly line, both of which are shown in Figure 3.20.

To see what Word thinks you should do (it offers the correct spelling of words or offers to help with your sentence structure), right-click or Control+click the underlined text. Select an option from the resulting pop-up menu to make a correction.

I can spelll really well.

I can spell more better.

3.20 Squiggly red and green lines indicate that Word thinks you've made a mistake in spelling or grammar.

Genius

If Word has never seen a word before it may flag it as being misspelled, even if you know better. To prevent the word from being flagged every time you use it you can add it to the Dictionary. Simply right-click or Control+click the word that Word believes is misspelled and select Add from the pop-up menu.

How Can I Spice Up My Documents?

A plain text document with basic Courier fonts is about as exciting as watching grass grow. That may have been able to cut it back in the heyday of typewriters, but in today's digital age you need documents that are going to grab the attention of readers through the deluge of information we have to contend with. Word 2011 comes with the tools necessary to help you make eye-catching documents and brochures. It is also equipped to help you quickly create documents through the use of wizards and applying graphics to them. Creative document construction has never been easier!

Simplify Document Creation Using Templates and Wizards

Sure, opening a blank document and banging away at the keyboard, manually laying out the contents as you go, is one way to go, but when you have the chance to make life a little easier why not take it? Word is happy to make your document creation simpler by giving you templates and wizards. Let's take a look at both and learn how to put them to work.

Using templates in your documents

I've referred to the kind folks at Microsoft often in this book, and templates are just one of the many reasons I hold them in such high regard. Templates are simply documents that have been preconfigured with fonts, colors, layouts, and so on. You can use these templates to create your own documents, inserting your text and graphics in place of those in the templates.

Word provides a plethora (one of my favorite words) of templates for you to use, and these templates can be modified to your liking. Templates are found in the Word Document Gallery, which opens automatically when first launching Word; if you already use Word, choose File ⇨ New From Template to open the Word Document Gallery. Figure 4.1 gives you a quick reference to the Word Document Gallery.

To begin using a template, follow these steps:

1. **Open the Word Document Gallery.**

2. **Select a template type from the Templates list on the left side of the window.**

3. **Browse the broad selection of preconfigured templates for the one that best suits your needs and click to select it.**

Genius

Don't see the template you need? Scroll down to the bottom of the Templates list in the Word Document Gallery and select Online Templates. Word will go to the Internet and dig up tons more templates for you to choose from!

4. **From within the template preview pane, click the Colors pop-up menu to deter-mine the colors that you want to use in the document (assuming the default range of colors for the template doesn't suit your tastes), as shown in Figure 4.2.**

5. **Also within the template preview pane, click the Fonts pop-up menu to change the default set of fonts, if you so desire.**

6. **Click Choose in the lower right to begin editing your new document.**

Templates list   Selection of templates   Template preview   Search field

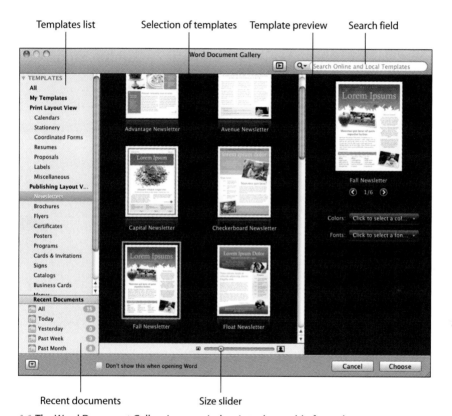

Recent documents   Size slider

4.1 The Word Document Gallery is your window into the world of templates.

Now that you have a new document you can begin to edit it.

Templates use placeholders to help you with the layout of your document. These place-holders are for text or images and are simple to edit.

To edit text placeholders, follow these steps:

1. **Click on a text placeholder to highlight it and show its blue size handles.**

2. **Click once more inside the placeholder and the box clears, allowing you to type whatever you like.** The text you type appears in the same color and font as the placeholder text, as shown in Figure 4.3.

3. **If the box isn't large enough, or you simply want to reconfigure it to fit your needs, click and drag the blue size handles to the necessary dimension.**

4. **When you finish editing, click anywhere outside of the placeholder box and the changes take effect.**

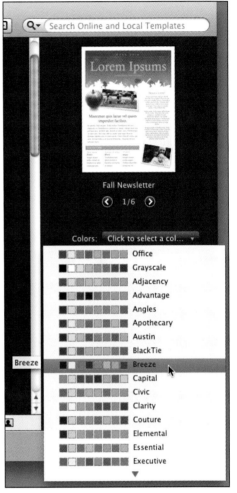

4.2 Choose your template's color range if the default isn't your cup of tea.

Genius

Don't feel constrained by the color palette or default fonts used in the template. If you want to use some other color or font, by all means do so. The default colors and fonts are there as much for inspiration as they are for guidance.

4.3 Your text appears in the same color and font as the placeholder text.

Editing an image placeholder isn't any more difficult than a text placeholder. Follow these steps:

1. **Click on an image placeholder to highlight it.** Again, you see the borders of the placeholder and its blue size handles.

2. **Right-click (or Ctrl+click if you have a one-button mouse) the image and select Change Picture, as shown in Figure 4.4.** The Choose a Picture window opens.

3. **Browse your Mac to find the picture you want to use, select the image, and click Insert.**

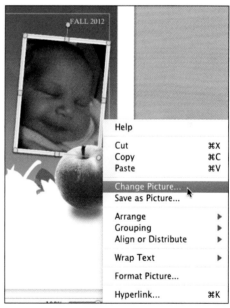

4.4 You can easily replace image placeholders with your own images.

4. **Should you need to resize the placeholder box, click and drag the blue size handles.** You can also click and drag the green rotation handle to rotate the image on the page.

5. **Click outside the image placeholder to finish editing it.**

Genius

Create your own templates! If you've become particularly enamored with a document that you created with your own hands you can save a copy of that document as a template, which allows you to use it to create future documents with the same layout. Simply choose File ⇨ Save As, and when the Save As dialog opens, select Word Template from the Format pop-up menu. See Chapter 5 for more information on saving your documents.

As you can see, you can easily build an entire document with very little fuss or muss using templates. Play around with the various styles; some of them may not jump out at you upon first glance, but if you apply a different color or font pattern to them they just might work better than you think.

Casting a spell on the mundane with wizards

Wizards are Word's way of holding your hand and walking you through the process of creating a document step by step. There are wizards to help you handle tasks such as creating envelopes, labels, and the standard letter.

Envelopes

Word can quickly create an envelope with the Envelope Wizard. You supply the delivery and return addresses and Word does the rest. Follow these steps:

1. **To open the Envelopes Wizard while already working within Word, choose Tools ⇨ Envelopes.** If you are launching Word from a cold start select the Envelopes Wizard from the Templates list.

2. **Type the address of your recipient in the Delivery address field, as shown in Figure 4.5.** If you already have the recipient in your Mac OS X Address Book or Office's Address Book just click the tiny Contacts button (it looks like a Rolodex card) and select the contact from the list.

3. **Click Font to modify the appearance of the delivery address text.** Click OK when finished modifying the text to return to the wizard.

4. **Click Position to tell Word where you want to place the delivery address on the envelope.** Use the Preview window to get a look at what your envelope might look like when printed. Click OK when finished.

5. **If you need a delivery barcode to be printed under the delivery address, select the Delivery point barcode check box.**

6. **Type your address into the Return address field either manually or using the Contacts button, and use the Font and Position buttons (as you did for the delivery address), respectively, to change the look of your return address text or to reposition it on the envelope.**

4.5 Type delivery and recipient addresses into the Envelope wizard for fast envelope creation.

7. **The Printing Options section is key to making sure the envelope prints correctly on the page.**

   - If you know that your printer supports the size envelope you are printing on, select the Use settings from your printer radio button, and then click Page Setup to select the envelope size and position.

   - If your printer does not officially support the envelope you are using, select the Use custom settings radio button. Click Custom to set the envelope's size as well as its position in the paper tray of your printer. If you need further help, contact technical support for the manufacturer of your printer.

8. **If you want to make this envelope a permanent part of your document, select the Insert this envelope into the active document check box.**

9. **Click Print to open the Print dialog and print your envelope.**

Labels

The Labels Wizard in Word is a thing of beauty, particularly when it comes to selecting label sizes and manufacturers. The wizard helps you type an address, choose a label size, select how many labels to print, and ultimately to print your labels — simply. Follow these steps:

1. **To open the Labels Wizard while already working within Word, choose Tools ⇨ Labels.** If you're launching Word for the first time today select the Labels Wizard from the Templates list.

2. **Type the address you want to appear on the labels in the Address box.** Click Font to change the appearance of the address text, if you want.

3. **The Labels Wizard defaults to Avery standard 5160 labels, so if that's not what you need click Options and choose from the following:**

   - Decide whether you're sending your labels to a dot-matrix (I kindly invite you to join us in the twenty-first century, if this is the case), laser, or inkjet printer.

   - Select the label manufacturer from the Label products pop-up menu. If this is a custom label or your label manufacturer is not in the list click New Label and type the dimensions of your label.

   - Choose the appropriate label style from the Product number list on the left side. Click Details if you need to see the dimensions of your label or to customize it to fit your needs (Figure 4.6).

   - Click OK to return to the Labels dialog.

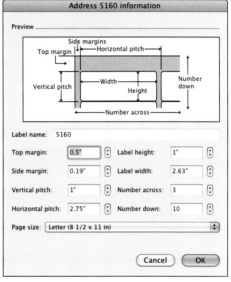

4.6 You can see the true dimensions of a label and even customize it if need be.

4. **Choose the number of labels you want to print, whether single labels or an entire page.**

5. **Click Customize in the Printing Options section to set the feed method that you use for loading labels into your printer's paper tray and click OK.**

6. **Click Print to open the Print dialog and print your labels.**

Letters

The Letter Wizard quite literally walks you through the steps to build a professional or personal letter, from specifying the recipient to detailing the format to standing in line at the post office for you (well, maybe not that far, but you get the gist).

1. **To open the Letter Wizard while already working within Word, choose Tools ⇨ Letter Wizard.** If you're just launching Word choose the Letter Wizard from the Templates list.

Note

Opening the Letter Wizard from within a Word document yields a slightly different result than by using the Word Document Gallery. The slight difference can be seen at the bottom of the wizard window. When opened from the Word Document Gallery you are offered Next, Back, and Finish buttons, and you take one step at a time. When opened from within an existing document, the Next, Back, and Finish buttons aren't there, but you are able to go to whatever step you want by clicking the tabs at the top of the window.

2. **Click the Letter Format tab, found at the top of the Letter Wizard window, to build the basic structure of the letter:**

   - The Choose a page design and Choose a letter style pop-up menus are your two main options. Click their respective pop-ups to see an entire list of templates designed to build the basic format of the letter.

   - Decide whether to include a date line, a header and footer (if using a page design), and let Word know whether you're printing on preprinted letterhead or not (and if so, where is the letterhead on the page, and how much room it needs).

3. **Click the Recipient tab (or click Next at the bottom of the window) to see options related to adding the letter recipient's information.** The following options are available:

   - If the recipient is already in your Mac OS X Address Book or your Office Address Book, simply click the Contacts button (remember, it's the tiny button that looks like a Rolodex card) and browse for him or her in the list.

   - Manually type the recipient's name and address information, and begin your letter with a salutation of your choosing.

4. **Click the Other Elements tab (or click Next) to add a reference line, mailing instructions, attention and subject fields, and to provide courtesy copies, as shown in Figure 4.7.**

5. **Click the Sender tab (or Next again) to add the information about the sender of the letter.** You can also add a complimentary closing if you like, along with a few other tidbits about yourself.

6. **Click OK (or Finish) to apply the settings to your new letter.** At this point, it is up to you to add your own contents to the body.

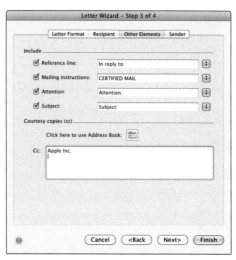

Inserting Images and Graphics Into Your Documents

Images, or pictures, really enliven a document. You almost can't do a newsletter or brochure without one, but even personal letters can benefit by the inclusion of a personal image (Memee would love to see a picture of her new grandson in your next correspondence).

4.7 The Letter Wizard helps you construct a letter from the ground up.

Adding graphics such as shapes, symbols, and clip art can help spice up a document, too.

Adding pictures to your document

You can either add pictures to a document by browsing your computer or another location (such as an external hard drive or a computer on your network), or you can insert a picture that's stored in your iPhoto or Photo Booth library.

Add a picture from your iPhoto or Photo Booth library

To add a picture from your iPhoto or Photo Booth library, follow these steps:

1. **Choose Insert ⇨ Photo ⇨ Photo Browser to automatically open Media Browser to the Photos tab.** You can also click the Media Browser icon in the toolbar and select the Photos tab.

2. **Choose a location for your photos from the pop-up menu (either iPhoto or Photo Booth).**

3. **Browse through the list of your pictures and find the one you want to add to the document.** If the pictures are too small for you to see well, simply drag the size slider underneath the picture list to increase their size.

4. **To add the picture, click to select it, and then drag and drop it into the document, as shown in Figure 4.8.**

5. **You can resize the document by dragging the blue size handles (if you don't see them just click the picture one time).** You can also rotate the document by dragging the green rotation handle at the top of the picture.

Add a picture by browsing your Mac

If you prefer to store pictures in a folder on your Mac or another computer, as opposed to using a photo cataloging application such as iPhoto, you can manually add those pictures to your document.

4.8 Click and drag your desired picture from the Media Browser window and drop it into your document.

1. **Choose Insert ⇨ Photo ⇨ Picture from File.**

2. **In the Choose A Picture window, browse your Mac, external drives, or your network to find the picture you want to use in your document.**

3. **When you find the picture, select it and click Insert to place it in your document.**

4. **Make adjustments and formatting changes to your picture as desired.**

Genius

If you have the screen real estate available, there's another option for adding a picture to your document. You can actually drag a picture straight from a Finder window or the desktop into your document and drop it in. Pretty nifty!

Formatting your pictures

There are many options available for formatting your picture, and these options shouldn't be overlooked here. They could affect the way your picture works with the rest of your document, such as your text. The best way to learn how these options will affect your work is to simply try them all out. You may find you will never need them, but that's not very likely, so it's a good idea to at least be familiar with them should they be needed sometime in the future.

To see the formatting options for a picture, right-click or Control+click the image and select Format Picture from the list. Choose an item from the list of settings on the left to apply formatting to your picture.

- **Fill.** Apply a solid, gradient, or pattern to the background of your picture.
- **Line.** Apply an outline to the picture box.
- **Shadow.** Add a drop shadow to the picture box.
- **Glow & Soft Edges.** Apply a glow to the outer edges of the picture box, or a soft edge to the picture itself.
- **Reflection.** Add a mirror reflection of the picture underneath it.
- **3-D Format.** Place a bevel around the image and adjust its depth and color.
- **3-D Rotation.** You can literally rotate the image three-dimensionally (this one's really cool!).
- **Adjust Picture.** Adjust the transparency, contrast, and make other color enhancements to your picture.
- **Artistic Filters.** Apply filters to your picture to change the look and feel of it. You can add textures, as shown in Figure 4.9, with the Light Screen filter and use the sliders to make variations in the effects. This is the closest to Adobe Photoshop a word processor can get.

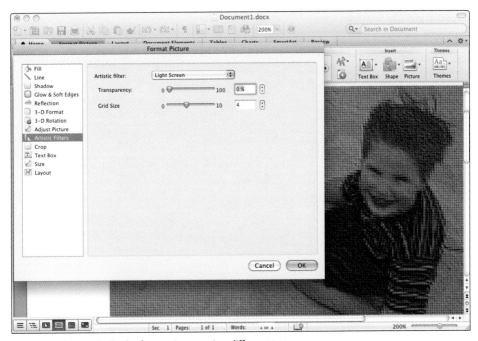

4.9 Filters change the look of your picture using different textures.

- **Crop.** Use these options to crop your picture box to a portion of the picture.

- **Text Box.** Make adjustments to a text box, such as its alignment and the direction of its text.

- **Size.** Manually change the size of the picture, as opposed to dragging the blue size handles. This technique is more exact in its measurements, to be sure.

- **Layout.** Adjust how the picture interacts with the text on your page, such as wrapping the text around the picture or placing the picture in the background behind the text.

Inserting graphics into your documents

Graphics, such as shapes and clip art, can be added using our trusty friend, Media Browser. The same techniques apply for graphics as for images. Follow these steps:

1. **Open Media Browser by clicking its icon in the toolbar.**

2. **Click the Clip Art tab, the Symbols tab, or the Shapes tab.**

3. **Find the item you want to add to your document and drag and drop it to the position you want it placed.**

4. **Adjust the size of the shape or clip art by selecting it and then dragging the blue size handles.** You can also rotate the item by clicking the green rotation handle and dragging in the direction you want to rotate it.

5. **You can also format a shape or clip art just as you would an image.** Simply right-click or Control+click the shape or clip art and select Format Shape or Format Picture from the list.

Putting Tables to Work

Tables are very useful for laying complex information out in a simple format, and they certainly make your document's appearance more professional. Word 2011 is a whiz at creating and formatting tables, thanks especially to the ribbon.

Adding tables to your document

Tables can be added to a document and the information filled in after the fact, or you can type your information in the document first and convert it to a table afterward.

The best way to add a table from scratch is by utilizing the ribbon:

1. **Click the Tables tab from within the ribbon.**

2. **Click the New button on the left side of the ribbon and create a table in one of two ways:**

   - Drag your cursor over the boxes, as shown in Figure 4.10, to quickly build a table and click the mouse after you select the desired number of columns and rows to create the table.

   - Select Insert Table from the pop-up menu and manually input the number of columns and rows you require.

If you prefer to type your information into the document first and then convert it to a table, follow these steps:

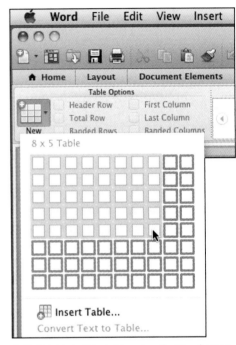

1. **Type your information into your document.** When typing your text be sure to use tabs (press the Tab key) between items in your columns so that Word knows where to automatically insert the columns. Press Enter at the end of each line of text to move to the next row, indicating to Word where a new row should be started.

4.10 Quickly build a table using the New button.

2. **Highlight all the text you want to convert to a table.**

3. **Click the Tables tab from the ribbon.**

4. **Click the New button and select Convert Text To Table.**

5. **After checking to make sure the information in the Convert Text To Table box is correct, click OK, and Word creates the table for you.**

Formatting tables

Formatting a table is actually fun with Word 2011. The ribbon makes it so simple to add columns and rows, and modify table styles and shading, that it feels almost automatic. To format a table, follow these steps:

1. **Click the table in your document.**

2. **Click the Tables tab in the ribbon.** When you select the Tables tab a new purple tab called Table Layout appears to the right of it (you learn more about it in a moment).

3. **You can make many cosmetic changes from within the Tables tab:**

   - Make certain columns and rows visible or invisible.

   - Select a style to apply to your table (see Figure 4.11).

   - Add or change colors for shading and border lines.

   - Draw or erase border lines.

4. **Click the Table Layout tab and you are rewarded with many ways to modify the contents of your table:**

4.11 Choose a table style from the within the ribbon.

   - The Settings section lets you make gridlines visible or invisible, and also allows you to change properties of the table, such as the way that text wraps around the table or how cells are aligned.

   - The Rows and Columns section lets you quickly add rows or columns to your tables. Place your cursor in the cell you want to work from and then use the Above, Below, Left, and Right buttons in the Rows and Columns section to add rows and columns to the table. Click the Delete button to quickly remove rows and columns from your table. How much easier can Microsoft make this?

   - The Merge section helps you merge two tables together, split a table into two, or split individual cells into even more cells.

   - The Cell Size section is great because you can easily resize cells automatically depending on the amount of text they contain, or you can make all rows and columns the same size regardless of content.

   - Place your cursor in a cell and use the tools in the Alignment section to align the text within the cell.

   - Use the items in the Data section to sort information automatically, total the numbers of cells you've selected, repeat header rows on every page of the document, or convert the table into text if you're tired of fiddling with tables.

AutoFormatting Can Handle the Dirty Work for You

Why do all the work when Word can do it for you? Word can automatically help you correct spelling mistakes, insert text into your documents to speed up their creation, or format your document in one fell swoop. Excessive use of these features may lead to the belief that everything in life should be this easy, so be judicious in your use of them. (I'm kidding, of course!)

AutoCorrect

AutoCorrect is the fancy name for Word's capability to detect words that you misspell and correct them on the fly. The concept is simple enough: If you type "teh," the AutoCorrect feature automatically changes it to "the." Some folks love this as it can save significant time over the course of a lengthy document, but still others find it annoying. It's simple enough to disable AutoCorrect should you fall into the latter category:

1. **Choose Tools ⇨ AutoCorrect.**

2. **Deselect the Replace text as you type check box.**

One function that most people overlook regarding AutoCorrect is that you can add words to the list that already comes with Word.

1. **Choose Tools ⇨ AutoCorrect.**

2. **Make sure that the Replace text as you type check box is selected.**

3. **Type the incorrect spelling of the word in the Replace field and type the correct spelling in the With field, as shown in Figure 4.12.**

4. **Click Add to add your new word to the list.** You can also delete words from the list by selecting the word and clicking Delete.

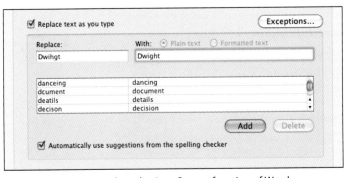

4.12 Add your own words to the AutoCorrect function of Word.

Genius

Do you like AutoCorrect, but wish that it would just leave some words alone? You can easily make exceptions to AutoCorrect. Choose Tools ➪ AutoCorrect, click Exceptions, click the Other Corrections tab and type the text you want to add as an exception to the Don't correct field. Click Add to finish making the exception.

AutoText

AutoText helps you quickly insert preconfigured text into your documents, such as a salutation, a closing, or pretty much anything else you want to add to your AutoText list.

1. **Place the cursor in your document where you want to insert the text.**

2. **Choose Insert ➪ AutoText.**

3. **From the AutoText submenu, select one of the preconfigured texts, as shown in Figure 4.13.**

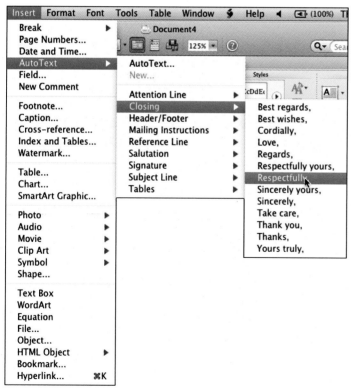

4.13 Choose an entry from the AutoText list to insert the text into your document.

As with AutoCorrect, you can add your own text to the AutoText list. Follow these steps:

1. **Choose Insert ⇨ AutoText ⇨ AutoText.**

2. **Click the AutoText tab in the AutoCorrect preferences window.**

3. **Type the text you want to add to the AutoText list in the Enter AutoText entries here field, and click Add.** You can also delete entries from the AutoText list by selecting them and clicking Delete.

AutoFormat

AutoFormat will do just what it says: format the text in your document automatically. Word can AutoFormat as you type, or it can perform the entire process at one time. AutoFormat is turned on by default, so if you notice Word beginning to insert bullet points out of the blue or add hyperlinks to Web addresses or e-mail addresses, AutoFormat is the culprit.

To AutoFormat a document

1. **Choose Format ⇨ AutoFormat.**

2. **In the AutoFormat dialog shown in Figure 4.14, you can select the AutoFormat now option to format the entire document now, or you can select the AutoFormat and review each change option.** I suggest the latter if you're not certain how the AutoFormat may affect the layout of your text.

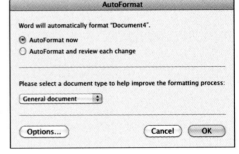

4.14 Choose to AutoFormat now or to review each change as it's made.

3. **Choose the type of document you want to format to help Word better understand how it should apply the changes.** Your choices are General Document, Letter, or Email.

4. **Click Options to further clarify what kind of elements you want Word to format.** For example, you can have Word automatically apply headings and bulleted lists to text or change fractions to actual fraction characters.

5. **Click OK to begin the automatic formatting of your document.** If you choose to review the changes, you are prompted to accept or reject all changes or you can click Review Changes to go through each change one at a time, giving your thumbs up or thumbs down as you go (see Figure 4.15).

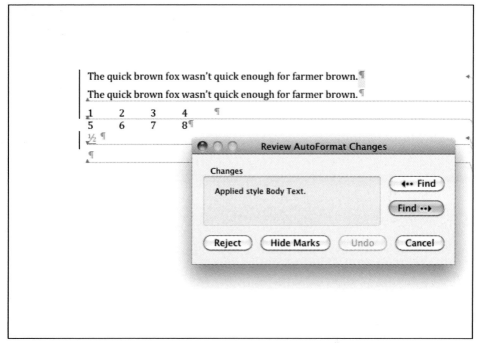

4.15 Review the changes made by AutoFormat one at a time to make sure everything looks the way you intend.

Using Themes, Styles, and Backgrounds

You're trying to make the perfect document, blending the right colors with the right fonts, but let's face it: You're no designer. Needless to say, this may take all night to complete. Have no fear; styles and themes are here!

Styles help you make quick changes to fonts and colors in your document, whether to single words or entire blocks of text. These styles can transform the look of text instantly and give your document that little added pop that gets the attention of your audience.

Themes help you to select a consistent look and feel across your document with just a single mouse click. Themes affect the fonts used for headings and body text, such as their color and style. Using the same theme across different types of documents, such as reports, newsletters, and brochures, gives them a professional and consistent look.

Applying styles to text

The ribbon makes it really easy to apply styles to the text in your document. Because the ribbon is within such easy reach, changing styles is quick and efficient, too. Applying styles to your document using the Toolbox is covered in Chapter 2, but here you use the ribbon exclusively. Note that it's not necessary to have text in your document in order to apply a style to it, but I would recommend it so you can immediately see what the style will look like.

1. **Highlight the text to which you want to apply a style, such as the title of your document.**

2. **Click the Home tab in the ribbon.** If you've not applied any styles to your document yet the Styles Gallery will show the Normal style. The Styles Gallery is found in the Styles section of the ribbon.

3. **Click the arrows on the right and left side of the Styles Gallery to scroll through the available styles.** Alternatively, click the arrow underneath the Styles Gallery to see a list of styles you can apply to the text you've highlighted, as shown in Figure 4.16.

4. **When you find the style you like, click it to apply the style to your text.**

To get the lowdown on the styles you're using in your document choose Format ⇨ Style. The Style dialog, shown in Figure 4.17, will tell you everything you need to know about the styles you've applied to your text.

- **The Styles pane shows you a list of styles you are using in your document.** Select one of the styles in the list and you will see previews for what the style looks like when applied to your document. The Description section gives you the scoop on fonts, line spacing, and more.

◉ **Click the Lists pop-up menu to only view the styles you are currently working with, view all available styles, or only those styles that you've created (see Chapter 2 for more on creating your own styles).**

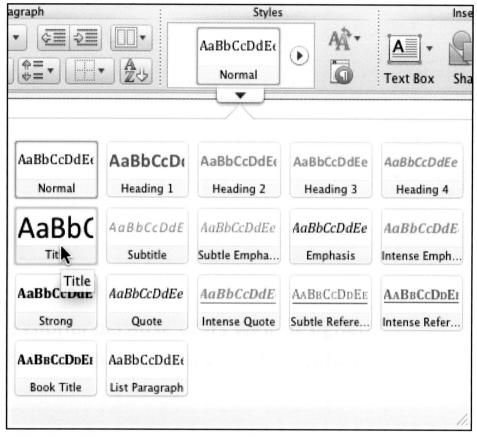

4.16 The Styles Gallery offers you many choices for adding some pizzazz to your document's text.

Choosing a theme for your document

Applying a theme to your document is so simple. Once again, the ribbon is there to make such tasks seem almost trivial, so let's get going.

To change the theme of your document, simply click the Themes button in the ribbon and select a theme from the Themes Gallery. The Revolution theme is selected in Figure 4.18. When you select the theme, the look of your entire document changes. Themes look at the styles in your document to determine how best to apply themselves. For example, if you have headings in your document Word knows which elements of the theme to apply to those headings.

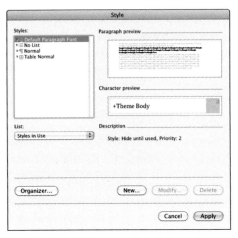

4.17 The Style dialog puts all the information you need about your styles in one easy-to-read window.

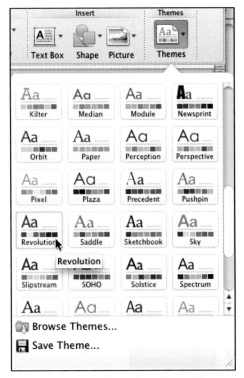

4.18 The Themes Gallery offers a host of themes for you to choose from.

Genius

Remember, a theme applies changes to your colors and fonts universally through-out your document. If you only want to change certain parts of your document, stick with using styles or manually make the changes you need.

You can make modifications to any theme and save them as a new theme if you like. Follow these steps:

1. **Change the layout view of your document to Publishing layout if it's not in Publishing layout already (click the Publishing button in the lower left of your doc-ument window).** If Word asks you if you want to create a new document or continue with the current, choose to continue.

2. **Click the Home tab in the ribbon.**

3. **Change the colors of your theme using the Colors button under the Themes section.**

4. **Change the fonts used in your theme using the Fonts button in the Themes section.**

5. **Click the Themes button and choose Save Theme.**

6. **In the Save Current Theme Window, give your theme a name, select a location in which to save it (Word's default folder, My Themes, is probably best), and click Save.**

7. **You can always apply your new theme by clicking the Themes button.** Your new theme will appear in the Custom section of the Themes Gallery.

Choosing backgrounds and fill effects

Another way to add splash to your documents is by using background colors. Sometimes a plain white background just won't do, so the ribbon comes through once again by giving you a really quick and easy way to apply colored backgrounds to your pages. You can also apply textures and other fills to your backgrounds and even use pictures as backgrounds. Follow these steps:

1. **Click the Layout tab in the ribbon.**

2. **Click the Colors button in the Page Backgrounds section to see a swatch of colors you can choose as your background color.** Select a color from the swatch and your entire page fills with that color.

3. **Select the More Colors option in the Colors button is you don't see the color you want in the Colors button.** You can create your own color using any of the tools in the Colors window. Click OK when finished to use your new color as the background.

You can add fill effects such as gradients and texture to your background by clicking the Colors button and choosing Fill Effects from the list. The Fill Effects dialog is chock full of fun tools to try:

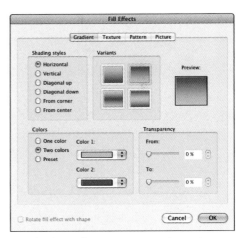

- **Gradient tab.** You can apply a two-color gradient to your background and adjust the directions and transparencies of the gradient, as shown in Figure 4.19.

- **Texture tab.** Change your background to look like marble or granite.

- **Pattern tab.** Add a neat pattern to the background. Experiment with both the Foreground and Background colors to get great combinations.

4.19 Apply gradients, textures, and more to your backgrounds using the Fill Effects dialog.

- **Picture tab.** You can actually use a picture as your background. Click Select Picture, browse the Mac for your picture, click Insert, and there you have it.

How Can I Use Word More Efficiently?

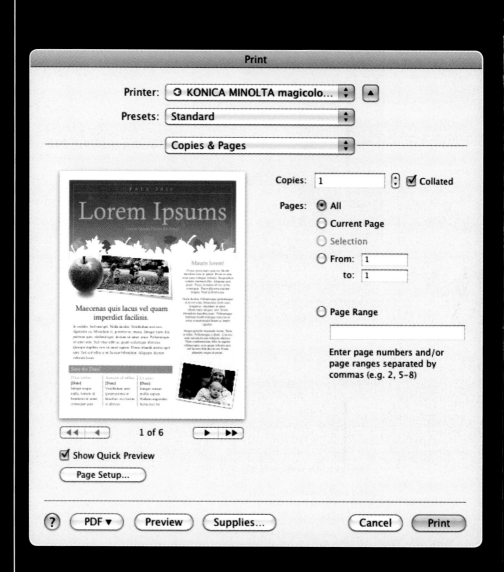

You have the basics and more advanced techniques of working with Word down pat by now. Next we're going to take a look at being more efficient with Word, including how-to's on viewing multiple documents, making toolbars that suit your needs, and saving and printing your Word files.

Viewing Different Sections of the Same Document

Sometimes when working with a lengthy document you may want to see two different sections to compare what you've written, check formatting continuity, or myriad other things. If your document is 20 pages long, scrolling from the top to the bottom to compare similar notes or quotes can be a time-consuming ordeal.

Word gives you a way to minimize, if not eliminate, this document hopping through the use of a split document. By splitting the document into two panes, you can view any two sections of it at one time, even copying and pasting elements between the two panes.

1. **Click the View menu to select Draft, Outline, or Print layout view, if you aren't using one of them already.** The split bar sits on top of the vertical scroll bar, as shown in Figure 5.1.

2. **Hold your mouse point over the split bar until the cursor changes to two arrows, one pointing down and the other pointing up.**

3. **Click and drag the split bar up or down to split the document into two panes.** You now have two panes and two sets of vertical and horizontal scroll bars, as shown in Figure 5.2.

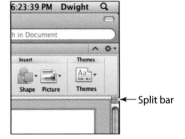

5.1 The split bar sits atop the vertical scroll bar.

4. **Scroll around within the panes to view the sections of the document you want to compare.**

5. **Go back to viewing a single pane by double-clicking the split bar.** You can also view the panes just as you left them by double-clicking the split bar again.

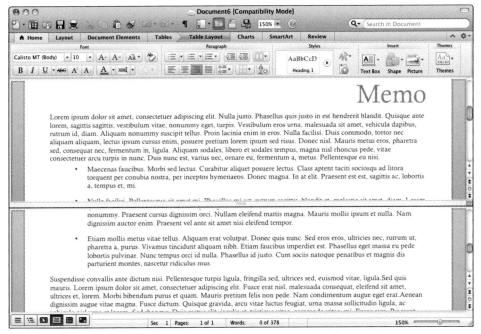

5.2 View different sections of the document at the same time by using the scroll bars in each pane.

Helpful Keyboard Shortcuts

Every computer user knows the old standby keyboard shortcuts such as ⌘+C for copying text, ⌘+V for pasting, and so on. Word certainly utilizes those shortcuts, as you know, but that's not even scratching the surface of the shortcuts that are available throughout the application. I'd like to show you some of the more popular shortcuts that apply to using Word functions more efficiently. Keyboard shortcuts may not seem like they help much if you're not proficient with them, but as you grow accustomed to using them and you memorize the necessary keystrokes, keyboard shortcuts can save you a world of time.

Tables 5.1–5.3 list commands and their keyboard shortcuts. The tables are divided into different types of tasks to make it easier to find a particular set of functions.

Note

Some of these keyboard shortcuts involve the use of function keys. If you have a laptop or compact keyboard, you may need to use the fn key to invoke some of these commands.

Table 5.1 Selecting and Editing Text and Graphics

Command	Keystrokes
Select one character to the right	Shift+Right arrow
Select one character to the left	Shift+Left arrow
Select one word to the right	Shift+Option+Right arrow
Select one word to the left	Shift+Option+Left arrow
Select text from cursor to the end of the line	⌘+Shift+Right arrow
Select text from cursor to the beginning of a line	⌘+Shift+Left arrow
Select one line down	Shift+Down arrow
Select one line up	Shift+Up arrow
Select text from cursor to the end of a paragraph	⌘+Shift+Down arrow
Select text from cursor to the beginning of a paragraph	⌘+Shift+Up arrow
Select all the text in a document	⌘+A
Select text from cursor to the beginning of a document	⌘+Shift+Home
Select text from cursor to the end of a document	⌘+Shift+End
Delete one character to the left	Delete
Delete one word to the left	⌘+Delete
Undo the last action you took	⌘+Z

Table 5.2 Formatting Text

Command	Keystrokes
Change a font	⌘+Shift+F
Increase font size	⌘+Shift+>
Decrease font size	⌘+Shift+<
Increase font size by 1 point	⌘+]
Decrease font size by 1 point	⌘+[
Change the case of a letter	Shift+F3
Change text to bold	⌘+B
Add underline to text	⌘+U
Add underline to only words (not spaces)	⌘+Shift+W
Change text to italic	⌘+I

Whoa! That's Not What I Expected to Happen!

Sometimes a keyboard shortcut in Word (or any other application, for that matter) may already be used by the Mac OS to perform tasks other than those intended by Microsoft, and when you press the keystrokes you get an outcome that isn't what you expected. You can correct this conflict by changing the key assignments for the Mac OS.

In Mac OS X 10.6 Snow Leopard, you can edit, add, or remove keyboard shortcuts in this manner:

1. **Click the Apple menu in the upper-left corner of your screen and select System Preferences from the list.**

2. **Click the Keyboard icon.**

3. **In the Keyboard preferences pane, click the Keyboard Shortcuts tab.**

4. **Find the shortcut you want to change, double-click it, and then press the key sequence you want to use for the shortcut.** You can also use the Add (+) and Delete (–) buttons, respectively, to add or remove keyboard shortcuts.

Table 5.3 Insert Special Characters

Command	Keystrokes
Insert a page break	Shift+Enter
Insert a line break	Shift+Return
Insert a copyright symbol	Option+G
Insert a trademark symbol	Option+2
Insert a registered trademark symbol	Option+R
Insert a column break	⌘+Shift+Return

Creating Customized Toolbars

The menu, Standard toolbar, and the ribbon combine to place many of the most-used features and tools in Word within easy reach for you, but you may want to customize the menus and toolbars to streamline them with the tasks that you perform most often.

To customize a menu, follow these steps:

1. **Choose View, hold your mouse over Toolbars, ⇨ Customize Toolbars and Menus.**

2. **Under the Toolbars and Menus tab, make sure the check box is selected next to Menu Bar.**

3. **Click the Commands tab.**

4. **Choose a category on the left side of the window.**

5. **Find the command you need from within the Commands pane and drag and drop it into the menu of your choice, as shown in Figure 5.3.** The Menu Bar editing window is found just beneath the actual Menu Bar.

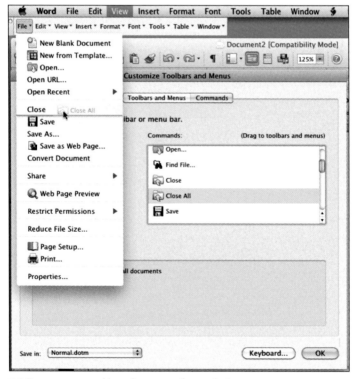

5.3 Drop a command into the menu of your choice.

6. **To remove a command from a menu, just drag and drop it outside of the menu, using the Menu bar editing window, of course.**

To customize the Standard toolbar, follow these steps:

1. **Choose View, hold your mouse over Toolbars, ➪ Customize Toolbars and Menus.**

2. **Under the Toolbars and Menus tab, make sure the check box is selected next to Standard.**

3. **Click the Commands tab and choose a category on the left side of the window.**

4. **Find the command you want within the Commands pane and drag and drop it onto the toolbar at the location you desire, as shown in Figure 5.4.**

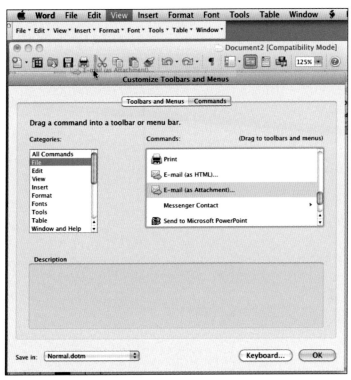

5.4 Place a new command between other command icons in the toolbar.

5. **To remove a command from the toolbar, just drag and drop it outside of the toolbar.**

Genius

By default, the Standard toolbar only displays icons for particular functions, and you can see what the icons represent by holding your mouse point over them. Microsoft does this to save screen real estate, but if you're just getting used to Word for the first time, or even if you're a Word veteran, you may rather see the names of the functions right along with the icons in the toolbar. To do so, choose View, hold your mouse over Toolbars, ➪ Customize Toolbars and Menus, click the Toolbars and Menus tab, and select the Show Icon and Text check box.

Saving Word Documents

Saving a Word document isn't quite as simple as it was back in the day. Now there are so many formats to be concerned with and compatibility issues to worry about that you have to have a good grasp of the options Word makes available for you. The following sections look at the options you have for saving a document as well as Word's capability to save your document as a Web page.

What format to use?

Once upon a time, only a small array of options was available when it came to saving your document. Now, saving your document can be a little like taking a shot in the dark, especially if you are sharing your document with others who may be using different versions of Word than you are or are using altogether different operating systems.

Table 5.4 lists the various formats in which you can save your document, the extension of the format, and a concise definition of each.

Table 5.4 File Formats in Word 2011

Format	Extension	Description
Word Document	.docx	The is the default document format for Word 2008 and Word 2011 for Mac, as well as Word 2007 and Word 2010 for Windows. This file is XML based.
Word 97-2004 Document	.doc	This is the format that's compatible with Word 98 through Word 2004 for Mac, as well as with Word 97 through Word 2003 for Windows.
Word Template	.dotx	Saves the document as a template that can be used to create new documents. This format preserves document content and settings and is XML based. This template version is compatible with Word 2008 and Word 2011 for Mac, as well as Word 2007 and Word 2010 for Windows.
Word 97-2004 Template	.dot	Saves the document as a template that can be used to create new documents. This format preserves document content and settings. This template version is compatible with Word 97 through Word 2003 for Windows and Word 98 through Word 2004 for Mac.
Rich Text Format	.rtf	This format is widely compatible with other text editors, and retains much of the generic formatting, such as fonts and colors.
Plain Text	.txt	Discards all formatting and saves the document as strictly plain text. Use this option only if you need to share the document with others who only have access to very limited text editors.

Format	Extension	Description
Web Page	.htm	Exports your document so that it will display in a Web browser.
PDF	.pdf	Saves your document as a PDF file, which is a cross-platform file format. PDF retains the look of your document, including formatting and graphics.
Word Macro-Enabled Document	.docm	This format preserves VBA macro code in your document. These XML-based documents only run in Word 2011 for Mac; they will not work in Word 2008 for Mac.
Word Macro-Enabled Template	.dotm	This format preserves VBA macro code in your document, and saves the document as a template. These XML-based documents only run in Word 2011 for Mac; they will not work in Word 2008 for Mac.
Word XML Document	.xml	Exports your document to an XML file, converting all formatting and text into XML. This version is compatible with Word 2007 and Word 2010 for Windows.
Word 2003 XML Document	.xml	Exports your document to an XML file, converting all formatting and text into XML. This version is compatible with Word 2003 for Windows.
Single File Web Page	.mht	Your document will be saved as a single HTML file that can be viewed with any Web browser and includes all elements of the page within it, such as graphics and fonts.
Word Document Stationery	.doc	Saves a document with the Finder flag set to Stationery Pad. This way, when the document is opened it opens as a new, untitled document.
Word 4.0-6.0/95 Compatible	.rtf	This saves your document in a format that is compatible with much older versions of Word, such as Word 4.0 through Word 6.0 for Mac as well as Word 6.0 and Word 95 for Windows.

Now that you have an understanding of the format choices available, here's how to save your document:

1. **Choose File ⇨ Save (or Save As, if the document has been saved before or you want to save it in a format different from the original).** The Save window opens.

2. **Give your document a title.**

3. **Choose a location in which to save your document.** If the arrow in the blue box next to the document title field is pointing down, you can select a location from the Where pop-up menu. If you'd like to browse your Mac for the location, as shown in Figure 5.5, click the blue box; the arrow will point up and you will see your Mac's hard drive on the left side of the window.

4. **Select a format from the Format pop-up menu.** Refer to Table 5.5 earlier to find the format that best suits your needs.

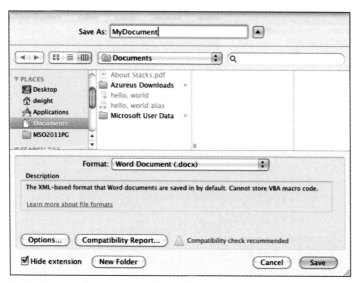

5.5 Saving your document can be an adventure if you're not familiar with your options.

5. **Click Options to open the Save preferences pane.** Here you can choose from a range of advanced save options, such as creating a backup copy of the file or saving a preview picture with the document. Click OK to return to the main Save window.

6. **Click Compatibility Report to have Word scan your document to see if there are any compatibility issues with older versions of Word, which is always a good idea if you need to share your document with others.** Should Word find some compatibility issues, you can click OK to check out its findings or you can click Continue Saving to do just that.

7. **Click Save to save your document to the specified location.**

Using the Save As Web Page feature

The Save As Web Page option in the File menu gets a special nod here because the options involved with saving a document as a Web page are a bit different than saving to all the other formats. That's why Microsoft makes it available in the File menu as a stand-alone selection, even though you could access the same options in the standard Save or Save As dialogs by selecting Web Page as your format.

1. **Choose File ➪ Save As Web Page.**

2. **In the Save As dialog, give the document a title and choose a location to save it.**

3. **Decide whether to save the entire file into HTML or only the display information by clicking the appropriate radio button.**

4. **Click Web Options to open the Web Options dialog, shown in Figure 5.6.** From there you can include a title for your Web page and any keywords that may help people find your page when doing a Web search with a search engine like Google or Yahoo!, decide a target screen size for your document, and determine the document's encoding. Click OK when ready.

5. **Click Save to save your document as a Web page in the location you specified.**

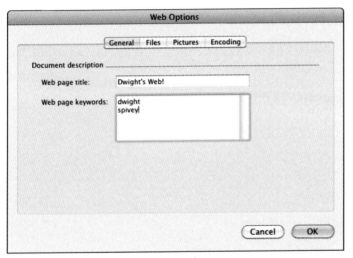

5.6 Saving your document can be an adventure if you're not familiar with your options.

Printing Your Word Documents

For many of us, good old-fashioned paper is still the way to share your documents with others, and that's where this section of the chapter comes in handy. Try as we might to fashion a paperless society, it just isn't going to happen any time soon. While it's okay for reports and the like to be digital only, books, postcards, and brochures may be better off in the far more personal mediums of paper and ink (or toner).

To print your document to your favorite laser or inkjet printer, follow these steps:

1. **Choose File ⇨ Print, or press ⌘+P to open the Print dialog, as shown in Figure 5.7.**

2. **Select a printer to print your document using the Printer pop-up menu.**

3. **Under the Copies & Pages pop-up menu, select the number of copies you want and determine which pages you want to print.** If you don't see the Copies & Pages pop-up menu, click the blue box containing the black arrow located just to the right of the Printer pop-up menu at the top of the dialog.

5.7 The Print dialog is where you set printing options for the document and send it on its merry way to the printer.

4. **Click Page Setup in the lower-left corner of the Print dialog to make sure you have the correct printer and paper selected, and the correct page orientation (see Figure 5.8).** Click OK to return to the main Print dialog.

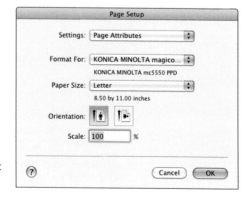

5.8 Page Setup is where you can select the paper options for your print job.

5. **On the left side of the Print dialog, Word offers a preview of what the document should look like when it prints.** If the preview doesn't look correct, click Cancel and try to resolve any issues you may have spotted.

6. **Click the Copies & Pages pop-up menu and you will see a list of all the printing options afforded by Mac OS X, Word, and your printer manufacturer (your options will most likely differ from mine).** For the purposes of our book, I stick to looking at the options offered by Word, so select Microsoft Word from the list to see options offered by Word (as shown in Figure 5.9).

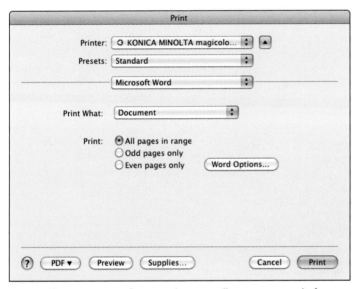

5.9 Word has its own set of options that you will want to peruse before sending your print job.

7. **Using the Print What pop-up menu, decide which elements of the document to print, such as printing the document only, printing the document with markups, printing only the properties of your document, and more.**

8. **Select whether to print all pages within the range you specified under Copies & Pages, or to just print even or odd pages.**

9. **Click Word Options to see the Print preferences pane.** From here you can make several options for printing your Word document such as reversing the print order of the pages, printing any hidden text, printing background colors and images, and more (refer to Chapter 2 for more information on these options). Click OK to return to the main Print dialog.

10. **Make any other settings you need that are specific to your printer, and click Print to print your document.**

How Do I Create Spreadsheets with Excel?

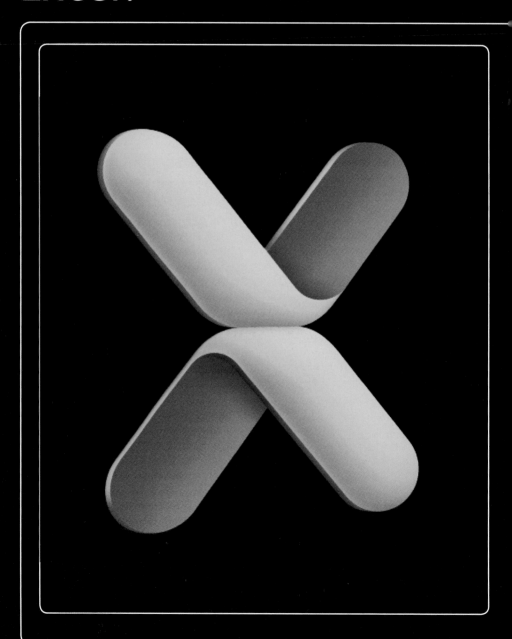

Excel is Microsoft's rock-solid Office application that has become an icon as much as a super-great spreadsheet factory. Excel is nearly the de facto tool for budgeting, reporting, accounting, analyzing, and tracking of data. In this chapter, I introduce you to Excel 2011 for Mac, and you get to know its interface and common functions. A bit of trivia: Excel made its debut in 1985, not on a Microsoft Windows operating system, but the Mac OS!

Getting Around in Excel

To know Excel is to know its interface and the tools that are at your disposal. Those tools are plentiful throughout Excel, and that's stating it lightly. Excel may be one of the most powerful and feature-laden applications of any kind on the market. Because Excel is such a huge application and its massive capabilities couldn't possibly be fully covered in this tome, I look at many of Excel's more common features so you can hit the ground running. Figure 6.1 points out the major elements of the Excel interface and Table 6.1 responds with brief explanations of each.

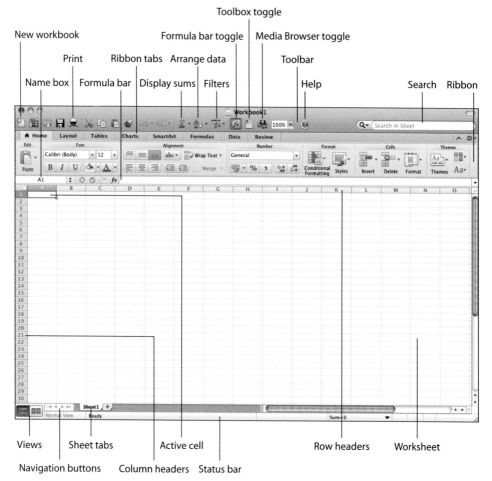

6.1 Get to know Excel's interface.

Note

Some items in the toolbar and ribbon function the same in Excel as they do in Word, and because these are covered in previous chapters they aren't duplicated here.

Table 6.1 Excel Interface Landmarks

Element	Function
New workbook	Create a new workbook.
Print	Print the currently active worksheet to your default printer.
Display sums	Displays the sum of cells you have selected in the worksheet.
Arrange data	Click to quickly sort your data according to criteria you set.
Filters	Click to view only the data that fits the criteria you select.
Formula bar toggle	Show or hide the Formula bar.
Toolbox toggle	Show or hide the Toolbox.
Media Browser toggle	Show or hide Media Browser.
Help	Open Excel's help system for instruction with various tasks.
Search	Type a search term to find an item in the currently active worksheet.
Formula bar	Displays the data or formula stored in the currently active cell. You can type or edit data, a formula, or a function in a cell using the Formula bar.
Name box	Displays the name of the currently active cell. For example, if the active cell is in row 2 and column C, its name would be C2.
Status bar	Keeps you informed of the status of the worksheet you are currently working in.
Views	Toggle between Normal and Page Layout views.
Sheet tabs	Click to select a sheet to work with.
Row headers	Identifies a row.
Column headers	Identifies a column.
Active cell	The cell you are currently working in.
Navigation buttons	Move back and forth among worksheets.

Setting Excel Preferences

Your attitude should be that this is your copy of Excel, darn it, and it will work the way you want it to! Okay, maybe you shouldn't cop an attitude with a piece of software, but you get the point that Excel should do what you need and you shouldn't be bending to its will. Excel has a large set of preferences that you can modify to fit your needs.

To open Excel's preferences, choose Excel ➪ Preferences, or press ⌘+, (that's the Command key combined with the comma key). The Excel Preferences window is divided into 16 tabs under three groups:

- Authoring
- Formulas and Lists
- Sharing and Privacy

Some options are discussed in greater detail later in this chapter and in upcoming chapters, but for now let's briefly take a look at each one.

Note

While some preferences may warrant more time than others, you can always get a quick definition of what an option is for in the preference panes. Hold your mouse pointer over a topic or option in a preference pane and a short description of it appears in the Description box at the bottom of the pane.

- **General.** The General tab (see Figure 6.2) handles just what it implies — general items that apply to Excel as a whole. Let's take a gander at some of the major points in this tab:

  - **Use R1C1 reference style.** Excel uses the A1 reference style by default, which is to say that cells are named by their column letter and row number, in that order. R1C1 uses numbers for both rows and columns and lists the row number before the column number.

  - **Provide feedback with sound.** This option enables sounds for errors, opening and closing files, and so on. The reason I mention this here is that if you enable or disable this option it is not specific to Excel; all Office applications are affected by this setting.

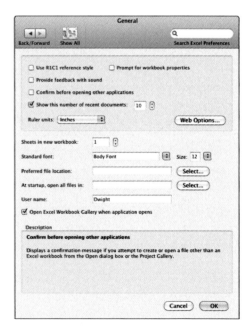

6.2 The General tab gives Excel good starting points when first launched and when creating new workbooks.

- **Web Options.** This button allows you to detail how Excel files will appear when viewed in a Web browser, such as Safari or Firefox.

- **Other options.** You can also set the default number of worksheets for new workbooks, define a standard font for new workbooks, specify a preferred file location, to open certain files immediately upon startup, and determine whether or not to open the Excel Workbook Gallery (more on that later) when Excel first launches.

- **View.** Tell Excel how you want workbooks to display on-screen, as well as what other elements join it.

  - **Settings.** Decide whether to show the formula bar and status bar by default, and whether to use Normal or Page Layout view as default.

  - **Window options.** Select the check boxes next to the items you want to appear within your new workbooks. The Color pop-up menu lets you choose a default color for gridlines (Automatic means gray).

  - **Comments and objects.** Indicate what types of comments and objects display in workbooks in the [For comments, show] and [For objects, show] sections.

- **Edit.** This tab determines some of Excel's behaviors while you are editing a workbook/worksheet. Each option affects editing in all Excel workbooks, and they are fairly self-explanatory, but there are a few that I want to touch upon:

  - **After pressing Return, move selection.** This option will cause an adjoining cell to become active when you press the Return key while in the currently active cell. For example, if you're working in cell A1 and press Return, one of the adjoining cells, A2 or B1, becomes active. Determine which cell is to become active by setting a direction in the Direction pop-up menu.

  - **Preserve display of dates entered with four-digit years.** Excel likes to display the last two digits in a year by default. For example, if you type 10/10/2010 the date will change to 10/10/10. Selecting this option makes Excel display 2010 as 2010. One example of when this option comes in handy would be if you are building a spreadsheet containing historical dates. If you typed a date of 10/10/1899, by default Excel would truncate it to 10/10/99, which would lead one to wonder which 99 you're talking about (1999, 1699, 2099?).

- **AutoCorrect.** This tab, shown in Figure 6.3, lets you customize how Excel corrects text automatically as you type. The Replacement list shows words that Excel will replace with another word should you misspell or type them a certain way. For example, if you type (c) Excel automatically transforms that text into a copyright symbol (©). I like that you can add your own words to the list so that when I constantly misspell my own name Excel replaces it with the correct spelling.

● **Chart.** Clicking this tab tells Excel how you want it to plot charts, such as how it should deal with cells that are invisible or contain no data. I cover these options in detail in Chapter 8.

● **Calculation dialog.** Use this to determine how Excel calculates formulas and data within a worksheet or an entire workbook. The available options are quite clear as to their functionality, but I want to touch on the two very visible buttons in the upper-right corner:

○ **Calc Now.** This is a nuke option for Excel, manually forcing it to calculate absolutely all formulas and data in all open worksheets. This button only works when you select Manually in the Calculate sheets section.

○ **Calc Sheet.** Clicking this button only calculates the currently active sheet, leaving all others to their own devices.

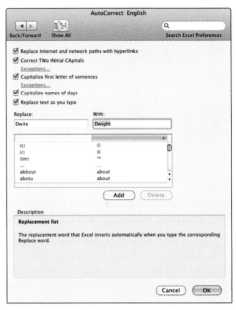

6.3 AutoCorrect helps Excel know which text it should automatically correct when you make a mistake.

Genius

If you don't want to have to come back to the Calculation preferences pane every time to perform a manual calculation, you will want to become familiar with the keyboard shortcut for Calc Now: ⌘-= (the Command key combined with the Equal key). If you're used to working with Excel on a PC you probably know that F9 is a popular shortcut for the Calc Now feature, but if you try that on a Mac you may be surprised when all your open windows display at once on your screen because F9 is a keyboard shortcut for Mac OS X's Exposé feature.

● **Error Checking.** This dialog, seen in Figure 6.4, allows you to modify how Excel checks your workbooks for errors.

○ You can enable or disable background error checking, reset errors that you've ignored, and change the alert color Excel uses to flag cells that contain those naughty little errors.

- The Rules section lets you apply all or some of the rules that Excel automatically looks for in your workbooks. While they are all enabled by default, you can disable any that you want (at your own peril).

- **Custom Lists.** This dialog shows lists that you created (maybe not yet, but in the near future) as well as a few that come standard with Excel. These lists are used when you need to automatically fill cells or sort data in various ways. For example, if you need to type the days of the week into a series of cells, don't manually type in every day for every cell; use the days-of-the-week list provided by Microsoft already. There's more on custom lists later.

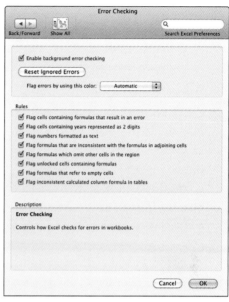

6.4 We all make mistakes, but Excel is all too happy to help you find them within your workbooks.

- **AutoComplete.** This is a timesaving feature of Excel that automatically completes items in cells for you as you type. AutoComplete uses information you typed into previous cells in a column to take an educated guess at what you want to type in the active cell. This dialog helps you control how AutoComplete goes about its tasks.

- **Tables.** This dialog lets you tell Excel how to behave when using tables in a workbook. Nothing magic about this one.

- **Filter.** The only option available in this dialog is Show dates in groups. When filtering columns in a worksheet that contain dates, the Filter dialog shows those dates as grouped by the year, month, and day when this option is enabled.

- **The Save dialog offers two options:**

    - **Save preview picture with new files.** When you save your workbooks, Excel also provides a preview picture that is helpful in recognizing the document when you go to open it or view it in the Excel Workbook Gallery.

    - **Save AutoRecover information after this number of minutes.** Set the number of minutes to have Excel save information about your workbook. This information doesn't replace the Save feature, but it does preserve documents at the specified interval so that they can be recovered in the event of a crash.

● **Compatibility.** This dialog, shown in Figure 6.5, helps your spreadsheets created in Excel 2011 play nice with earlier versions of Excel for Mac or Windows. The following sections are included:

○ **Compatibility Report.** This section lets you enable a compatibility check. Clicking Reset Ignored Issues causes Excel to check the active workbook for issues you may have ignored in previous compatibility checks. Click Reset All Issues to force a completely new compatibility check on the currently active workbook.

○ **Transition.** This section allows you to set the default format for saving your spreadsheets. Select the Transition formula evaluation check box to help Excel open Lotus 1-2-3 documents without destroying the data they contain.

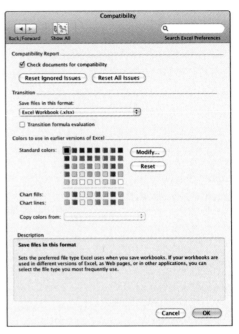

6.5 Make sure that your Excel 2011 spreadsheet will play nice with older versions of Excel.

○ **Colors to use in earlier versions of Excel.** Earlier versions of Excel may not be able to display the same colors that you used in the creation of a spreadsheet in Excel 2011. You can still determine how those colors display in older versions of Excel using the options in this section.

● **Security.** This dialog is where you tell Excel whether you want your personal information saved within spreadsheets you create and whether to warn you if a spreadsheet you are opening contains macros. If the file contains macros you are given the option to turn them off before opening the file.

● **Feedback.** This dialog allows you to enable or disable the Customer Experience Improvement Program. Enabling this program allows Microsoft to anonymously collect information about your Mac's hardware and how you utilize your software. As I say for all Office applications that offer this program, please read the information in this dialog carefully before enabling or disabling it.

- **Ribbon.** This dialog is where you can enable or disable the ribbon, determine whether it opens in expanded form when a workbook opens, and customize its appearance.

What Are Worksheets and Workbooks?

Sometimes folks use the terms *worksheet* and *workbook* interchangeably (including many who are longtime Excel users), but they are not one and the same. Let's get a quick understanding of their differences and then see a couple of ways to create new workbooks.

A worksheet is a single sheet containing data, formulas, and functions. This is where you do all your legwork in Excel. When you first open an Excel file the window you see containing all the gridlines is a worksheet (sometimes referred to as just a sheet).

A workbook contains multiple worksheets, much like a regular book contains multiple pages. You cannot have a worksheet without a workbook to contain it. Workbooks generally pertain to a certain subject, while the worksheets it contains are geared to specific topics within that subject. For example, you may have a workbook for your personal budget, and contained within that workbook you have separate worksheets for bank accounts, bills, and other financial considerations.

Create a blank workbook in one of three ways:

- **Click the New workbook button in the toolbar.**
- **Press ⌘+N.**
- **Choose File ➪ New Workbook.**

You can also use the Excel Workbook Gallery to create new workbooks. The Excel Workbook Gallery contains tons of ready-made templates that you can plug your own data into to generate instant professional spreadsheets. The Excel Workbook Gallery, seen in Figure 6.6, opens automatically by default when you first launch Excel 2011.

Templates list

Recent workbooks   Selection of templates

Search field

Template preview

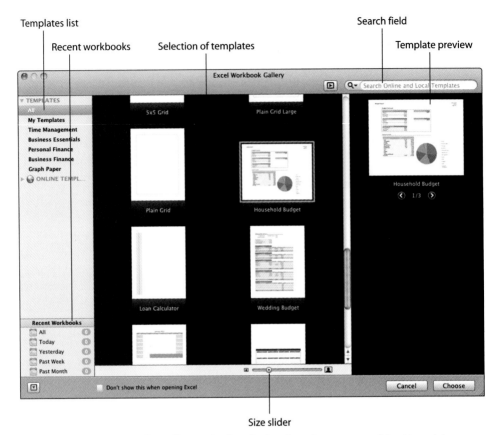

Size slider

6.6 The Excel Workbook Gallery offers scads of professional, ready-to-go spreadsheet templates you can use.

To create a new workbook using the Excel Workbook Gallery, follow these steps:

1. **If you aren't launching Excel for the first time today, press ⌘+Shift+P to open the Gallery.**

2. **Browse the Gallery for just the right template for your project.** Use the size slider to get a closer view of the templates listed.

3. **Select the template that strikes your fancy and view its preview.**

4. **Click Choose in the lower-right corner of the Gallery window to open your new workbook.**

Genius Don't see a template that strikes your fancy? Click the arrow next to Online Templates and you will see dozens of new templates that reside on Microsoft's servers and are accessible via the Internet. You are free to use these templates just as you are those that came in the box with Excel.

Using Cells, Rows, and Columns

One thing is for sure: You won't have much of a spreadsheet without cells, rows, and columns. Whether you're a longtime Excel user, a switcher from Windows to Mac, or you've never seen a spreadsheet in your life, learning how to implement data into cells (or getting a refresher) is a must.

Adding information to a cell

Blank cells are actually useful in some spreadsheets, but chances are you didn't purchase Excel so you could create beautiful spreadsheets with no information in them. A cell can contain anything you want in terms of numbers and text. Follow these steps:

1. **Click the cell in which you want to add information.**

2. **Type the information you want to add to the cell.**

3. **Press Return to finish adding information to the cell and move to the next cell.**

You can also type information in a cell by using the formula bar. Follow these steps:

1. **Click the cell in which you want to add information.**

2. **Click inside the formula bar, type the required information, and press Return.**

Genius You can type more than one line of text in a cell using line breaks. To create a line break within a cell, press Control+Option+Return.

That's just about as simple as anything can get when it comes to working with a computer. How about typing dates and times in cells or using decimal points? Those get a tad more complicated, but they're certainly nothing to fret about.

Typing dates and times in a cell is a snap. Follow these steps:

1. **Click the cell in which you want to add the date or time.**

2. **Type the date or time in the following manners:**

   - **Type the time (example: 3:00) followed by a space, and then type a or p to specify AM or PM.** If you are basing your time on a 12-hour clock, Excel defaults to AM unless you tell it otherwise.

   - **Type dates using slash marks or hyphens to separate the month, day, and year of the date.** For example, for January 1, 2001, type 1/1/2001 or 1-Jan-2001. If you type a full date, such as January 1, 2001, into the formula bar and press Return, Excel automatically renders it as 1-Jan-01.

Genius

Type the current date into a cell by pressing Control+; (semicolon), and the current timeby pressing Contol+Shift+; (semicolon).

What if you want to use a different format than 1-Jan-01 or 1/1/2001? Follow these steps:

1. **Right-click the cell containing the date you want to format.**

2. **Select Format Cells from the resulting pop-up menu.**

3. **In the Format Cells dialog (see Figure 6.7), click the Number tab.**

4. **Select Date from the Category list on the left side of the dialog.**

5. **Scroll through the list of formats in the Type box.**

6. **Select the format you want to use and click OK.**

Genius

What if you want the dates and times in your cells to reflect the current date and time? To display today's date, type =TODAY() in the cell and press Return. To display both today's date and time, type =NOW() and press Return. These values are updated each time the worksheet is recalculated; recalculation happens each time you open a worksheet or manually recalculate by pressing the ⌘+= (Equal).

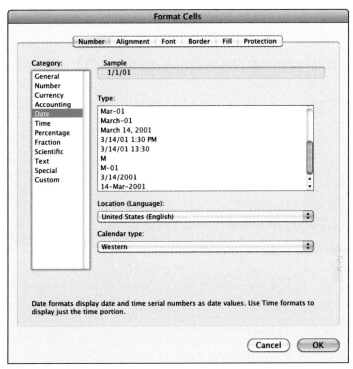

6.7 Change the format for dates and times in the Format Cells dialog.

Moving and copying cells

If you type information into the wrong cell, how do you resolve it? If you need to copy information from one cell to another, how do you do that? Both issues are easy enough to resolve.

To move the information from one cell to another, follow these steps:

1. **Click the cell containing the informa-tion you want to move.**

2. **Hold your mouse pointer over the cell's borders until you see the pointer turn from a cross hair into a hand.**

3. **Click and drag the cell from its current location to the new one and drop it (let go of the mouse button), as shown in Figure 6.8.**

6.8 Move information from one cell to another by dragging and dropping it.

113

To copy information from one cell to another, simply perform the same steps but hold down the Option key while clicking, dragging, and dropping the information.

Of course, you can always revert to common Cut, Copy, and Paste commands to perform these tasks as well.

Genius

You can quickly copy data in a cell to an empty cell immediately to its right or immediately below it. Select the empty cell to the right or below the cell whose data you want to copy. Press Control+R to copy the data to the right, or press Control+D to copy data to the cell below.

Moving around within a worksheet

You can move around in your worksheet by pointing and clicking your mouse, but that's not always the most efficient way of moving from cell to cell or from the end of a spreadsheet to the top. Keyboard shortcuts help you keep your hands on the keyboard so you can quickly enter information into cells. Table 6.2 lists keyboard shortcuts that will help you navigate a worksheet with ease.

Table 6.2 Keyboard Shortcuts for Fast Worksheet Navigation

Keyboard shortcut	To move...
Left arrow	One cell left
Right arrow	One cell right
Up arrow	One cell up
Down arrow	One cell down
Control+Home	To top of worksheet (cell A1)
Control+End	To last cell containing data
Control+Down arrow	To end of data in a column
Control+Up arrow	To beginning of data in a column
Control+Right arrow	To end of data in a row
Control+Left arrow	To beginning of data in a row
Tab	One column to the right
Shift+Tab	One column to the left

Finding and replacing information in cells

If you have a huge spreadsheet, finding information can be a lengthy and trying process if you simply scan every cell with the naked eye. Give your pupils a break and let Excel do the work, if you know what you are looking for, that is. Here's how to find items within a spreadsheet, and even replace them with other information if you want. Follow these steps:

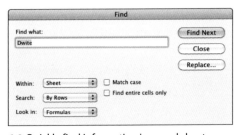

1. **Open the workbook in which you want to find information.**

2. **Press ⌘+F to open a Find dialog, much like the one in Figure 6.9.**

6.9 Quickly find information in a worksheet or the entire workbook.

3. **Type the information you want to search for in the Find what field.**

4. **Use the pop-up selections at the bottom left of the window to direct your search.** You can use the following options to break down your search:

    ● **Within.** You can search within the currently active sheet or the entire workbook.

    ● **Search.** Search by rows or columns.

    ● **Look in.** You can direct your search to look in formulas, values, or comments.

5. **Click Find Next to find your search term within the workbook or worksheet.**

To find information and automatically replace it with new data, follow these steps:

1. **Open the workbook in which you want to find information.**

2. **Press ⌘+F to open a Find dialog.**

3. **Click Replace to transform the Find dialog into a Replace dialog, as shown in Figure 6.10.**

4. **Type the information you want to search for in the Find what field, and type the information you want to replace it with in the Replace with field.**

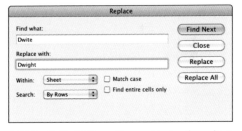

6.10 Easily find information and instantly replace it with new data using the Replace dialog.

5. **Use the pop-up selections at the bottom left of the window to direct your search:**

    ● **Within.** You can search by rows or columns.

    ● **Search.** You can direct your search to look in formulas, values, or comments.

6. **Click Find Next to find your search term within the workbook or worksheet.**

7. **Automatically replace it with the new information by clicking Replace.**

8. **If there are multiple instances of the information you're searching for you can replace all instances at one time by clicking Replace All.** If the nuclear option isn't for you, simply click Find Next to find the next instance of the information and decide whether to replace it by clicking Replace. Click Find Next again to continue the process.

9. **Click Close when you finish your hunt.**

Editing and deleting cells, rows, and columns

Editing a cell isn't complicated, I promise, and neither is deleting a cell, but neither is quite as simple as waving a magic wand.

You can edit a cell in a couple of ways:

- **Double-click within the cell and type the new information as needed.**

- **Click the cell you want to edit, click the formula bar, and begin adding the new information. Boom! Done.**

Deleting a cell can be the tiniest bit more difficult than editing one. Follow these steps:

1. **Right-click the cell that's about to get the axe and select Delete from the pop-up menu to open the Delete window.**

2. **Determine how the deletion of the cell will affect the rest of the spreadsheet using the four options available:** shift cells up, shift cells left, delete the entire row, or delete the entire column the cell is contained in.

3. **Click OK to delete the cell according to the option you choose in the Delete window.**

Caution Be alert when deleting a cell! Make certain this is the cell, row, or column you really want to delete. If you delete the wrong cell, row, or column you could throw the rest of the spreadsheet completely out of kilter, especially if information in that particular cell is used to calculate data for other cells.

Inserting additional cells, rows, and columns

Don't be a hater and just delete stuff all the time. Expand your horizons and your spreadsheet by adding new cells, rows, and columns.

To insert a cell into your worksheet, follow these steps:

1. **Click the cell where you want to insert a new one.** You can also select a range of cells. Note that the number of cells you select will be the number of cells you will be adding during this exercise. If you need to insert three new cells then be sure to select three cells in the worksheet.

2. **Choose Insert ⇨ Cells.**

3. **Select an option for placement of your new cell(s) from the Insert window, as shown in Figure 6.11, and click OK.**

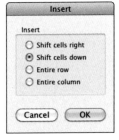

6.11 Choose one of these placement options when adding a new cell or group of cells.

To insert new rows or columns, follow these steps:

1. **Decide where you want to insert the new row or column and select the row or column that already exists there.**

2. **Choose Insert ⇨ Rows or Insert ⇨ Columns.**

Note

New rows or columns are placed either above or to the left of the cell you selected in the worksheet. If there are other cells in the worksheet that referenced the cells that were moved when you inserted the new row or column, the references are updated with the new position of the cells. For example, if the E10 cell in your worksheet referenced C1, but C1 changed to D1 when you inserted a new column, the reference in E10 is automatically changed to D1.

Using AutoFill

Excel's AutoFill function allows you to automatically fill worksheet cells with data. AutoFill can fill cells with many different types of data, whether it's data that is stored in other cells already or data that follows a pattern, such as the days of the week or a series of numbers (1,2,3, and so on.).

Here are some of the more common ways to utilize AutoFill:

- **To automatically repeat data that already exists in a column:**

  1. **In a blank cell, type the first few characters that match existing data within the same column.**

  2. **Excel displays a list of entries that match the characters you typed.** Use the down arrow on your keyboard to scroll down to the selection that you want to use.

  3. **To use the proposed entry, press Return.**

Note Excel can only AutoFill using data that contains text or some combination of text and numbers. Data that contains only numbers, dates, or times cannot be used for AutoFill.

● **Use the fill handle to fill data in adjacent cells:**

1. **Select a cell or series of cells.**

2. **Click and drag the fill handle, as shown in Figure 6.12, over the adjacent cells that you want to fill with the same data.** The fill handle is the little blue box you see in the lower-right corner of a selection. To drag the fill handle, position your mouse pointer over the fill handle until the pointer looks like a black cross hair, and then click and drag.

Fill handle

6.12 The fill handle is the tiny blue box in the lower right of a selection.

3. **Click the Auto Fill Options button that appears in the lower right of the cells into which you just copied the data to determine how the selected cells will be filled.** Make a selection from the pop-up list (the options in the list depend on what type of data is being copied) and press Return.

● **Fill in a series of information, such as numbers or months:**

1. **Click the cell that contains the first item you want to begin with.** For example, select a cell containing a date, time, or day of the week.

2. **Click and drag the fill handle to the right or below the selected cell for as many cells as you want to the data to occupy.** For example, if your first cell has 3:00 for its data

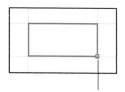

6.13 Select Fill Series in the AutoFill Options button to create a series of times in the selected cells.

and you want to add cells for 4:00 and 5:00, click the fill handle in the 3:00 cell and drag it two cells to the right.

3. **Click the AutoFill Options button in the lower right of the cells into which you just copied data.** Decide how the cells will be filled by making a choice from the pop-up menu. To continue with the time example, choose Fill Series, as shown in Figure 6.13.

Formatting cells

By now you're probably begging for a little color in your cells. Or how about some way to change the text to a different font within cells? What about putting borders around a cell instead of leaving its data to run wild? If any of those is the case, then you desire to perform a task Excel calls formatting cells. Formatting cells allows you to give cells a customized look and feel.

To begin formatting cells, follow these steps:

1. **Click a cell or a group of cells you want to format.**

2. **Press ⌘+1, or choose Format ⇨ Cells to open the Format Cells dialog.**

The Format Cells dialog contains lots of options that you can tinker with. The tabs at the top of the window dictate what element in a cell or cells that you are going to format. Let's take a quick look at each tab and see what options they afford:

- **Number.** You briefly saw this tab earlier in the chapter when you wanted to modify how dates appear in a cell. That's exactly what the options in this tab are for: modifying how numbers are displayed within a cell or group of cells. To use this tab, do the following:

  1. **Choose a category from the Category list to tell Excel what type of numerical data you want to modify.** You are presented with a host of options for the particular category you select.

  2. **Make adjustments to the options as necessary.** If you select a cell or group of cells already containing data you can see a preview of what your numbers will look like in the Sample field.

  3. **Click OK when you are ready to apply the changes.**

- **Alignment.** Click this tab (see Figure 6.14) to make changes to how your text is aligned within the cell.

  - In the Text alignment section, determine the horizontal and vertical positions of your text within the cell.

  - In the Text control section, tell Excel how the text should behave within the cell when moved or resized.

  - The Orientation section is where you can get funky with the text a bit. Click the vertical bar to align your text vertically within the cell, or angle the text anywhere from 90 to -90 degrees.

  - Click OK when finished.

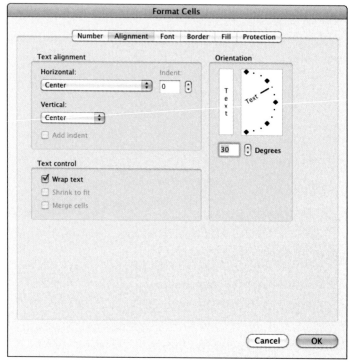

6.14 Change the alignment of text within a cell using the Alignment options in the Format Cells dialog.

- **Font.** The Font tab offers the basic font modifications that you know and love.

- **Border.** Most spreadsheets use borders to organize the data they contain, and this tab is where you go to apply borders to cells.

  - Use the buttons in the Presets section to apply preset borders to a cell or selection of cells.

  - Use the buttons in the Border section to customize borders within one or more cells.

  - Choose a style of line to use for your borders in the Line section.

  - If you want something other than the default black, use the Color pop-up menu to define a color for your borders.

- **Fill.** This tab allows you to add a big splash of color to cells.

  - Choose a background color using the Color pop-up menu in the Background section.

  - Select a foreground color in the same manner, using the Color pop-up menu in the Foreground section.

- If you desire, apply a pattern to the foreground color, as shown in Figure 6.15. You can view the effects of your changes in the Sample area.

- Click OK when you are ready to apply your changes to the selected cell(s).

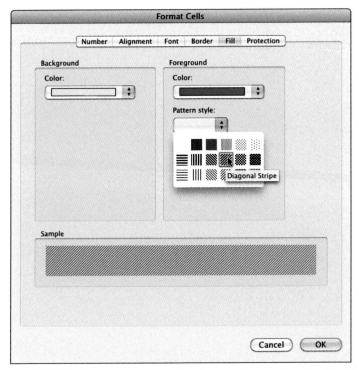

6.15 The Fill tab helps you spice up those boring old spreadsheets cells with vivid color!

Printing Your Excel-lent Spreadsheets

Printing your spreadsheets is a great way to share your information with others, such as in a meeting or with someone who doesn't have access to a computer (believe it or not, there are some holdouts out there). In some instances, you may need information in hard-copy form as opposed to only digital, so printing is the only way to go. Follow these steps:

1. **Open the workbook you want to print.**

2. **Press ⌘+P to open the Print dialog, as shown in Figure 6.16.**

3. **Select a printer from the Printer pop-up menu.**

4. **Type the number of copies you need and select which pages to print using the options in the Copies and Pages sections.**

5. **The Print What section allows you to print only a selection you've made in the spreadsheet, just the currently active worksheet, or the entire workbook.**

6. **Use the Scaling options to fit your spreadsheet onto a certain amount of pages.**

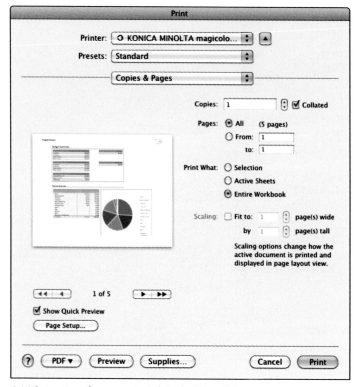

6.16 Set options for your print job in the Print dialog.

7. **Check the preview on the left side of the Print dialog to make sure your data looks like it will print the way you want it to.**

8. **Click Print when ready to send your job to the printer.**

How Can I Use Excel Formulas?

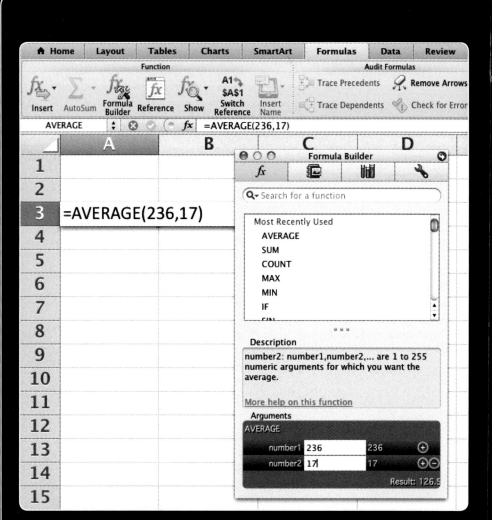

This chapter is one that delves a bit into the mathematical side of Excel, tinkering with formulas and their components. I endeavor to keep this chapter simple enough for the "I hate math" camp, detailed enough for those in the "math ain't so bad" camp, and entertaining enough to hold the attention of the "when is he going to get to the complex variable calculus?" camp. Whichever group you fall into, this is need-to-know stuff if you want to use Excel for calculations of any kind, so here we go.

What Are Formulas?

The formulas you're concerned with don't have as much to do with lethal chemicals as they do with good old-fashioned mathematics (which for some folks there may be very little difference).

A formula is an equation that Excel uses to make calculations in your spreadsheet based on data that you type into its cells. These equations can calculate all manner of numerical data and are used for anything you deem necessary: create a family budget, organize business trip expenses, tally church collections over the past decade, show how funds are being spent in the school system, or anything else you can think of.

A few cool things about using formulas

- If the data changes in your spreadsheet, formulas are designed to detect those changes and update their calculations.
- Formulas can use data found in other worksheets, not just the one that's currently active.
- Formulas can be as simple or as complex as you need them to be in order to calculate your data.

There are four basic components formulas can utilize:

- Functions
- Constants
- References
- Operators

Figure 7.1 shows an example of a formula that contains all four components, and Table 7.1 gives you a quick reference to what these components can do for you.

Note A formula must begin with an = (Equal) sign. Why? Because this tells Excel to sit up and take notice: You want to perform an equation in a particular cell. If your formula doesn't begin with = you don't have a valid formula and Excel will disappoint you mightily.

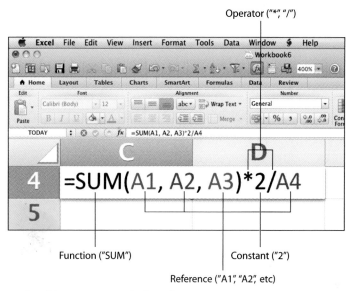

7.1 Possible components of a formula.

Table 7.1 Possible Components of a Formula

Component	Function
Functions	Functions are preset formulas, a great many of which are included with Excel, that take values, perform operations on those values, and give you a different value based on the operation performed. Functions can keep a complex formula manageable by eliminating the need for repetitive entries. In Figure 7.1, the function is SUM().
Constants	Values in a formula that do not change. Examples of constants would be a fixed number, such as 2, or fixed text, such as Monthly Income. The constant in Figure 7.1 is the number 2.
References	References point to cells within a spreadsheet. For example, if you want to utilize the data found in cell B2 for your formula, the reference would be B2. References in Figure 7.1 would be A1, A2, A3, and A4.
Operators	Signs and/or symbols that specify what type of calculation to perform in a formula. There are several types of operators, including reference, comparison, and mathematical. Examples of operators in Figure 7.1 are * (multiply) and / (divide).

Understanding References

References are necessary for Excel to know where it should look for data because they identify cells or ranges of cells within your spreadsheet. Excel uses these references to know where it should look for information that it needs.

References can point Excel to cells anywhere within a workbook, even other worksheets. You can even refer to cells in completely separate notebooks.

Getting to know the A1 reference style

You may recall from Chapter 6 that the default reference style for Excel is the A1 reference style. This means that a cell is referred to by its column, which is represented by letters (A, B, C, and so on), and its row, represented by numbers (1, 2, 3, and so on). For example, C3 refers to the cell that intersects with column C and row 3. Simple.

Table 7.2 shows how to use references for different scenarios, such as referring to all cells in a row or all cells in a range of columns.

Table 7.2 Examples of References

To refer to:	Type reference:
The cell in column B and row 2	B2
The range of cells in column B and rows 2 through 8	B2:B8
The range of cells in row 2 and columns A through C	A2:C2
The range of cells in columns A through C and rows 2 through 8	A2:C8
All cells in column B	B:B
All cells in columns B through D	B:D
All cells in row 2	2:2
All cells in rows 2 through 8	2:8

Genius

To refer to a cell or range of cells in another worksheet than the one you're currently working in, use the name of the worksheet followed by an exclamation point (!), type the cell or range of cells within that worksheet you need, and enclose the whole thing in parentheses. For example, if you want to refer to cells 2 through 8 of column B in a worksheet called Budget, type (Budget!B2:B8).

Working with relative, absolute, and mixed references

There are three types of references that need to be discussed: relative, absolute, and mixed.

A relative reference is one that adjusts itself automatically when copied to another cell. Let's say you have a formula, =A1*B1, in the cell address of E1, and then you copied that formula into E2. A relative reference automatically updates itself to change the cell references to reflect the change, resulting in the formula in E2 now reading as =A2*B2.

But what if you don't want the cell addresses to change when a formula is copied to a different cell? If that's the case, you want an absolute reference, which is one that never changes no matter how much you beg and plead with it (kind of like my bank account). However, I must let you know that there is a magical tool that you must invoke in order to change a relative reference into an absolute reference. That tool is the always-powerful dollar sign ($).

Placing $ in front of both the column and row of a cell address tells Excel to keep its hands off of this reference because it's not changing for anybody. For example, if you had made the formula in the previous example read as =A1*B1, that formula won't change, no matter what cell you copy it to.

Sometimes you have a formula that may require a relative reference in conjunction with an absolute reference: These are called mixed references. In a mixed reference, you place $ in front of either the column or the row, but not both.

If you had used a mixed reference in the previous example to keep the columns the same but the rows could change, the formula would have read like so, =$A1*$B1. Then, no matter where you copy the formula the columns remain A and B, but the rows change to correspond to the row number of the cell you copied the formula into.

Getting Familiar with Formulas

Let's get your feet wet by creating a simple formula using constants and operators, and then take more-detailed looks at some of the components of formulas, such as operators and references.

You're going to jump into formula creation by using addition, subtraction, multiplication, and division. To create a formula, follow these steps:

1. **Open a workbook into which you want to enter a formula.**
2. **Double-click the cell in which you want to create the formula.** Your cursor should be blinking in the cell to let you know Excel is ready for you to input some information.
3. **Type = (equal sign).**
4. **Type the formula.** Table 7.3 gives you some examples of simple formulas you can enter using constants and operators.

Table 7.3 Examples of a Simple Formula Using Constants and Operators

Example formula	What happens
=1+2	Adds 1 and 2.
=2-1	Subtracts 1 from 2.
=1/2	Divides 1 by 2.
=1*2	Multiplies 1 times 2.

5. Press Return when finished to perform the calculation.

I realize this is pretty basic stuff, but it's very important to get a grasp of this so you can better understand how formulas affect your spreadsheet.

This next formula is also simple, but gives you a bit more interaction with the rest of the spreadsheet. This time, instead of simply typing numbers, your constants are cells in a spreadsheet, such as A1, B2, and so on.

1. **Double-click the cell in which you want to create the formula.**

2. **Type =.**

3. **Click the cell that contains the value that you want to use in the formula, type the operator that you want to use, and then click another cell that contains a value.**

4. **Press Return to complete the formula.**

Figure 7.2 shows you that C10 is selected to hold the formula, A7 is the first constant, addition is the operator, and B7 is the second constant. Table 7.4 shows some of the forms this type of formula may have taken if other operators were used.

7.2 Cells A7 and B7 are added to populate the C10 cell.

Table 7.4 Examples of Formulas Using Cells as Constants

Example formula	What happens
=A7+B7	Adds the values in cells A7 and B7.
=A7-B7	Subtracts the value in cell B7 from the value in A7.
=A7/B7	Divides the value in cell A7 by the value in B7.
=A7*B7	Multiplies the value in cell A7 times the value in B7.

Using Operators

In Excel, an operator is one of those little signs and symbols that specify what kind of calculation you want to perform within a formula. The data the calculations are being performed on are called operands. For example, in 1+2, the + is the operator while 1 and 2 are the operands.

There are four kinds of operators: arithmetic, reference, comparison, and text concatenation. The following sections look at all four and explain exactly how to use them within an Excel formula.

Arithmetic operators

You've already seen some arithmetic operators in previous examples. Arithmetic operators help you do the basic mathematical calculations using numerical operands: addition, subtraction, and the like. These operators can certainly be used in conjunction with one another, too.

Table 7.5 lists arithmetic operators and Figure 7.3 shows what a formula using several arithmetic operators might look like.

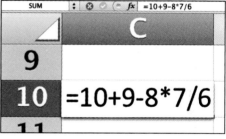

7.3 You can simultaneously use as many different arithmetic operators as necessary to reach the calculation you need.

Table 7.5 Arithmetic Operators

Function	Operator	Example
Addition	+	1+2
Subtraction	-	2-1
Multiplication	*	1*2
Division	/	1/2
Percent	%	10%
Exponentiation	^	4^2

Reference operators

There are three reference operators: the range operator, the union operator, and the intersection operator. These guys are used to combine ranges of cells so that you can perform calculations on them.

Table 7.6 lists the reference operators and gives an example of their use in a cell.

Table 7.6 Reference Operators

Operator	Operator Type	Example
: (colon)	Range	A1:A5
, (comma)	Union	SUM(A1:A5,B1:B5)
(space)	Intersection	C12:D14 D13:E17

Here's how the trusty reference operators work:

Range operators are used to join two cell references to make a range reference. For example, the range A1:A5 would represent the rectangle that is drawn between the two operands. Anything within that rectangle is fair game for your calculations. Figure 7.4 shows a better visual representation of what the range A1:A5 encompasses.

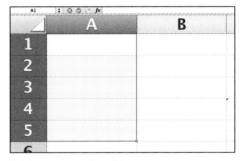

7.4 A representation of the range operator combined with the operands A1 and A5.

People can become quickly confused when it comes to distinguishing between a union operator and an intersection operator, so I'll try to clear it up quickly.

A comma represents the union operator. The union operator combines the contents of the ranges it's given and returns that value. For example, say you have two sets:

- **Set A contains 1, 3, 5, 7, and 8.**
- **Set B contains 1, 2, 4, 6, and 7.**

The union of these two sets would be 1, 2, 3, 4, 5, 6, 7, and 8. All the elements from both sets are combined.

Genius

Union operators are usually used within parentheses to separate them from other elements of the formula, which also may use commas.

The intersection operator is represented by a (space). Intersection operators combine only the elements that a range has in common and reports those values. Following are two more sets to illustrate how intersection operators work their magic:

- **Set A contains 2, 5, 6, 7, 10, and 14.**
- **Set B contains 1, 4, 5, 10, 14, and 16.**

Invoking an intersection operator returns the result of 5, 10, and 14, because those are the only three elements common to both sets. If the two sets don't contain information that intersects, or is common, Excel reports a #NULL! error value.

Figure 7.5 illustrates what cells in your spreadsheet would be affected when using a union operator of (C12:D14,D13:E17) and an intersection operator of (C12:D14 D13:E17).

7.5 Green represents the cells affected using (C12:D14 D13:E17) and (C12:D14,D13:E17).

Comparison operators

As their name indicates, comparison operators work by comparing values. When Excel compares two values using comparison operators it can only arrive at one of two logical conclusions: The result is true, or it is false. For example, if you have cell A1 containing the value of 1 and cell B1 contains the value of 2, Excel uses the following formulas to arrive at a conclusion:

- A1 > B1 returns a value of false.
- A1 < B1 returns a value of true.
- A1 = B1 returns a value of false.

Table 7.7 shows all the comparison operator possibilities within Excel.

Table 7.7 Comparison Operators

Function	Operator	Example
Greater than	>	A1>B1
Less than	<	A1<B1
Equal to	=	A1=B1
Not equal to	<>	A1<>B1
Greater than or equal to	>=	A1>=B1
Less than or equal to	<=	A1<=B1

Text concatenation operator

Notice the title indicates a single operator, not "operators" like the others. That's right, there is only one very lonely text concatenation operator.

The text concatenation operator is represented by an ampersand (&), and its sole purpose in life is to join text from multiple sources into one text string.

For example, say that you want to list the first name of a person in one column of the spreadsheet, the last name in another column, and combine the two in still a third column. Follow these steps:

1. **Open a new spreadsheet.**

2. **Type** First Name **in A1,** Last Name **in B1, and** Full Name **in C1.**

3. **Click C2 and type the formula for adding the first name and last name to complete the full name:** =A2&B2

4. **Click the fill handle in the lower-right corner of C2 and drag down the C column for as many names as you want to use.** This causes the formula to apply to other rows in the spreadsheet. =A2&B2 in C2 becomes =A3&B3 in C3, and so on.

5. **Begin typing names in the First name and Last name columns.** As you type, the Full name column should populate accordingly, as shown in Figure 7.6.

Notice how the text string in A2 is added to the text string in B2 to complete the famous author's name in C2. But there's something awry, isn't there (and I don't mean the name of the author in C2)? The first and last names in the Full Name column are scrunched together.

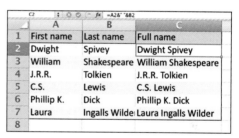

7.6 The trusty text concatenation operator hard at work in your list of famous authors.

You can correct that by adding a space to the formula. Follow these steps:

1. **Double-click C2 to edit the formula.**

2. **Insert a space between your two operands like so: =A2&" "&B2**

3. **Press Return to invoke the change and apply the space between the two names in C2.**

4. **Next, make this apply to all the names in the list.**

5. **Click the fill handle in the lower-right corner of C2.**

6. **Drag the fill handle all the way down the C column until you come to the end of your list.** The change is auto-matically applied and the Full name column instantly becomes more read-able, as shown in Figure 7.7.

7.7 Now the list of famous authors is suddenly readable. Amazing what one single space can do.

Understanding the order of Excel calculations

The order in which Excel performs calculations can make a huge difference in the final value of an equation. If one little operator is out of place or not grouped properly then all heck will break loose in your spreadsheet. It's very important to understand the order that Excel uses to perform calcula-tions so you can avoid some potentially big mishaps.

Excel calculates your equations running from left to right. Excel sees your = at the beginning of the formula and goes from there, using what is termed as *operator precedence* to calculate the oper-ands based on the operators that separate them.

Table 7.8 lists the operators in the order that Excel calculates them. If there are two operators with the same operator precedence, such as a + (addition) and – (subtraction), Excel calculates from left to right.

Table 7.8 Operator Precedence in Excel

Function	Operator
Reference operators	: (colon)
	, (comma)
	(space)
Negation (negative numbers)	Example: -4
Percent	%
Exponentiation	^
Multiplication and Division	*
	/
Addition and Subtraction	+
	-
Text concatenation	&
Comparison operators	=
	<
	>
	<=
	>=
	<>

Utilizing the mighty parentheses

Parentheses are big players when it comes to operator precedence and the order in which Excel calculates your formulas. They can literally force Excel to perform one calculation and take its value before performing the next calculation.

For example, take the following formula and analyze it just a bit:

=9-2*3

It looks like the final value results in 21, right? Wrong. Remember that little thing called operator precedence (look back at Table 7.7 if you need a quick refresher)? The multiplication operator takes precedence over the subtraction operator, so it is performed first. In other words, instead of 9 minus 2 equaling 7, and therefore 7 multiplied by 3 equaling 21, what you really have is Excel calculating 2 multiplied by 3 first and then subtracting the resulting 6 from 9. The result Excel gives from your formula is quite correctly 3.

Now, change things a bit using the mighty parentheses:

=(9-2)*3

You still have the same operands, but a couple of interlopers — parentheses — are inserted into the mix. In this scenario, you are bludgeoning Excel into submission and forcing it to calculate the operands and operator contained within the parentheses first, and then applying the result of that calculation to the rest of the formula. In this instance, 2 is subtracted from 9, and the resulting 7 is multiplied by 3, resulting in the grand total of 21, as you originally anticipated.

How Can I Augment My Spreadsheets?

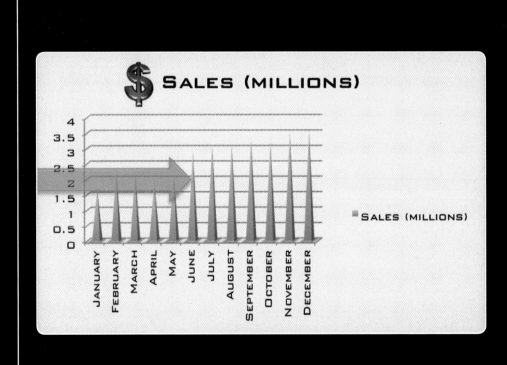

You just completed the four-hour task of entering all the data necessary for your spreadsheet. The information is there, it's organized to perfection, and it's ready to be given to the stockholders. But, while containing the pertinent information your stockholders need, your spreadsheet is incredibly bland. If the stockholders make it all the way through your report without nodding off it will be a miracle. There's no denying that a good presentation can make even the most boring information tolerable. In this chapter, I look at how to add charts and graphs, how to use custom lists, and how to use a few special effects.

Why Use Charts and Graphs?

Information, when presented in row after row, column after continuous column, can get to be pretty tedious stuff. The very reason that the right and left sides of your brain work differently is so you can appreciate all things in the world, both the beauty and the data. Why else do you think that magazines and newspapers throughout the world use charts and graphs to convey the data they present? You retain information much better when it appeals to both the right and left hemispheres. Take a look at Figure 8.1. The same information in the table is also shown in the graph, but which one captures your attention the fastest?

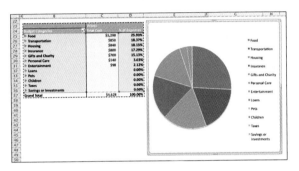

8.1 Compare the table without any formatting to the chart representing the same information.

Understanding Different Types of Charts

Creating a chart is simple; if you have the data, Excel has the chart to suit your needs. If there's something Excel has no shortage, it is types of charts you can use to disseminate information graphically.

There are several types you can use for plotting your data:

- **Column.** These charts are the most typical, and they are helpful when you need to compare items or when you need to show how data has changed over a span of time, as with a monthly sales comparison.

- **Line.** Line charts help you to see how things trend over a set equal amount of time. For example, if you need to show how sales have trended over the years spanning 2001 to 2010.

- **Pie.** These charts are great for displaying how individual items comprise a whole set of items. And they are also great at causing pizza cravings.

- **Bar.** Bars are helpful when comparing individual items. You could almost think of them as column charts that have been knocked over on their sides (I like to throw in some technical jargon from time to time).

- **Area.** Area charts help you to convey the difference between two or more sets of values over a given time period.

- **Scatter (or XY).** If you remember plotting graphs in school with graph paper, you'll get the idea behind a scatter plot. In a scatter plot, both the X and Y axes contain numeric data, and each set is displayed together.

- **Stock.** You don't have to work on Wall Street to get what this type of chart is used for, but I'll tell you anyway: It's a great tool for illustrating the fluctuation of stock prices over a given period.

- **Surface.** These charts are pretty darn cool. They can convey, in true 3-D, the interaction of three sets of data on one another. Surface charts are great for conveying topographical information (longitude, latitude, and elevation).

- **Doughnut.** These are very similar to pie charts, beyond the fact that they both make you hungry. The advantage that doughnut charts have over pie charts is that they can convey more than one set of data, making it easier to see changes over time to a percentage distribution.

- **Bubble.** Bubble charts are akin to scatter charts, except that they use three data points as opposed to two. This causes the data to form a bubble, which represents the value of the third data point, as shown in Figure 8.2.

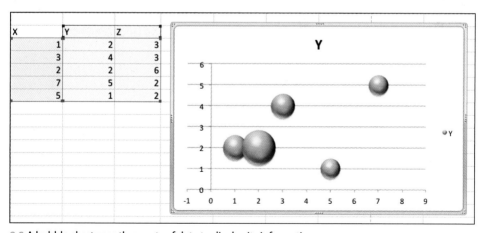

8.2 A bubble chart uses three sets of data to display its information.

A Word Regarding 3-D Charts

As you peruse the many charts available in Excel you will notice some are labeled 3-D (such as 3-D Scatter, 3-D Bubble, and so on). They are hard to miss because they are so appealing to the eye. However, I find that they may not be the best choice for delivering hard data. Many times the data may be lost behind other 3-D bars, and other times the data may be hard for some to process, especially if they aren't used to viewing these kinds of charts and graphs. There is really only one truly 3-D chart in Excel, and that's the surface chart. If you want to use 3-D charts, by all means, be my guest, but if you're shooting for good looks while retaining clarity, I'd stick with the more traditional forms of charts.

● **Radar.** Radar charts can sometimes be called *spider charts* based on their resemblance to webs. They are typically used to represent data from several categories, with each category having its own value axis that is drawn from the center of the chart. The more categories you have, the more sides you will have in your chart.

Note

Make sure that the information you want to convert to a chart is set up in the spreadsheet in the proper way for the type of chart you are creating. Should you find that your data isn't populating a chart quite like you thought it would, the formatting may be wrong.

Creating a Simple Chart

Let's create a chart, already. Follow these steps:

1. **Open a workbook.**

2. **Select the worksheet and data within the workbook that you want to convert to a chart.**

3. **Click the Chart tab in the ribbon.**

4. **In the Insert Chart section, click a chart type and then select the chart you want from the resulting pop-up menu (the Clustered Pyramid is shown as the selected chart in Figure 8.3).** Excel creates your chart using the data you select.

5. **If the chart isn't in the correct place in your spreadsheet you can easily move it.** Hold your mouse pointer over the chart until it turns into four arrows, and then click the

chart, move it to the position you desire for it, and drop it into place.

6. **You can resize your chart if its size isn't what you need.** Click the chart to highlight it. A blue border (which for some reason reminds me of something out of a *Star Wars* film) appears around the chart. The blue border contains size handles in each corner and on each side. Click and drag these handles to resize the chart to the dimensions you prefer.

Your chart is ready to go.

Excel remembers the table from which your chart received its data, and it links that data to the chart. Whenever you make a change to that data, Excel automatically updates the chart to reflect it.

On the other hand, though, making a change in the chart doesn't affect the data. The only things you can change in the chart are the titles and labels anyway.

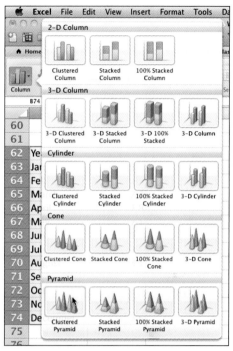

8.3 The list of charts you can choose from is bountiful indeed, but some are simply cooler than others.

Formatting Information for Charts

It's important to understand how to format the information you use in your spreadsheet in order to create a chart. If you don't match the proper formatting of your data to the type of chart you are using, you will end with a chart Frankenstein of sorts.

Let's take a closer look at the types of charts available in Excel and how to best format, or structure, your data for each type.

- **Area, bar, column, line, doughnut, surface, and radar charts.** Information for these types of charts needs to be formatted in simple columns or rows, as shown in Figure 8.4.

143

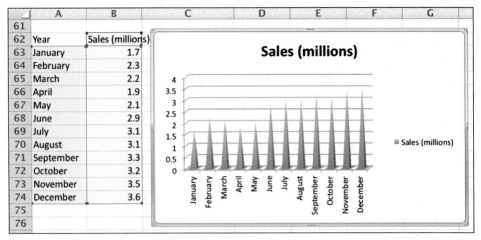

	A	B	C	D	E	F	G
61							
62	Year	Sales (millions)					
63	January	1.7					
64	February	2.3					
65	March	2.2					
66	April	1.9					
67	May	2.1					
68	June	2.9					
69	July	3.1					
70	August	3.1					
71	September	3.3					
72	October	3.2					
73	November	3.5					
74	December	3.6					
75							
76							

8.4 Proper formatting makes this column chart turn out just right.

- **Pie chart.** Data needs to be laid out in one column or row of values and another column or row of labels (such as Sales, Marketing, Engineering, and so on). Figure 8.5 gives you a good idea of this format.

	A	B
1		Sales
2	January	10000
3	February	13000
4	March	12500

8.5 Pie charts need information in one column of values and a second column of text or labels.

- **Bubble chart.** It's best to format your data in columns. Place the X-axis information in the first column, the Y-axis information in the second, and the size of the bubbles in the third, as shown in Figure 8.6.

- **Scatter charts.** These are similar to bubble charts, except they don't require the third column for size.

	A	B	C
1	X	Y	Size
2	1	3	2
3	2	4	5
4	2	5	7

8.6 Bubble charts are best formatted using columns.

- **Stock charts.** These must be arranged in the proper order, using names and dates for your label text, as shown in Figure 8.7.

Following these parameters when arranging the information for your chart will make your life much simpler, I promise. I speak from cruel, cruel experience.

	A	B	C
1		12/13/70	12/14/70
2	Open	11	10
3	High	14	99
4	Low	8	10
5	Close	10	99
6			

8.7 Arrange data in precisely this format if you want to create a proper stock chart.

Enhance Your Chart's Visual Appeal

Okay, you have at least one chart to work with by this point. You need it to work along while I show you how to apply some fireworks to your charts.

Adding colors and textures to your chart

Charts are just boring with one color, don't you think? You may have one color for your bars of columns, but the rest of the chart is pretty dreary. You can brighten things up a bit by using a different theme or by customizing the chart to your own liking.

When you first create a chart, Excel applies the default Office theme to it (refer to Figure 8.4) if you aren't working within a different theme already. You can change the entire look of a chart by simply changing the theme. Follow these steps:

1. **Open the spreadsheet that contains the chart to which you want to apply a theme.**

2. **Click the Home tab in the ribbon.**

3. **In the Themes section on the right side of the ribbon, click the Themes button, browse the list of available themes, and presto, you've got a new look for your colors and fonts (compare Figure 8.4 with Figure 8.8).**

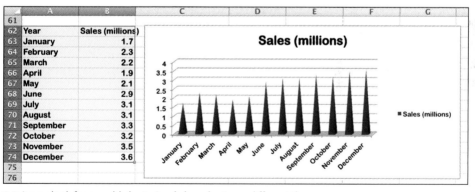

8.8 A new look for our old chart, simply be selecting a different theme.

Genius

What if you don't want to change the entire theme, but want to change the colors? Simple: Open the spreadsheet and click the Home tab, then click the Colors button and choose a themes color palette. This changes the colors of your chart, but doesn't mess with any other formatting.

Let's really get down to business with modifying your chart's appearance. That theme stuff can change a few basic colors, but what about transforming the entire chart? There are several parts in a chart, and you can modify each part individually. First, let's modify the chart's area:

1. **Right-click, or Control+click, an empty space in the chart to open a contextual menu.**

2. **Select Format Chart Area from the menu.** If you don't see Format Chart Area, try clicking a different part of the chart. The Format Chart Area window opens and offers a ton of options for making your chart a little more unique in appearance.

3. **Click the Fill category from the list on the left side of the Format Chart Area dialog.** From here you can click the following tabs to change how the background of the chart looks:

   - **Solid.** Click this tab to apply a solid color to the background, as shown in Figure 8.9. Choose a color from the pop-up menu, and you can use the slide to apply a transparency.

   - **Gradient.** Click this tab to apply a gradient of color to the background. Gradients can look pretty cool if you know what you're doing.

   - **Picture or Texture.** Click this tab to place a picture or a texture in the background of your chart.

   - **Pattern.** Click this tab to add a pattern to the background. The pattern uses the color you selected in the Solid tab.

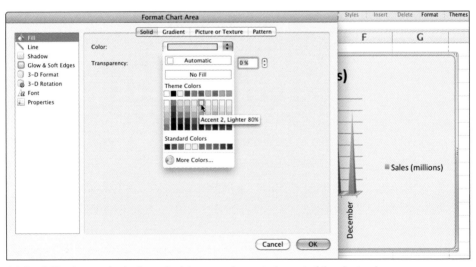

8.9 A solid background color is applied that complements the rest of the chart colors.

4. **Click Line in the category list to modify the outline of the chart.** The following tabs are available:

- **Solid.** Click this tab to apply a color to the outline. Choose a color and adjust its transparency.

- **Gradient.** Click this tab to apply a gradient to the outline. Choose a style and the direction of the gradient, and then select the colors to use with it.

- **Weights & Arrows.** Click this tab to make a huge impact on the outline, mainly by changing its size. Apply a Line Style and then adjust the weight of the line to your liking. You can also change the dashing of the line, as well as its endpoints.

5. **Apply a shadow.** Sometimes a shadow adds just the right effect to make your chart pop off the spreadsheet. If you think one might help you, click the Shadow category from the list on the left side of the window. Select the Shadow check box to enable the shadow, and then make adjustments to the style, color, angle, and other elements, as shown in Figure 8.10.

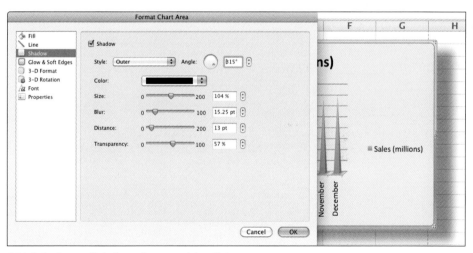

8.10 A shadow really helps a chart pop right off the page.

6. **If you really want your chart to stand out against a dark backdrop, apply a glow to it using the Glow & Soft Edges category.** Choose a color and size for the glow, which is seen around the outer edges of the chart.

7. **Give your chart that *Avatar* feel by giving it a 3-D appearance using the 3-D Format category.** The following tabs are available:

- **Bevel.** Click this tab to apply a bevel around the edges of your chart. Imagine the bevel on a picture frame and you will get a good idea of how this will affect your chart's appearance.

- **Depth & Surface.** Click this tab to adjust the depth of the bevel, depending on the bevel you selected in the Bevel tab, and to modify the appearance of the surface (metal and plastic are just two of your options).

8. **For a little more 3-D fun, use the 3-D Rotate category to actually rotate the chart to give it a 3-D look and feel.** Select a rotation type and a chart scale to make your chart look as if it has rotated.

9. **Changing fonts can make some of the most dramatic changes to a chart, and that's what the Font category allows you to do.** Click the Font tab to change the font characteristics, as shown in Figure 8.11, and click the Character Spacing tab to change the spacing between characters.

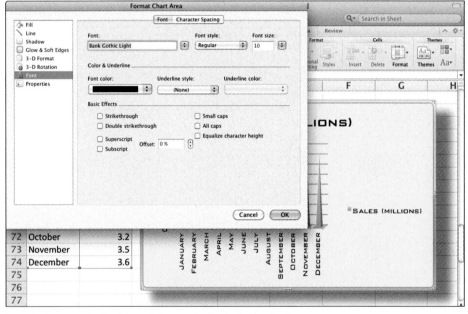

8.11 Fonts can make the biggest changes to the look of a chart.

10. **Click the Properties category to tell Excel how to handle this chart when other items in the spreadsheet change.** You can use the following options:

- **Object positioning.** Select this option to determine whether the chart will move within the spreadsheet as other items within it move.

- **Print.** Select this check box to allow the chart to be printed along with the rest of the spreadsheet.

- **Locked.** Select this check box to prevent the chart from being removed.

- **Lock Text.** Select this check box to prevent the text in the chart from being altered.

11. **Click OK when you finish applying the formatting to your chart's area.**

The chart area is only the beginning of formatting changes you can make to a chart. If you right-click on different parts of the chart you are offered different selections to choose from in the contextual menu. For example, when you right-click the X-axis at the bottom of your chart and select Format Axis, the Format Axis dialog appears, as shown in Figure 8.12. This dialog contains formatting categories that are specific to modifying the X-axis.

When you right-click other parts of a chart, and dialogs appear that allow you change to format the legend, chart title, major and minor gridlines, data series, and text. Each formatting option provides categories specific to the area of the chart you are working on.

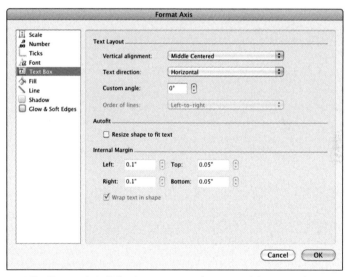

8.12 The Format Axis dialog lets you control aspects of the particular axis you selected in your chart.

Adding shapes and images to your chart

Formatting and color changes aren't the limit to making your chart even better. On the contrary, you still need to look at how shapes and images can help liven up things. You might want to add a shape that points out certain information in a chart that you feel is critical, or perhaps a background of the family will enhance a chart detailing your family budget. As with Word and the other members of the Office 2011 family of applications, Excel uses Media Browser to afford these options to you. Follow these steps to add shapes and images to your charts:

1. **Open the spreadsheet containing the chart you want to work with.**

2. **Click the Media Browser button in the toolbar to open Media Browser.**

3. **Click the Shapes button to apply a shape to your chart, Clip Art to insert a piece of clip art, or Photos to place a photo from your iPhoto or Photo Booth library into the chart.**

4. **Click and drag the item you want to insert from Media Browser and drop it into the area of the chart where you want to place it, as shown in Figure 8.13.**

5. **If the item doesn't fit properly into the chart, click it once to see its size handles and then click and drag the size handles to resize the item.**

6. **Should you need to make any formatting changes to the item, right-click (or Control+click) it and select Format Shape or Format Picture, whichever suits the type of item you're formatting.**

7. **Click any area outside of the chart to apply the shape or picture.**

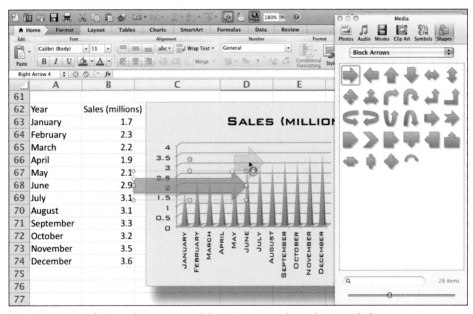

8.13 Drag an item from Media Browser and drop it into your chart where needed.

How Do I Create a PowerPoint Presentation?

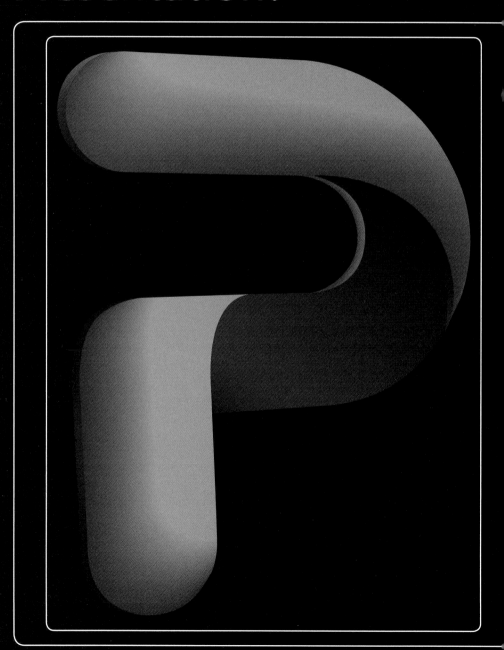

t's the biggest project you've ever been tasked with. Do you just shove a fin-
shed product across a table to them, or simply send an e-mail with the barest
of information about the product? No way! You want to make them anticipate
he product. You need … a really great PowerPoint presentation! This chapter
provides the basics of using PowerPoint 2011 so that when the time comes to
dazzle the world with your presentation, you'll be ready to roll.

PC, it's a good idea to get the lay of the land. The following sections identify the fundamental land-marks of PowerPoint 2011 to see where your favorite tools may reside in Microsoft's latest offering of this perennial presentation-making favorite. Fortunately, as with Word and Excel, some items are universal across each of Office 2011's applications, so you don't have to get into every little detail, but focus on those that are specific to PowerPoint.

Let's get started by actually opening PowerPoint! Simply double-click the large orange P icon found in your Microsoft Office 2011 folder and PowerPoint will launch (see Figure 9.1).

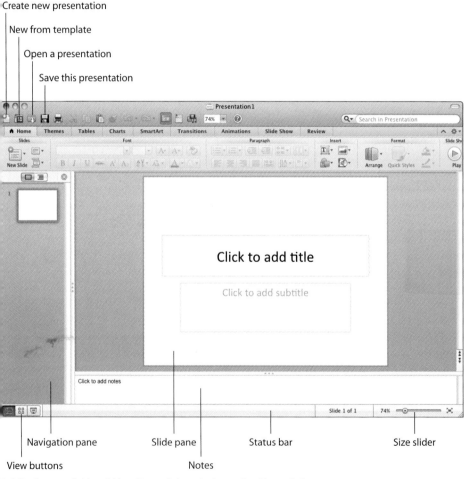

9.1 Options available within a PowerPoint window using Normal view.

Also, like Word and Excel, by default PowerPoint opens to a window containing document templates, in this case called the PowerPoint Presentation Gallery. Select PowerPoint Presentation in the Gallery and then click Choose to open a new presentation window. If the PowerPoint Presentation Gallery doesn't open, you can create a new presentation by pressing ⌘+N.

Table 9.1 offers brief explanations of the popular points of interest.

Table 9.1 Options Available Within a Standard PowerPoint Window

Button/Option	Description
Create new presentation	Create a new blank presentation.
New from template	Opens the PowerPoint Presentation Gallery so you can select a template to begin a new presentation.
Open a presentation	Allows you to browse your Mac for PowerPoint presentations you want to read or edit.
Save this presentation	Opens the Save dialog, where you can select where to save your current presentation.
Expand/minimize ribbon	Increase or decrease the size of the ribbon.
Navigation pane	Click the Slide button to see previews of each slide in order, or click the Outline button to see slides in outline form.
Slide pane	This is where you view and edit individual slides.
View buttons	Click Normal to view the presentation in a standard window, click Slide Sorter to see a preview of all your slides in order (you can rearrange the order of slides here), or click Slide Show to view your slides as they would appear during a presentation.
Notes	Type notes to yourself here to help you with your presentation. These notes do not appear to others viewing the presentation.
Status bar	Displays the number of the slide you're currently working in, the number of slides in your presentation, the template or background in use, or the current view (Normal, Slide Sorter, or Slide Show).
Size slider	Drag the slider to the right or left to increase or decrease the size of the slide on your screen.

Setting PowerPoint's Preferences

PowerPoint's a great tool, but like any tool worthy of the title it needs to be honed to your liking. Preferences help streamline the application to your working environment and give you greater control over the default behaviors of PowerPoint.

To open PowerPoint's preferences, choose PowerPoint ⇨ Preferences, or press ⌘+, (that's the Command key in conjunction with the comma key). The PowerPoint Preferences window is divided into ten sections, each one designed to handle a specific set of actions in PowerPoint. Let's briefly take a look at each one, being sure to take a little more time for some subjects if need be.

● **General tab.** Track the documents you've recently opened in PowerPoint, determine whether the PowerPoint Presentation Gallery opens upon launch of the application, enable macro virus protection, and more. You can also set options for the playback of movies that are embedded into your slides by clicking the Movie Options button. From within the Movie Options dialog (see Figure 9.2) you can set several options, including the ability to add credits to the movie, include a background soundtrack, have the movie play at the same screen resolution as your Mac, and more. There's more to be found on these topics in Chapter 10.

Movie Options

Movie Settings | Credits

Size and quality

Optimization: Automatic (Normal)

Movie dimensions:
◉ 640 x 480   ○ Current screen size
○ Custom   40   X   80

Media settings

Slide transitions: Follow Slide Show settings

Background soundtrack: [None]

☐ Loop Movie
☑ Show movie player controls

Save

◉ Apply these settings to all new presentations
○ Apply these settings to the current presentation

Cancel   OK

9.2 Modify how movies embedded in your slides behave with the Movie Options window.

● **View tab.** As you might imagine by the title, you can alter the default view (Normal, Slide, or Outline) for PowerPoint here, but you can do more, too:

○ **Enable the vertical ruler and designate the units of measurement you prefer.**

○ **Let PowerPoint warn you when opening a linked file, application, or macro.**

○ **Tell PowerPoint to end each presentation with a black slide.**

○ **Use a pop-up menu button for slide navigation.**

● **Edit tab.** There's not a lot going on here, so depending on your point of view that may be good or bad. From Edit you can tell PowerPoint to use smart cut-and-paste, to automatically choose an entire word when selecting, to allow drag-and-drop text editing, and finally to set a limit on the number of times you can undo edits in each presentation.

Caution   I would advise you to not set the number of times you can undo edits to a small number. If you're mistake-prone, this might be a hindrance you should avoid. You can max out at 150 and minimize to just 3.

- **Save tab.** There are quite a few options here, but most are self-explanatory. There are two that I particularly want to draw your attention to, though:

  - **Warn before saving in a format where presentation elements are removed.** I would advise against turning this off as it gives you a heads-up should you have elements in your presentation that won't be saved if you convert it to a different format. At least this way you won't be surprised to find that some of the items in your presentation won't be there when you get ready to share it.

  - **Save AutoRecover info every *X* minutes.** AutoRecover is PowerPoint's way of backing up your presentation's data every few minutes so that at least some of it, if not all, can be recovered should something untoward happen while working on it (power failure, spilling soda all over your MacBook, your 2-year-old deciding to play piano with your Mac's keyboard, and so on). You might not want to set this to every minute, but you also don't want to go to the other extreme (9,999 minutes).

- **Spelling tab.** These are just basic spell-check options that even the least of the inexperienced can understand.

- **Ribbon tab.** There's some good stuff here, as shown in Figure 9.3. You can enable or disable the ribbon (why you'd disable is beyond me) and have it be expanded upon opening PowerPoint, or change its appearance from PowerPoint Orange to Graphite. My favorite part, though, is the ability to turn on or off a variety of tabs within the ribbon, such as the Themes, Tables, and Developer tabs. You can also drag the tabs in the list into the order you want them to appear in the ribbon.

- **AutoCorrect tab.** Good, old AutoCorrect is always ready to help out when you make that critical spelling error. You're familiar with AutoCorrect's features based on previous chapters in this book dealing with Word. The same features pretty much apply for PowerPoint, such as replacing words as you type and automatically capitalizing the first word in a sentence.

- **Compatibility tab.** This little tab doesn't have a lot of options, but it can play a big role. The only check box in the pane offers you the chance to enable or disable compatibility checks for your presentations. The Reset Ignored Issues and Reset All Issues buttons are there to provide you with the chance to start over with your compatibility checks, just in case you missed something the first time around.

- **Advanced tab.** The options offered here don't seem all that advanced, but we'll go with it. You have the ability to specify the default location in which PowerPoint loads or saves your presentations and to edit the user information for them.

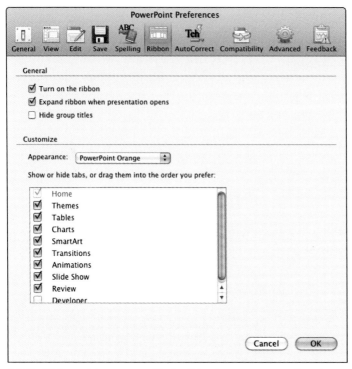

9.3 The Ribbon tab lets you modify the ribbon's appearance, or have it not appear at all.

● **Feedback tab.** From here you can enable or disable the Customer Experience Improvement Program. If you enable this program, Microsoft anonymously collects information about your Mac's hardware and how you use its software. Read the information in this tab carefully before enabling or disabling this program (it's disabled by default).

Creating a Simple Presentation

Enough dilly-dallying. Let's learn how to make presentations! There are two methods for making a presentation — starting from scratch with an unspoiled slide, or with the help of a template. The aim of this book is not to cover the ABCs of how to build professional presentations from a content standpoint (meaning I won't tell you how to analyze your subject matter and break it down into manageable parts or how to match it to your audience), but I'll show you the tools that are available to you and how to utilize them in the creation of your slides.

Starting from scratch

I've often heard that the best place to start something is from the beginning, and so it sometimes is with presentations. Beginning with a blank slate can be intimidating for some, but at times it's necessary because a template may not be formatted the way you want. Of course, templates are great and make life much easier, but it's a good idea to see how presentations are built from the ground up, too.

To start from scratch, you need a new presentation. As you learned earlier in this chapter, pressing ⌘+N gives you a new canvas with which to work. The slide pane shows your new slide ready for input.

You may notice that your new slide isn't exactly blank. While a blank slide is possible (more on that in a bit), PowerPoint gives you a tiny head start by supplying placeholders. A *placeholder* is a text or image box that you can modify for your own use. For example, the first slide in a new presentation contains placeholders called "Click to add title" and "Click to add subtitle." Microsoft assumes you want to begin your new presentation with a title page, and this is the default. To edit a placeholder, simply click it and begin typing your own text.

Adding and deleting slides

One slide does not an effective presentation make. If you look in the Navigation pane on the left side of your window, you'll note that there's only one lonely slide there. To give it some company, simply press ⌘+Shift+N or choose Insert ➪ New Slide.

If you have a slide in your document that you'll be using often, you can duplicate that slide by pressing ⌘+Shift+D.

You may also add slides from other PowerPoint presentations. Follow these steps:

1. **Choose Insert ➪ Slides From ➪ Other Presentation.** You can browse your Mac for the presentation from which you want to import slides.

2. **Click the appropriate radio buttons in the lower left of the Choose a File dialog to import all or only a portion of the slides in the presentation.**

3. **Click Insert to begin importing slides from a previously created presentation into the new one.** If you choose to import only some of the slides in the presentation, the Slide Finder dialog appears, as shown in Figure 9.4. Use the Slide Finder to browse and select the slides you want to import (hold down the Shift key while clicking to select multiple slides), and then click Insert.

Deleting slides is a fairly simple task, but be careful that you don't accidentally delete a slide you want to keep. To delete a slide, follow these steps:

1. **From within the Navigation pane (left side of the window), select the slide you want to delete.**

2. **Choose Edit ⇨ Delete, or simply press the Delete key on your keyboard.** The unfortunate slide simply disappears into the ether.

Slide and title masters

Every presentation uses a design template. This is a file that contains the styles used in a presentation, which include the following:

- A slide master and optional title master
- Type and size of fonts and bullets
- Placeholder sizes and positions in the slide
- Background design and fill colors

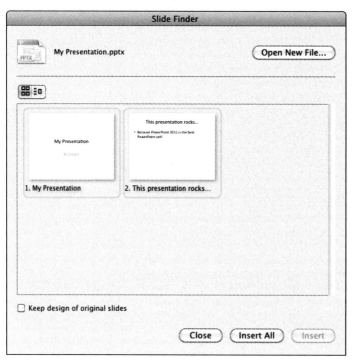

9.4 Insert single slides from other presentations into your new presentation to save yourself a lot of unnecessary work.

The slide master is the basic design that all slides in the presentation duplicate. The main purpose of the slide master is so that you can easily make global changes, such as a different font, to your presentation in one place (the slide master) as opposed to changing the font in every individual slide. Changing fonts in every slide can get a bit tedious and time consuming, to say the least.

Title masters are similar to slide masters, except they are intended only for the title page of your presentation.

To see your slide master, and to edit it if necessary, follow these steps:

1. **Choose View ⇨ Master ⇨ Slide Master.** Take a moment to check out the Master View window, as shown in Figure 9.5. You see the following:

   ● The Navigation pane shows you a list that includes a slide master and layouts (more on those in the next section of this chapter).

   ● The slide master is visible in the Slide pane.

   ● A new purple tab appears in the ribbon, called Slide Master. Click this tab to make edits to the slide master, add a new master, or add a new layout.

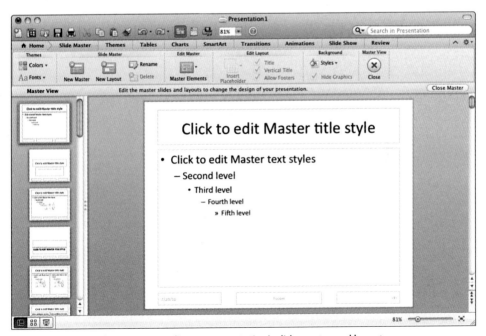

9.5 Master View is where you can edit your presentation's slide master and layouts.

2. Use the tools in the Slide Master tab of the ribbon to do the following:

● **Themes section.** You can change the colors and fonts associated with the slide master.

● **Slide Master section.** This area helps you to create a new master slide, a new layout, and rename or delete selected items.

● **Edit Master section.** You can change elements of the master slide. This button is not available unless you select the slide master in the Navigation pane (it's grayed out if you're viewing a layout).

● **Edit Layout section.** You can only change elements of a layout. To add a place-holder, click the Insert Placeholder button, select a type of placeholder from the list (such as a chart, text box, picture, and the like), and then click and drag the cursor (looks like a +) to draw the placeholder where you want it. Select the Title check box to put a title placeholder at the top of the slide. Select the Vertical Title check box to put a title placeholder on the side of the slide; the text is vertical, too. Select the Allow Footers check box to place footers at the bottom of the slide.

● **Background section.** You can add a custom background to your slide master and layouts. Click the Styles button to choose a background included in the theme, or insert and format your own background (using a single color, gradient, picture, or pattern) by selecting the Format Background option. Click the Hide Graphics button to hide any graphics that may be part of a themes background, if you want.

● **Master View section.** One, and only one, option is offered here: to close Master View.

3. Click a placeholder in the slide master or a layout. A new purple tab called Format appears next to the purple Slide Master tab in the ribbon. The Format tab, shown in Figure 9.6, affords the following editing tools:

9.6 The Format tab helps you modify elements of a placeholder in the slide master or a layout.

● **Shape Styles section.** Choose a color theme, add a fill color to the text or image placeholder, add an outline to the text or image placeholder, apply effects to the con-tents of the placeholder (such as 3-D rotation, shadows, and reflections), and adjust the transparency of the fill color.

● **Text Styles section.** Choose from a list of Quick Styles to format text, select font and outline color themes, and apply special effects to your text.

- **Arrange section.** Make placement adjustments to the objects within a placeholder. Group objects in a placeholder together so they can be treated as a single object, rotate objects 90 degrees to the right or left or flip them vertically or horizontally, and align the edges of an object. You can also rearrange the placement of objects in a slide master or layout by clicking the Reorder button and selecting Reorder Objects. This opens a really cool new screen, shown in Figure 9.7, that displays the objects of a slide master or layout in a 3-D grid. Click an object and move it to the left or right to reorder it among the other objects, and click OK when finished.

4. **Click the Close Master button on the right side of the yellow Master View strip to exit Master view.**

Note You can quickly jump to Master view from Normal view by holding down the Shift key while clicking the Normal view button in the lower left of the window. To return to Normal view, simply click the Normal view button.

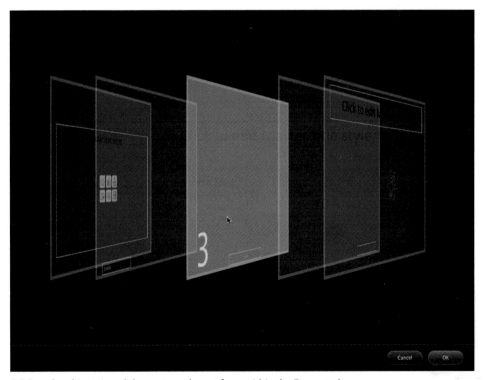

9.7 Reorder objects in a slide master or layout from within the Format tab.

Selecting a slide layout

Layouts are simply the arrangement of elements, such as pictures, titles and subtitles, tables, bullet lists, charts, and movies, on a slide. Every slide master has a set of preconfigured layouts for you to choose, and you can edit the layouts to create your own.

To add a new slide layout to your presentation, follow these steps:

1. **Click the Home tab in the ribbon.**

2. **Click the tiny arrow next to the New Slide button to see the list of available layouts, as shown in Figure 9.8.**

3. **Browse the list of layouts and select the one you want to add to your presentation by clicking it.**

If the layout you chose for a particular slide no longer suits your fancy, just change it:

1. **Select the slide you want to change from within the Navigation pane.**

2. **Click the Home tab in the ribbon.**

3. **Click the small button called Change the layout of the selected slide.** This button is located immediately up and to the right of the New Slide button.

4. **Browse the list of layouts and select the one to which you want to change your slide.**

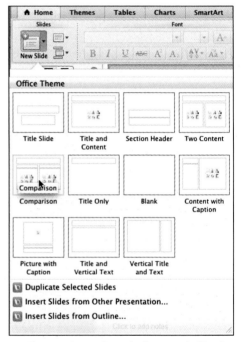

9.8 Choose a layout from the list provided by the New Slide button in the ribbon.

Genius

You can see the title of a slide master, slide, or layout by simply holding your mouse pointer over it in the Navigation pane, whether in Normal or Master view. After a second or so a small yellow window appears with the name of the layout.

Inserting and formatting text in a slide

Typing text into a slide's text placeholders is as simple as clicking the desired placeholder and tapping merrily away on your keyboard. Your text appears in the default font and color of the slide master.

Getting just slightly more complicated, you can easily change the appearance of text in a place-holder just as you would in other Office apps, like Word. Follow these steps:

1. **Click the Home tab in the ribbon.**

2. **Choose the slide you want to modify.**

3. **Highlight the text within the slide that you want to change.**

4. **Use the tools in the Font, Paragraph, Insert, and Format sections of the Home tab to spruce up your text any way you please.** I suggest you go all out and use Wingdings as your default font…or not!

Moving and resizing placeholders

PowerPoint 2011 allows you to move placeholders to a different area within the slide, and to also resize them. Follow these steps:

1. **Choose a slide you want to modify from within the Navigation pane.**

2. **Click on a placeholder to select it.** You will see eight blue sizing handles on the corners and sides of the placeholder and a green rotation handle slightly above it.

3. **Click and drag the blue sizing handles to adjust the width and height of your place-holder in the slide.** The items within the placeholder will resize to fit the new dimensions.

4. **Click and drag the green rotation handle, as shown in Figure 9.9, to rotate the placeholder within the slide.** The items within the placeholder will rotate with it.

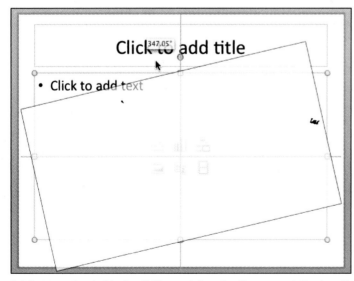

9.9 Rotate a placeholder by clicking and dragging its green rotation handle.

Creating a presentation from a template

You've already had a little peek at the wonder that is the PowerPoint Presentation Gallery, but you do more now than just dip your toe in. The PowerPoint Presentation Gallery is loaded with precon-figured templates that you can use to dazzle the office, teachers' conference, church group, or knitting class. One look at the available templates and it becomes more than obvious that Microsoft has put its graphic designers through their paces.

What template to choose?

The obvious answer to this question is that it's entirely up to you. While all the templates are pro-fessional and well designed, some templates fit certain situations better than others. Something tells me that the SOHO template would not translate well to a group of teenage football players trying to review their playbook, while Black Tie might not be the best choice for a PTA meeting.

To go about browsing and choosing a template, follow these steps:

1. **Open the PowerPoint Presentation Gallery.** Figure 9.10 provides a map of the Gallery's landmarks.

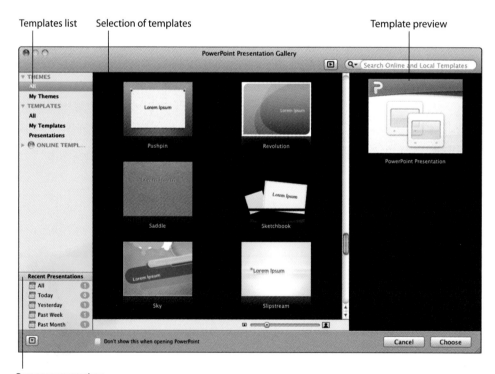

Templates list   Selection of templates   Template preview

Recent presentations

9.10 The PowerPoint Presentation Gallery is chock full of great preconfigured templates or themes.

- If PowerPoint is already running, press ⌘+Shift+P, or choose File ➪ New from Template.

- If PowerPoint isn't running, double-click its icon in the Microsoft Office 2011 folder to launch it, and the Gallery should open by default (unless you've changed that behavior in PowerPoint's preferences).

2. **Under Themes on the left side of the Gallery window, select All to access the Templates list.**

3. **Browse the selection of templates until you find the one that sings out to you, and click to select it.**

4. **Click Choose in the lower-right corner to open the template in PowerPoint.**

Genius

You can see even more of a template than a preview of its title master when using the PowerPoint Presentation Gallery. Move your mouse pointer over a template preview and you can see what the other slide layouts contained within it look like (move slowly so you don't miss any). This way you can see more of the template to better make a decision on which one to use for your presentation.

Editing information in the template

Editing placeholders in a template is no different than when creating a presentation from scratch. To edit a text placeholder, click the placeholder and let your fingers do the walking on your trusty keyboard. Of course, the text appears in the default font and color of the template, and yes, you are free to change them if you want.

Editing an image placeholder requires a tad more work, but it's certainly not going to make you break a sweat. Follow these steps:

1. **Add a new slide that contains a picture placeholder, as shown in Figure 9.11.**

2. **There are a couple of ways in which you can add your own image to the placeholder:**

   - **Drag an image from the desktop or a Finder window into the picture placeholder.** You will need a bit of screen real estate to pull it off, but if you can position your Slide pane so that you can see the desired image file on your desktop or within a Finder window, literally just drag and drop the image from the desktop or Finder into the picture placeholder in your slide.

   - **Click the Picture icon in the middle of the placeholder to insert an image from a file.** When the Choose a Picture dialog opens, browse your Mac or your network for the image file you need and select it. Click Insert to situate the file in the picture placeholder.

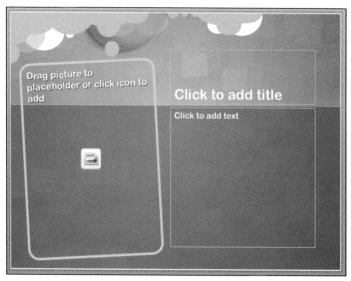

9.11 Drag an image into the picture placeholder or click the picture icon to browse your Mac for a file.

Using Notes and Handouts with Your Presentation

A presenter will only bore an audience to tears if he or she simply reads the contents of each slide in the presentation verbatim. Everyone knows that all good public speakers use notes to remind them of talking points, and PowerPoint is more than capable of providing a way for you to add notes to your presentation that only you, the presenter, are privy to. Your audience will simply think your dazzling wit and humor are byproducts of a truly personable public speaker and will be none the wiser that even you need a little prompting.

Also, you can't just walk into a meeting and start giving a presentation filled with information and statistics to your boss and colleagues; they want to be able to have that info handy during and after the presentation. That's why the folks at Microsoft knew it was a good idea to provide a hand-outs feature, which allows you to print your presentation using the same design themes.

Adding notes to your slides

There are a few ways to add notes to your slides in PowerPoint, but this is my favorite method:

1. **Select the slide to which you want to add notes.**

2. **Choose View ⇨ Notes Page to display the image of the slide and a text box for your notes.** The page may appear too small, but you can zoom in using the size slider in the lower-right corner of the window, as shown in Figure 9.12.

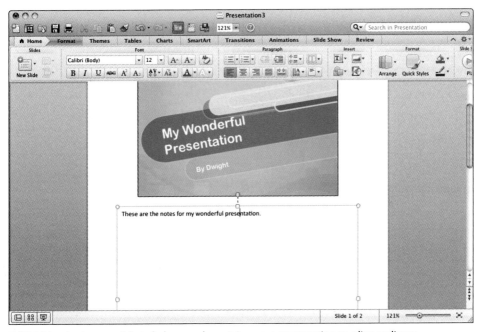

9.12 Add notes to your slide to help you when giving your presentation to a live audience.

3. **To edit the notes, click the text box and type the text you need.** You can change fonts and colors using the ribbon, just as you would in a text placeholder in the slide itself.

4. **To change the size and position of the slide and notes placeholders, click the place-holder and drag the sizing handles to the new positions.**

5. **To finish adding notes to your slide, click the Normal view button.**

Note

When resizing a placeholder, hold down the Shift key while dragging a corner sizing handle and the placeholder expands or contracts proportionally. This tip works when resizing any placeholder in any view, not just within the Notes view.

Note

Yes, you can add notes to your slide while in Normal view, but I prefer to do so in Notes view because that is the view I see when giving the presentation.

Just like for slides, you can modify how notes appear throughout your document. And because there are slide masters for your slides, it stands to reason that there is a notes master for your notes. To edit the notes master, follow these steps:

1. **Choose View ⇨ Masters ⇨ Notes Master.** The purple Notes Master tab appears in the ribbon (see Figure 9.13).

2. **Click the Notes Master tab to access the Notes Master tools for modifying the layout of your notes.**

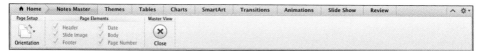

9.13 Notes Master view gives you options to modify the notes on-screen and in print.

3. **PowerPoint keeps it simple with only three sections in the Notes Master tab:**

   - **Page Setup.** You choose to view your notes in portrait or landscape modes.

   - **Page Elements section.** You can enable or disable objects within the notes, such as the date and headers and footers.

   - **Master View section.** This has one very important option: Click the button to close the Notes Master view.

Creating handouts from your presentation

Handouts allow you to print your presentation for your audience so they can take your great information with them. These handouts are especially useful if you teach classes using presentations. As with slides and notes, you can modify how a handout will look when it's printed by making adjustments to the handout master.

To create a handout of your presentation, follow these steps:

1. **Choose View ⇨ Masters ⇨ Handout Master.** The purple Handout Master tab appears in the ribbon next to the Home tab.

2. **Click the Handout Master tab to see options for modifying your handout's appearance.**

3. **PowerPoint still keeps it simple, but this time with four sections for your perusal:**

- **Page Setup.** Choose to view and print your handout in portrait or landscape mode.

- **Page Elements section.** You can enable or disable four objects within the handout: headers, dates, footers, and page numbers.

- **Slides Per Page section.** This gives you the flexibility to print from two to nine slides per page (see Figure 9.14), as well as print an outline of your slides.

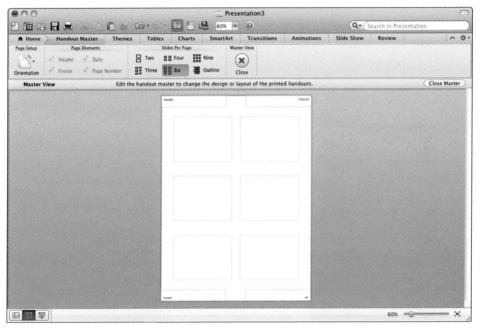

9.14 Modify the number of slides that are printed per page for your handouts.

- **Master View section.** This gives you the option to close out of the Handout Master View by clicking the button.

How Can I Add Some Pizzazz to My Presentations?

f you're a whiz at the basics of creating a presentation, working with slides, and using placeholders, it's time to kick it up a couple of notches. Bare-bones presentations just won't do in some situations, so in this chapter you learn how to add images and graphics to your slides to give them a personal touch. You also learn about adding images and movies, which may be just the pizzazz your presentation needs. PowerPoint isn't only functional; it's pretty cool, too!

ey, I love a plain, white background in a slide as much as the next person, but adding a touch of lor and throwing in an image or two can only serve to sweeten the deal. In this section, I look at plying and changing themes, using background colors to brighten, or in some cases darken, a de; the ABCs of inserting images and clip art with the help of Media Browser; utilizing objects d charts within a slide; and touching up text with SmartArt graphics.

pplying and customizing a theme

ou can apply your own background to a slide or use one of the predefined themes that ships with werPoint. Many themes use a graphic containing an illustration of some sort, while others use a mple background color. Of course, themes don't affect just the backgrounds and colors in your esentation, but also the fonts used within it.

ie great thing about themes is that they look great without you having to hardly lift a finger, and if ere isn't a theme that's exactly what you need you can customize elements of a theme as you go.

oplying a theme to a slide is easy. Follow these steps:

1. **Create a new slide, or select a slide in an existing presentation that you want to modify.**

2. **Click the Themes tab from within the ribbon.**

3. **Browse the available themes found in the Themes section in one of two ways:**

   - Click the arrow on the right or left side of the themes browser to scroll through the themes.

aution

If you apply a theme to one slide in a presentation it is applied to all the slides in the presentation. If you decide to make such a change in the middle of putting together a presentation, be sure to go back and look at all of the slides in your presentation to make certain they weren't adversely affected.

- Hold your mouse pointer over the themes browser and an arrow appears just beneath it. Click the arrow and you see a drop-down menu, like the one shown in Figure 10.1, which allows you to see the themes together in a larger window.

4. **Click the theme you want to use with your slide and it is instantly applied.**

Now that you've picked a theme (the example uses one of my favorites, Sky), let's mess with it a bit. You can change its default colors, fonts, and backgrounds.

The following steps show you how changing the default colors in a theme can make a drastic impact on its appearance:

10.1 Browse the list of themes to find the one you want to apply to your presentation.

1. **Select a slide in the Navigation pane.** Again, the example uses the Sky theme, but you can pick your own theme if you want.

2. **Click the Themes tab from within the ribbon.**

3. **In the Theme Options section, click the Colors button to see a list of all the precon-figured theme colors that ship with PowerPoint 2011.**

4. **Make a selection from the list of theme colors, preferably a color palette that is markedly different than the theme you're currently using, and click to apply it to your theme.** Newsprint has been applied to this example, and you see the vast difference it makes in the Sky theme in Figure 10.2.

Changing the color palette of a theme can make a major difference to the way your presentation appears. You can also change fonts and backgrounds for your slides in the same manner, both from within the Theme Options section of the Themes tab in the ribbon.

10.2 Compare the Sky theme's original look to the custom one using Newsprint's theme colors.

Genius

Do you like the new theme you've created? If so, and you think you might want to use it again, save it. Just click the Save Theme button (found in the Themes section of the Themes tab in the ribbon), give the new theme a name, and click the Save button.

Adding background colors and fills

Backgrounds are colors, and in some cases images, that decorate the very back portion of a slide. The background color or image sits behind the information in the slide and is meant to enhance the information, not distract from it.

Fills are simply background colors or images that reside within a placeholder. You can add, edit, and remove fills as easily as you can backgrounds.

To add a background to a slide, follow these steps:

1. **Select a slide from within the Navigation pane.**

2. **Click the Themes tab in the ribbon.**

3. **In the Theme Options section, click the Backgrounds button.**

4. **Browse the list of available backgrounds and click to select the one you want to use.** The color palette of backgrounds depends on the theme you are using.

Now try your hand at a placeholder fill. Follow these steps:

1. **Select a slide from within the Navigation pane that you want to work with.**

2. **Select a placeholder within the slide.** A new purple tab called Format appears in the ribbon next to the Home tab.

3. **Click the Format tab to peruse its wares.**

4. **In the Shape Styles section, click the arrow next to the Fill button to see a list of available colors.**

5. **Choose a color from the pop-up list by clicking on it.** The colors are divided into Theme Colors and Standard Colors. The Theme Colors also list shades of the individual colors beneath their original swatch. Hold the mouse pointer over a shade swatch and it displays the percentage that it is lighter or darker than the original, as shown in Figure 10.3. The placeholder is now filled with the color you selected. You can change the color if you want by simply clicking the Fill button again and selecting something different from the options.

6. **If you don't care for any of the colors in the Fill pop-up list, select the More Colors option to open the Colors window.** Click one of the buttons at the top of the window and you can select any color that the screen of your Mac can reproduce:

10.3 You can select shades of Theme Colors as well as Standard Colors by clicking the Fill button.

- **Color Wheel.** Click anywhere in the color wheel to select a color and use the slider on the right to adjust its shade.

- **Color Sliders.** Click the pop-up menu to choose which kind of slider to use: Gray Scale, RGB, CMYK, or HSB. Drag the sliders under each kind to mix a new color.

- **Color Palettes.** Click the Palette pop-up menu to select a color palette, and then browse the color list to select a color.

- **Image Palettes.** Click the Image pop-up menu to select a palette (Spectrum is the one and only choice until you add a new palette from the Palette pop-up menu). Click in the color window to select a color.

- **Crayons.** Choose a color from the crayon box and click OK to select it.

Genius

You can assign a color, or ICC, profile to colors created with the Color Slider section of the Colors window. Click the tiny multicolored box to the left of the slider pop-up menu and choose a color profile from the list. The profiles differ depending on the color slider used.

A simple fill is all well and good, but your fill isn't quite ready for prime time in my opinion. Follow these steps to jazz up a fill:

1. **Select the placeholder containing the fill you want to spiffy up.**

2. **Select the Format tab in the ribbon.**

3. **Click the arrow next to the Fill button and select Fill Effects from the list to open the Format Shape window to the Fill tools.**

4. **Click the Solid tab to choose a new color or adjust the transparency of the color using the slider provided.**

5. **Click the Gradient tab to apply a gradient to the placeholder using the fill color and a second color of your choosing.** There are several tools here:

   - Choose a style for your gradient and apply an angle or direction to it.

   - Drag the sliders under the color bar in the Gradient section to adjust the levels of colors in the gradient.

   - Change the colors in the gradient by clicking a slider and choosing a color from the Color pop-up menu.

   - Add or delete colors from your gradient by using the Add Color or Delete Color buttons. When you click Add Color, a new slider appears under the color bar. To delete a color, select the slider for the color you want to delete and click the Delete Color button.

   - Adjust the transparency of a color using the Transparency slider.

   - Select the Rotate gradient with shape check box to have the gradient maintain its angle and direction even if you decide to rotate the placeholder in which it resides.

6. **Click the Picture or Texture tab to use an image or a texture as a fill instead of using a color.**

   - To use an image as your fill, click Choose Picture to browse your Mac for the image you want to use and then click Insert to place the image in the placeholder.

   - If you'd rather use a texture, click the Choose Texture pop-up menu, browse the list of textures (see Figure 10.4), and select the one that you like.

   - Drag the transparency slider to adjust the picture or texture transparency.

   - Select the Rotate with shape check box to have the image or texture move in concert with the placeholder should you decide to rotate it to one angle or another.

   - Select the Tile check box if the image you select doesn't entirely fill the placeholder. This causes PowerPoint to tile multiple copies of the image to fill the space as required.

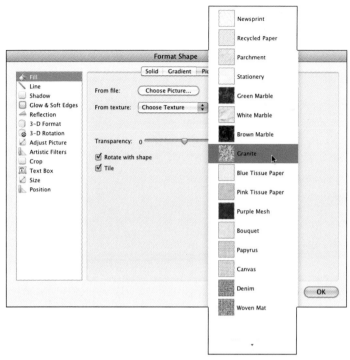

10.4 There is a long list of textures you can utilize as a fill as opposed to using a color.

7. **Change your solid color to a pattern using the Pattern tab.**

- Choose a pattern from the large selection.
- Choose foreground and background colors from the appropriate pop-up menus.

A fill looks pretty good in a placeholder, don't you think? Now it's time to add a line to the placeholder, which acts as a border. Follow these steps:

1. **Select the placeholder to which you're going to apply the line.**

2. **Click the Format tab in the ribbon.**

3. **Click the arrow next to the Line button and select a color from the list.** You probably want to choose something that's complimentary to the fill color. If you don't see something that strikes your fancy in the selection offered, select the More Colors option to use the Color Window to find a color.

4. **Click the arrow next to the Line button again and position your mouse pointer over the Weight option.** Select a weight for your line from the resulting submenu.

5. **Click the Line button's arrow again, hold your mouse pointer over the Dash option, and choose a style for your line from the submenu.**

Great, you have a line! Now, what to do with it? You might be wondering: "A line is a line is a line, right?" Well, yes, but it doesn't have to be, not in PowerPoint 2011. Follow these steps:

1. **Select the placeholder whose line you want to monkey around with.**

2. **Click the Format tab's Line button and choose Line Effects from the pop-up to open the Format Shape dialog to the Line tools.**

3. **Click the Solid tab to change the color of your line and to change its transparency, if you want.**

4. **Believe it or not, you can add a gradient to a line, too, by clicking the Gradient tab, as shown in Figure 10.5.** The same options used for a fill gradient apply here, as well.

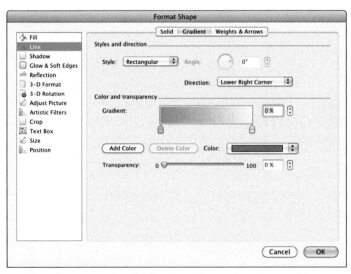

10.5 A gradient can make a line border really stand out in your slide.

5. **Click the Weights & Arrows tab.** From here you can bump up the weight of your line (which is usually necessary when using a gradient so that one can actually make out the line) and change the style of your line using the Style, Dashed, Cap type, and Join type pop-ups.

Genius

What if you want to make a background or fill universal throughout your presentation? If that's the case you need to modify the slide master using the same techniques discussed so far. See Chapter 9 for more on slide masters.

Inserting your own images

When you have a personal or family project to do, using your own images is one great way to go when creating backgrounds of fills for your slides. Media Browser remains the easiest way to add pictures from your iPhoto or Photo Booth libraries. To utilize it, follow these steps:

1. **Choose the slide to which you want to add the picture.** You can place a picture as the main background of a slide or you can add it to a placeholder in the slide; you'll need to decide which you want to do when selecting a slide.

2. **Open Media Browser by clicking its button in the toolbar.**

3. **Click the Photos button at the top of the Media window.**

4. **Choose either iPhoto or Photo Booth as the location for the picture you want to use.**

5. **Scroll through the list of pictures until you see the one you want to use.** If you can barely make out the pictures due to their small size in the list, drag the size slider to the right a bit until they are large enough to see clearly.

6. **Click and drag the picture you want to use from the list of pictures to the place you want to use it in the slide (on the background or in a placeholder), as shown in Figure 10.6.**

You may need to make some minor (or major) adjustments to an image before you think it's ready to star in your presentation, and if that's the case PowerPoint 2011 is surprisingly loaded with several very powerful image-editing tools. When you click a picture that you've added to a slide the purple Format Picture tab appears next to the Home tab in the ribbon, and that's where the action takes place when it comes to sprucing up a picture. The following options are available:

- **Corrections.** Click this button to see the many corrections that PowerPoint can make for you automatically, including sharpening or softening a picture, and adjusting its brightness and contrast. If you want to do the driving yourself, select the Picture Correction Options selection and manually tweak the picture's color settings.

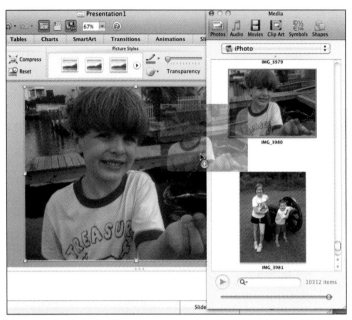

10.6 Just drag a picture from the list and drop it into your slide. Nice and easy, isn't it?

- **Recolor.** Click the Recolor button and PowerPoint offers to automatically correct your colors or simply change them altogether. Make a selection from the list to apply the change to your slide.

- **Filters.** Click the Filters button to apply an artistic filter to your picture, such as Paint Brush, Blur, and Glass.

- **Remove Background.** This has to be one of the coolest features in PowerPoint. It allows you to remove the background of an image and crop to just the portion of the picture you want, as shown in Figure 10.7. The purple shaded area is the part of the picture I want to remove. I can add or remove items in the picture by dragging the sizing handles on the selection boxes or by clicking areas on the picture.

Genius

The busier the background of an image, the tougher it is to crop the image accurately. You may need to take a bit more time, and even increase the size of the slide in the Slide pane, in order to accurately crop busy pictures.

🔘 **Crop.** Click the Crop button to place cropping handles on the corners and sides of the image. Drag the handles to crop the picture to your liking. Alternately, you can click the arrow next to the Crop button and choose to crop the image to fit a particular shape (Mask to Shape), crop it to fit the slide or placeholder, or crop it to fill the slide or placeholder.

10.7 PowerPoint makes it easy to remove a background from a picture.

Adding Clip Art or Symbols to Slides

Add clip art or symbols to your slides in the same manner as you add images, with the help of Media Browser:

1. **Select a slide to which you want to add the object.**

2. **Click the Media Browser button within the toolbar.**

3. **Click the Clip Art or Symbols button at the top of the Media window.**

4. **Scroll through the list of images or symbols until you see the one you want to use.**

5. **Drag the clip art or symbol you want to use from the list to the location you want to use it in the slide.**

- **Compress.** Some images are very large in terms of file size, and they can bloat the size of your presentation. PowerPoint provides the Compress option so that you can make adjustments to the image that ultimately result in a smaller file size for the presentation. The original file isn't touched, only the copy used by PowerPoint. I love this feature.

- **Reset.** Have you butchered your picture beyond recognition? That's exactly why Microsoft provided this little gem. Click the Reset button and your picture returns to its original glory. I love this feature, too, for obvious reasons.

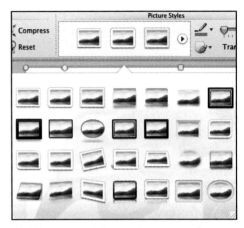

10.8 You can apply frames, borders, shadows, and more effects to your pictures using Picture Styles.

- **Picture Styles.** Frame your image, and even angle it, using the options in the Picture Styles section. Click the arrow under the list of options, as shown in Figure 10.8, and select an option to apply a frame and/or angle an image. Apply a border to the image with the Line button. Add a shadow, reflection, glow, bevel, or 3-D rotation effect to the image using the Visual Effect button, and use the Transparency slider to adjust transparency of the image.

- **Arrange.** Use the options in this section to make alignment changes to the image, flip or rotate the image, change the order of objects, or group objects together.

- **Size.** Manually make size adjustments to your pictures with the Height and Width selectors in this section.

Drawing shapes

Shapes can perform all kinds of functions within a slide, from simply adding a little fun to actually performing an action, such as playing music or jumping to another slide. To draw a shape, follow these steps:

1. **Choose the slide to which you want to add a shape.** You can place a shape anywhere in the slide.

2. **Open Media Browser by clicking its button in the toolbar.**

3. **Click the Shapes button at the top of the Media window.**

4. **Click the pop-up menu if you're looking for a particular type of shape, or leave it at All to see all the available shapes at once.**

5. **Add a shape to the slide in one of two ways:**

   - Drag the shape from the list and drop it into the slide.

   - Click the shape you want to add one time; your cursor changes to a cross hair (+). Point the cross hair to a position within your slide, click and drag the mouse to draw the shape to the desired size, and let go of the mouse button when finished.

   If you draw an action button, the Action Settings dialog, seen in Figure 10.9, opens. Set options to customize the actions taken when this button is clicked while working within the presentation. For example, place a Home button (looks like a house) in a slide; clicking this button should take you back to Home, which is the first page of the slide. A button's default behavior can be changed easily from the Action Settings dialog, too.

10.9 The Action Settings dialog is where you choose what will happen when an action button is clicked in a slide.

6. **Use the sizing handles on the shape's box to adjust the size, or drag the rotation handle to rotate the shape.**

7. **Click the purple Format tab in the ribbon to make any desired changes to the shape:**

   - In the Shape Styles section you can choose a color theme for your shape, add a fill color to it, add an outline using the Line button, apply effects to the shape (such as 3-D rotation, shadows, and reflections), and adjust the transparency of the fill color.

   - The Text Styles section won't apply to your shapes.

• The Arrange section helps to make placement adjustments to all objects within the slide. Group objects together so they can be treated as a single one, rotate objects 90 degrees to the right or left or flip them vertically or horizontally, and align the edges of an object. You can also reorder objects within a slide.

8. **Manually adjust the size of your shapes using the Height and Width selectors.**

Genius

Have you noticed the little yellow handles in some of the images? If you have, those handles allow you to modify a particular part of a shape. For example, if you place a smiley face shape in your slide, click to highlight it and you will notice the yellow handle on the mouth of the smiley face. Click and drag the handle to change that smile to a frown. Other shapes can be manipulated in much the same way.

Adding charts to presentations

A PowerPoint presentation without a chart is bit like a Steve Jobs without his trademark jeans and black turtleneck; it just wouldn't seem right. Charts have been an integral part of presentations for as long as, well, forever! PowerPoint 2011 doesn't disappoint in its implementation of charts, either; the ribbon excels at it.

1. **Choose a slide to add a chart to.**

2. **Click the Charts tab in the ribbon.**

3. **Under the Change Chart Type section, choose a chart from one of the options, as shown in Figure 10.10.**

4. **The first time you select a chart Excel opens so that you can enter your chart's data.** As you type the data in the spreadsheet, Excel uses it to build the chart in PowerPoint. Close the spreadsheet when finished to return to PowerPoint. Now that's what I call teamwork!

5. **If you don't quite get the data right in the chart, click the Edit button under the Data section to reopen the data in Excel and make any necessary changes.**

6. **If you don't like the layout of the elements in your chart, or you're not too keen on the colors, use the Chart Quick Layouts section and the Chart Styles section to spruce things up a bit.** Simply click the arrow button beneath each one to see your options, and then choose one.

7. **Make further changes to your charts by clicking the purple Chart Layout and Format tabs in the ribbon (the chart must be selected within the slide for these tabs to be visible):**

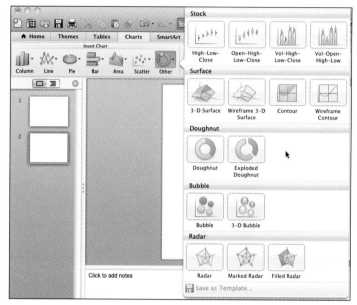

10.10 PowerPoint offers a huge choice of chart types to represent your data graphically.

- **Chart Layout tab.** This allows you to modify how data appears in the chart. Add or edit labels in the chart, change the format and layout of each axis in the chart, add analyses to the data (such as a trendline), and if the chart supports it you can rotate the chart three-dimensionally.

- **Format tab.** This helps you change the colors and effects used in the chart, arrange objects within the chart, and add special effects to the chart's text.

SmartArt graphics

A SmartArt graphic is a really cool way to represent information on your slide using some of PowerPoint's great graphics. The graphics represent different ideas, such as hierarchies, relationships, processes, and lists. All you have to do is select a graphic type, choose the art, and add your text; done! Follow these steps:

1. **Select a slide to which you want to add the SmartArt graphic.**

2. **Click the SmartArt tab within the ribbon.**

3. **In the Insert SmartArt graphic section, choose a graphic from one of the graphic types.**

4. **When the graphic is inserted into the slide, the Text Pane appears, as shown in Figure 10.11.** Type the text in the areas provided in the Text Pane, and use the buttons at the top of the Text Pane to modify its contents, such as the text position in the graphic, and adding or removing text boxes. Click outside the graphic to close the Text Pane, and click inside to reopen it.

10.11 Add and edit text in a SmartArt graphic using the Text Pane.

5. **Edit the shapes used in the SmartArt graphic, shift items to the left or right, and arrange shapes in an organizational chart by utilizing the tools in the Edit SmartArt section.**

6. **Change the colors and appearance of the SmartArt graphic using tools in the SmartArt Graphic Styles section.** Click the Colors button to change the color palette of your graphic. Click the arrow below the styles bar to see all the available styles for the type of graphic you're using.

7. **Click the purple Format tab to make adjustments to the appearance of your graphic's text.**

Slide Transitions

Slide transitions have come a long way, baby. Transitions are simply effects that can be applied to the way you move from one slide to another within a presentation. The effects offered in

PowerPoint 2011 are just flat-out awesome! I remember back in the day when one slide fading out while another faded in was a pretty cool trick; nowadays you can shred, ripple, dissolve, and even warp into a vortex. Technology rocks.

1. **Click the Transitions tab in the ribbon.**

2. **In the Transition to this Slide section, choose a transition from the transitions bar, as seen in Figure 10.12.**

3. **Some transitions offer options that you can configure for their effects.** Click the Effects Options button to see what's available, because it differs for every transition.

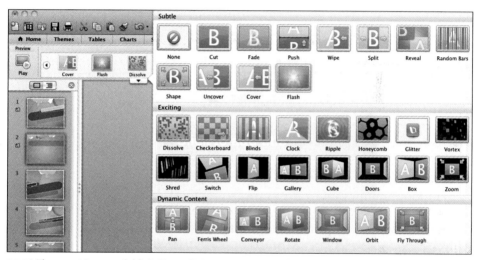

10.12 The transitions available in PowerPoint 2011 are so cool...

4. **Choose how long the transition effect should last between each slide using the Duration option.**

5. **Add a sound to the transition by clicking the Sound pop-up menu.** If you don't like what you hear choose Other Sound, browse your Mac for the sound file you want, and click Insert.

6. **Determine whether to advance the slides in your presentation with a mouse click in the Advance slide section.**

7. **Click the All Slides button in the Apply To section to make the transition universal across all slides in the presentation.**

Genius

Don't go crazy applying nonstop dazzling transitions to your presentation. Remember the old axiom: Less is more. Keeping it simple by using the same transition between every slide for consistency is the best advice I can offer.

Note

Transitions made in PowerPoint 2011 may not work in older versions of PowerPoint. If you find yourself trying to run a PowerPoint 2011 presentation using an earlier version of PowerPoint, transitions that aren't compatible will revert to the default of that version of PowerPoint.

Adding Sounds and Movies to Your Presentation

Yes, Virginia, you really can add sounds and movies to your PowerPoint presentations. Add some music to your presentation, or show a movie of the kids playing with their new puppy for the family reunion slide show. Media Browser once again shows up to help you add yet another cool item to your slides. To add sound to your slide, follow these steps:

1. **Choose a slide to which you want to add a sound.**

2. **Click the Media Browser button from within the toolbar.**

3. **Click the Audio button at the top of the Media window.**

4. **Choose the location of your sound file from the pop-up menu at the top of the window.**

5. **Find your sound file in the list, and drag and drop it into the slide.**

6. **The sound file appears in the slide using a sound speaker icon.** Click the icon to play the audio from within the slide.

7. **Select the speaker icon and then click the purple Format Audio tab in the ribbon.**

8. **Use the tools in the Audio Options section to determine when to play the sound file and other playback options.**

To add a movie to your slide, follow these steps:

1. **Click the Movie button at the top of the Media window.**

2. **Select the location of the movie on your Mac using the pop-up menu.**

3. **Scroll through the list of movies until you find the one you want to use.** Use the size slider at the bottom of the window to make the movie previews larger.

4. **Click to select a movie and click the Play button at the bottom of the window if you want to watch the clip before inserting it into the slide.**

5. **Drag and drop the movie from Media Browser into the slide, as seen in Figure 10.13.**

6. **With the movie selected in the slide, click the purple Format Movie tab in the ribbon to make changes to the way the movie appears in the slide.**

7. **Click the Play button to see a preview of the movie within the slide.**

8. **Use the Start pop-up menu to determine whether the movie plays as soon as the slide displays or when you click it.**

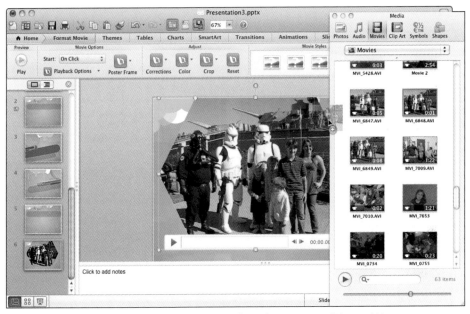

10.13 Drag a movie file from the Media Browser and just drop it onto a slide to add it to your presentation.

9. **Click the Playback Options button to force the movie to play full screen, to rewind the movie back to its beginning, to loop the movie until you stop it, or to hide the movie from view while it's not being played.**

10. **Use the options in the Adjust section to make minor corrections to the movie's brightness and contrast, adjust colors, and crop the movie to fit your slide or a shape.**

11. **Apply a frame, a border, or a special effect to your movie using the Movie Styles section.**

How Do I Give a Presentation?

After weeks of laboring on your most important presentation, it's time to deliver it to an audience. How do you deliver the presentation to your audience? PowerPoint 2011 is ready, willing, and able to jump in with both feet to help you deliver this masterpiece to the eager throngs.

by which you get the information contained within your slides into the minds and hands of an audience is just as important as the hard work you put into creating them. Whether you just show viewers the presentation on your Mac's screen, another monitor, or with the aid of a projector, the following sections explain the options you can use to get your presentation from your Mac to your addressees.

Playing a presentation

Playing a presentation means to begin showing the presentation in full screen mode, viewing it one slide at a time. You can feel free to follow the order in which you created the slides, or get all spontaneous and flit around from slide to slide with abandon.

There are five ways to launch a presentation from the first slide:

- Use the Play button in the ribbon's Home tab:
    1. **Click the first slide in your presentation from the Navigation pane.**
    2. **Under the Home tab of the ribbon, click the Play button on the right side (under the Slide Show section).**
- Click the Slide Show view button in the lower left of the window.
- Press ⌘+Shift+Return.
- Choose Slide Show ➪ Play from Start.
- Click the From Start button in the ribbon's Slide Show tab:
    1. **Click the Slide Show tab from within the ribbon.**
    2. **Click the From Start button located in the Play Slide Show section (see Figure 11.1).**

11.1 Click the From Start button in the ribbon's Play Slide Show tab to launch your presentation from the first slide.

I'm sure you noticed that you could also play the presentation beginning with a slide other than the first one. If not, here are a few ways to do it:

- Use the Play options in the ribbon's Home tab.
    1. **In the Navigation pane, click the slide from which you want to begin the presentation.**
    2. **Go to the Home tab in the ribbon.**

3. **Click the tiny arrow next to the Play button under the Slide Show section and choose Play from Current Slide.**

- In the Navigation pane, select the slide you want to launch from and press ⌘+Return.
- Select the slide you want to start with from within the Navigation pane, and choose Slide Show ➪ Play from Current Slide.

Basic movement from slide to slide is a breeze once within a slide show. You can move to the next slide in one of the following ways:

- Click the right arrow.
- Click the slide you're currently viewing.
- Press N.

There are two ways to go to the previous slide in the show:

- Click the left arrow key.
- Press P.

There are lots of other keyboard shortcuts you can use to maneuver within a slide show. Table 11.1 points them out. Many of the tasks listed have several keyboard shortcuts, so take your pick. Other shortcuts listed are discussed later in this chapter.

Table 11.1 Keyboard Shortcuts for PowerPoint Slide Shows

Task	Keyboard shortcut(s)
Move to the next slide or animation	Right arrow, Return (or Enter), Page Down, Down arrow, N, Spacebar
Move to the previous slide or animation	Left arrow, Up arrow, Page Up, P, Delete
End the slide show	Esc, Hyphen, ⌘+. (period)
Jump to a slide number	Press the number of the slide and press Return (or Enter)
Play from the first slide	⌘+Return
Play from currently selected slide	⌘+Shift+Return
Display a black screen, or return to slide show from a black screen	B or . (period)
Display a white screen, or return to slide show from white screen	W or , (comma)
Stop/restart an automatic slide show	S or + (plus)

continued

195

Table 11.1 continued

Task	Keyboard shortcut(s)
Erase annotations made on-screen	E
Go to the next hidden slide	H
Show a hidden pointer and change the pointer to a pen	⌘+P
Show a hidden pointer and change the pointer to an arrow	⌘+A
Hide the pointer immediately	⌘+Control+H
Hide the pointer in 10 seconds	⌘+U
Show or hide arrow pointer	A or = (equal)
Show the contextual menu	Hold Control and click the mouse button (the right mouse button if using a two-button mouse)

Note If you have a laptop or use a keyboard layout other than U.S., these shortcuts may be different. Consult Apple for information regarding keyboard shortcuts for your device or keyboard layout.

Set up a slide show

There are several options that you can set before running your slide show that will make it behave the way you want it to. For example, you may want to run the slide show this time without narration, whereas by default it contains a narrative. To quickly set up a slide show, follow these steps:

1. **Click the Slide Show tab in the ribbon.**

2. **In the Set Up section, click the Set Up Show button to open the Set Up Show dialog, as shown in Figure 11.2.**

3. **Determine the type of show you want to deliver under the Show type section.**

4. **The Show options section gives you extended control over content.** The available options include

   - **Loop continuously until 'Esc'.** Select this check box to allow the slide show to play nonstop until you press Esc.

   - **Show without narration.** Select this option to play your slide show without the narration track you may have recorded.

- **Show without animation.** Select this check box to disable any animations you may have included in your slides.

- **Annotation pen color.** Click this pop-up menu to choose a different color for your pen while making on-screen notes during your presentation.

5. **Play all the slides or only a select few using the options in the Slides section.**

6. **Determine whether to progress through your presentation manually or with timers you've already set within the slides in the Advance slides section.**

Using Presenter View

Anyone who has given a presentation comes to be most thankful for Presenter View after using it a time or two. Presenter View allows the presenter to see the presentation on the computer screen alongside other information such as how much time has elapsed during

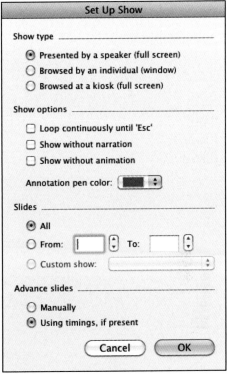

11.2 The Set Up Show dialog allows you to make a few adjustments to playback before launching a slide show.

the presentation, notes, and the next slide in the presentation. Meanwhile, the audience simply sees the slide show on a second display. It's a very helpful way for the presenter to keep tabs on what's going on while maintaining the audience's focus on the presentation. Of course, you can also use Presenter View while using only one monitor if you want.

To begin using Presenter View, follow these steps:

1. **Click the Slide Show tab within the ribbon.**

2. **In the Navigation pane, choose the slide you want to begin the slide show with.**

3. **Click the Presenter View button in the Presenter Tools section to see the Presenter view.** Figure 11.3 gives you a quick tour of Presenter View and its amenities, and Table 11.2 gives a quick rundown of what each does for the presenter.

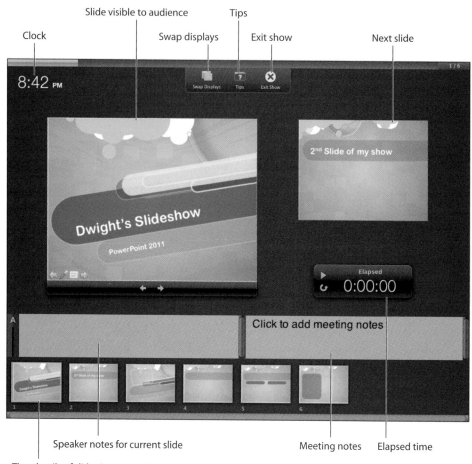

Clock

Slide visible to audience

Swap displays

Tips

Exit show

Next slide

Speaker notes for current slide

Meeting notes   Elapsed time

Thumbnails of slides in presentation

11.3 Presenter View in all its glory.

Table 11.2 Functions Available Within Presenter View

Feature	Function
Clock	Displays the current time.
Slide visible to audience	This is the slide that the audience is currently viewing.
Next slide	This is the next slide up in your presentation. Seeing the next slide will help you make sure that the upcoming slide is what you intend.
Elapsed time	Click the Play button to start the timer. It shows the amount of time your presentation is taking. Click the Reset button to reset the timer.

Feature	Function
Speaker notes for current slide	These are the notes you added to your slides while in the process of creating it.
Meeting notes	This field allows you to take notes on the fly during the presentation.
Swap displays	You can click the Swap Displays button when using two monitors to move Presenter View to the other monitor, and the audience's view appears on your display.
Tips	Click the Tips button to see a window listing keyboard shortcuts you can use for navigating your slides.
Exit show	Click the Exit Show button to quit the presentation.

Genius

You can also jump from one slide to another in your presentation quite quickly in Presenter View. Drag your mouse pointer to the bottom of the screen and your slides will "pop up." Simply click the slide you want to jump to next.

Rehearse a presentation

Practice makes perfect, or so it's said. While it may not make you a perfect presenter, practice will certainly get you closer to flawlessness than sitting on your duff watching television. Practicing your presentation will help you get a better handle on the material, and will give you a good idea of the time you'll need to present your slides. To practice your presentation, follow these steps:

1. **Click the Slide Show tab within the ribbon.**

2. **In the Navigation pane, choose the slide you want to begin the slide show with.**

3. **Click the Rehearse button in the Presenter Tools section.**

4. **The Rehearse View looks almost identical to Presenter View with one key difference: the elapsed time timer.**
   Notice in Figure 11.4 that the timer now shows you not only the total time elapsed in the presentation, but also the time elapsed on the current slide.

11.4 The Format tab helps you modify elements of a placeholder in the slide master or a layout.

5. **Rehearse your presentation.** Click the right or left arrow to advance to the next or previous slide.

199

6. **Press Esc to stop rehearsal.** PowerPoint will ask if you want to save the timings of each individual slide to the presentation. The answer is up to you. The effect of answering yes is that you can use the timings when running the presentation automatically.

Genius

Did you think of something you wanted to add to your speaker notes during your rehearsal? If so, you can easily add it to your existing notes. Click the Pause button to pause the timer, and then click inside the notes pane on the right side of the window. Type your new thoughts, and when you exit rehearsal they will be added to the notes that were already in the slide.

Record a presentation

When you record a narrative in your slide show PowerPoint also records the timings for each slide, just as in Rehearsal mode, and for the same reason. Add a narrative to your slide show by following these steps:

Note

Your computer must have a microphone in order to record narration. This won't be a problem for many newer Macs, but older models may not come so equipped.

1. Click the Slide Show tab within the ribbon.

2. In the Navigation pane, choose the slide you want to begin with.

3. **Click the Record button in the Presenter Tools section to open the Presenter View window.** Be aware that recording automatically starts as soon as you enter Presenter View.

4. **Click Pause to pause recording, Play to continue, and the Reset button to rerecord the slide.**

5. **When finished recording a slide, move to the next by clicking the right or left arrows under the current slide.**

6. **Press Esc when your recording is completed.** PowerPoint again asks you if you want to save the timings for each slide, and again the answer is up to you. Each slide for which you've recorded a narrative appears with a speaker icon in the lower-right corner, but this icon won't be visible to the audience during a show.

Technical Tips for Delivering an Effective Presentation

While I'm sure you're perfectly adept at giving a presentation, there are a couple of things that some folks may fail to consider when it comes time to deliver. These are just a few technical foibles you'll want to avoid that will help the entire presentation go much smoother:

- **Make sure your equipment and presentation work correctly before you begin.** Don't assume it will work today just because it happened to yesterday!

- **If you're using a projector make sure that its resolution is the same as the computer you used to create it.** This way you can avoid some slides potentially being cropped.

- **If you have a screen saver turned on, turn it off.** If you linger too long on a slide your screen saver may kick in, totally throwing off your audience's focus.

Draw on slides during a presentation

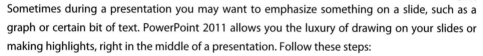

Sometimes during a presentation you may want to emphasize something on a slide, such as a graph or certain bit of text. PowerPoint 2011 allows you the luxury of drawing on your slides or making highlights, right in the middle of a presentation. Follow these steps:

1. Click the Slide Show tab within the ribbon.

2. In the Navigation pane, choose the slide you want to begin with.

3. Click the From Start button in the Play Slide Show section.

4. Right-click (or Control+click if you have a one-button mouse) the slide you want to draw on to open the contextual menu.

5. Hold your mouse over Pointer Options and select Pen from the submenu (**Figure 11.5**). Use the Pen Color menu to select a color for your drawings.

6. Click and hold your mouse button to draw on your slide, releasing the button when finished drawing.

7. Press E to erase drawings from your slide.

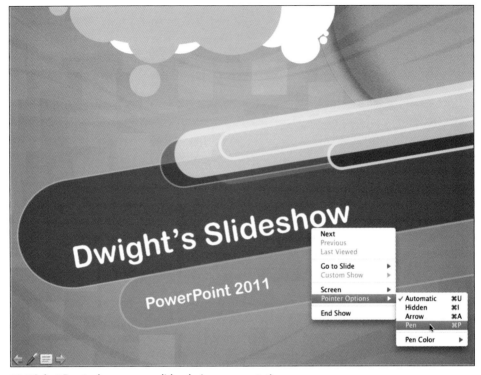

11.5 Select Pen to draw on your slides during a presentation.

Broadcast a live presentation

What can you do when your audience is scattered in different locations about the country? Sure, you could record the presentation and send it to them later, but why do that when PowerPoint allows you to broadcast your presentations (live I might add) over the Internet?

Best of all, this is a free service Microsoft offers to users of PowerPoint 2011. You simply broadcast the presentation using the PowerPoint Broadcast Service, send a URL to those you want to attend, and they can view your presentation live via the Internet using any Web browser on any operating system. Gotta love it.

Note

You must have a Windows Live ID to use the PowerPoint Broadcast Service. If you don't yet have a Windows Live ID, you are given the opportunity to acquire one during the setup process for broadcasting your presentation.

1. **Open the presentation you want to broadcast.**

2. **Click the Slide Show tab in the ribbon.**

3. **In the Play Slide Show section, choose Broadcast Show.**

4. **Click the Connect button in the Broadcast Slide Show dialog.** Your presentation will be uploaded to the PowerPoint Broadcast Service. You may be prompted to type your Windows Live ID and password. If you don't have one yet, click Get a Live ID. PowerPoint Broadcast Service creates a URL for you to distribute to your intended audience, as shown in Figure 11.6.

5. **Click Send in E-mail to open a new e-mail in your default mail application (Outlook, anyone?).** Alternately you can click Copy Link and then paste the link into an e-mail; this is especially helpful if you use browser-based e-mail.

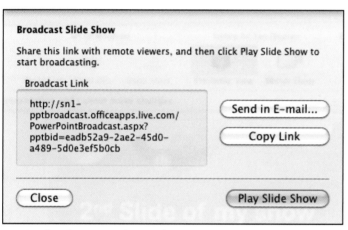

11.6 Send a URL to your cohorts to broadcast your slide show worldwide via the Internet.

6. **After your audience has received the URL, click Play Slide Show to begin your slide show broadcast.** The audience is able to watch your slide show only; they cannot see anything else you may do on your Mac, such as access a different application.

7. **When your presentation is complete, press Esc on your keyboard or click the End Broadcast button in the yellow bar and your slide show broadcast ends.**

Genius You may have quit your broadcast, but PowerPoint still has you logged on to your Windows Live ID account. You must quit PowerPoint (press ⌘+Q) in order to completely log out of Windows Live.

Making a PowerPoint Movie

Let's say you have to send your presentation to someone who doesn't have PowerPoint; how can that person view your presentation? One cool alternative is to save your presentation as a QuickTime movie (.mov), which can be played by any application that supports the format.

A few things to be aware of when saving to a movie

● **Each slide in the presentation will display for a default amount of time unless you set individual timings for each slide.**

● **Some transitions between slides may not look the same in the movie as they do when playing the presentation from within PowerPoint.**

● **Animations you may have added to your slides will simply not play at all.**

With those caveats in mind, follow these steps to save your presentation as a movie:

1. **Open the presentation you want to save as a movie.**

2. **Choose File ⇨ Save as Movie.**

3. **Give the new movie a name in the Save As field and select a location on your Mac in which to save it.**

4. **Click the Movie Options button to open the Movie Options dialog, as shown in Figure 11.7, and add one or more of the following to your movie:**

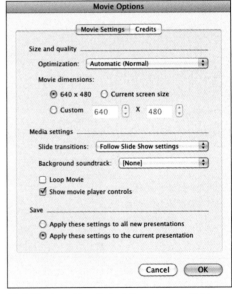

11.7 Movie options help tailor your movie to your audience's needs.

- **Size and quality section.** You can set the dimensions of the movie using the radio buttons and optimize the movie for best playback using the Optimization pop-up menu.

- **Media settings section.** Decide whether to use slide transitions, add a background soundtrack, and allow the viewer of the presentation to control the movie with play-back controls.

- **Save section.** You can determine whether these settings apply to all movies in the future or just to this current movie.

- **Credits.** Click the Credits tab to add credits to the movie.

5. **Click OK when finished adding options to your movie.**

6. **Click Save to save the presentation as a QuickTime movie.**

Printing Your Presentation

Printing slides seems pretty straightforward, and indeed it can be, but only if you simply want to print your slides. What if you want to print your speaker's notes, too, or want to create handouts from your presentation? Printing gets more involved when those are the cases.

To print a presentation, follow these steps:

1. **Open the presentation you want to print.**

2. **Choose File ⇨ Print to open the Print dialog, as shown in Figure 11.8.** You can also press ⌘+P.

3. **If you simply want to print your slides click Print and wait by your printer for the job to finish printing.** If this print job is a bit more involved, please continue.

4. **Click Page Setup to determine the size and orientation of your slides when printing them.** Click the Header/Footer button to add these items to the final output, or click options to select a paper size to print on. Click OK to return to the main Print dialog.

5. **To print handouts of your slides, click the Print What pop-up menu and choose one of the handouts options (2 slides per page, 3 slides per page, and so on).** These handouts print your slides and provide space for your audience members to take their own notes.

6. **To print your presenter's notes along with the slides, click the Print What pop-up menu and select Notes.**

7. **Click Print to send your job to the printer.**

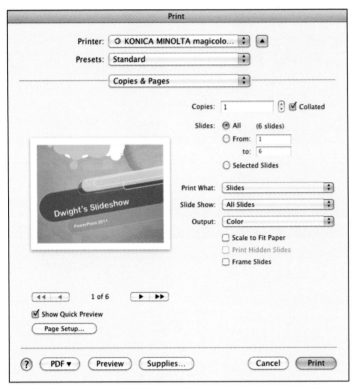

11.8 PowerPoint's Print dialog options let you decide what to print for your audience.

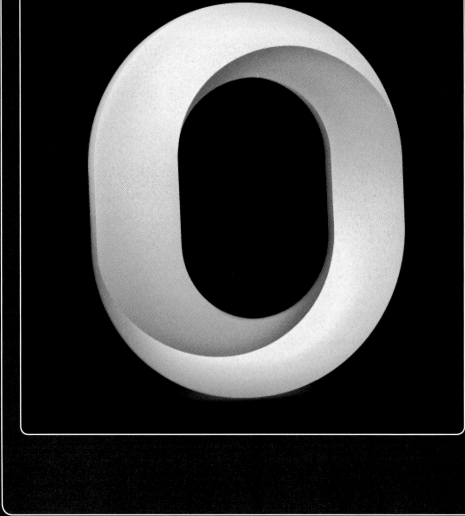

Welcome back, Outlook! There was a time, long ago (around 2001, I believe), when Outlook was present on many a Mac, sending and receiving e-mail with and sometimes without an Exchange server. Then there was a dark period in Microsoft/Apple history when there was no Outlook equivalent for the Mac to speak of (no, I'm sorry, Entourage didn't quite cut it). Now Outlook is back and ready to send and receive messages, and help you arrange schedules.

Getting Around in Outlook

Most of us are familiar with a typical e-mail application, but when faced with a new version of something you've used before, it's a good idea to get to know your surroundings before diving in too deep. Let's take a quick stroll around Outlook's interface and see what there is to discover.

You guys are experts at this by now, so I believe it goes without saying that if you haven't already done so, launch Outlook by double-clicking its icon within the Microsoft Office 2011 folder (or single-click its icon if one resides in the Dock).

When Outlook launches, you see a window that looks remarkably like that in Figure 12.1. This figure points out the major functions in Outlook's interface, while Table 12.1 offers a brief description of what these functions can do for you.

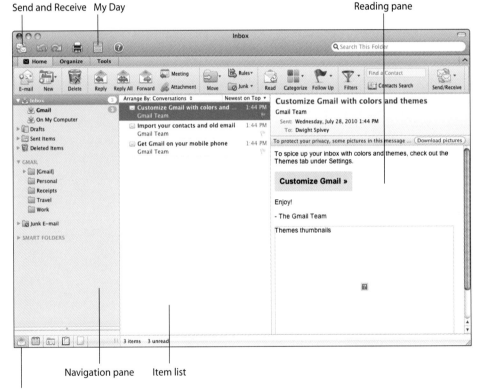

12.1 Outlook's major landmarks are both plentiful and plenty helpful.

Table 12.1 Outlook's Main Interface Elements

Item	Function
Send and Receive	Click to force Outlook to send e-mails that are in your Outbox and to receive any e-mails waiting for you on the e-mail server.
Undo and Redo	Use these buttons to undo and redo tasks you've performed in Outlook.
Print	Print selected items instantly.
My Day	Opens My Day (more on My Day in Chapter 14).
Help	Click to open Outlook's Help system.
Search	Type a subject you want to search for into this field and Outlook does its due diligence to find it for you.
Create new e-mail	Click to open a new e-mail message window.
Create new item	Click the arrow to the right of the button to create a new e-mail, meeting, appointment, contact, contact group, task, note, or folder.
Delete	Click to delete a selected item, such as an e-mail or folder.
Reply	Click to reply to the sender of the e-mail you're currently viewing.
Reply All	Click to reply to all the participants in an e-mail.
Forward	Click to forward a copy of an e-mail to a contact.
Meeting	Click to create a meeting based on an e-mail.
Attachment	Click to forward an e-mail as an attachment.
Move	Click to move or copy an item to another folder.
Rules	Click to apply a rule to an e-mail or to edit the rules.
Junk	Click to mark an e-mail as junk or to modify junk e-mail protection settings.
Read/Unread	Click to toggle an e-mail's state between read and unread.
Categorize	Click to classify an e-mail as a specific category, such as Family or Work.
Follow up	Click to flag a message so that you can follow up on it at a later time.
Filters	Click the arrow next to the Filters button to filter messages in the item list using the criteria in the pop-up menu.
Contact search	Type the name or e-mail address of a contact to find him or her in your Address Book.
Send/Receive	Click the arrow to send and receive messages, just send all messages (don't receive), or synchronize the current folder with your e-mail server.
Navigation pane	Peruse the folders of your e-mail accounts.
View switcher	Change the view to Mail, Calendar, Contacts, Tasks, or Notes.
Item list	Displays the items contained within a folder.
Reading pane	Displays the contents of the item selected in item list.

Now that you have the lay of the land, there's one piece of information that you simply cannot continue without: keyboard shortcuts. As with all other applications, Outlook is much easier to work with if you come to friendly terms with its keyboard shortcuts, which are explained in Table 12.2.

Note

I'm skipping the obvious shortcuts, like ⌘+P for print and ⌘+C for copy, and concentrating on those keyboard shortcuts that are specific to Outlook's functionality within Mail view. Also, remember that these shortcuts may differ if you are using a keyboard layout other than U.S. and/or if you're using a laptop.

Table 12.2 Keyboard Shortcuts Specific to Mail View

Function	Keyboard Shortcut
Create a new e-mail message	⌘+N
Send the e-mail you're working in	⌘+Return (or Enter)
Send and receive	⌘+K
Send all e-mails in the Outbox	⌘+Shift+K
Add an attachment to an e-mail	⌘+E
Reply to an e-mail's sender	⌘+R
Reply to all participants in an e-mail	⌘+Shift+R
Forward an e-mail	⌘+J
Mark e-mail as junk	⌘+Shift+J
Mark e-mail as not junk	⌘+Shift+Option+J
Move an e-mail to a folder	⌘+Shift+M
Delete an e-mail	Delete
Mark e-mail as read	⌘+T
Mark e-mail as unread	⌘+Shift+T
Mark all e-mail in a folder as read	⌘+Option+T

Setting Outlook's Preferences

Outlook's preferences allow you to make important customizations to the way it works specifically for you in your environment. These options tailor your Outlook experience so that you can optimize workflow for your day-to-day activities. The layout of Outlook's Preferences window, seen in Figure 12.2, is very much like the System Preferences in Mac OS X; items are categorized according to the functions they serve. Some preferences are discussed in more detail later in this chapter and in upcoming chapters, such as Accounts and Rules.

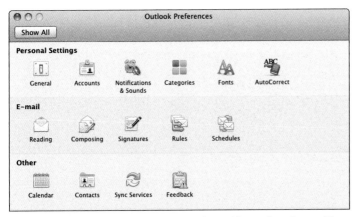

12.2 Outlook's preferences are categorized according to function, making them easier to find and decipher.

The Personal Settings section of the Preferences window lets you personalize items such as your accounts, alert sounds, default fonts, and define categories. Let's take a brief look at each available pane:

- **General.** Group similar folders from different accounts, such as combining Inboxes, make Outlook your Mac's default e-mail application, and hide folders within the Navigation pane that reside on your Mac.

- **Accounts.** Add or remove e-mail accounts from Outlook. More on this later in the chapter.

- **Notifications & Sounds.** The following options are available.

  - Tell Outlook to alert you when a new e-mail arrives by showing an alert on your desktop and/or bouncing the Outlook icon in the Dock.

  - You can also set up default sounds for when you receive an e-mail, send an e-mail, get a reminder, run into a problem syncing mailboxes, don't have any new messages, and even receive a welcome sound when Outlook opens.

  - The Reset Alerts button deselects any Don't show this message again check boxes that you have selected while working within Outlook.

- **Categories.** Create or delete categories using the + or − buttons under the Categories list (see Figure 12.3). Select the Show new categories in navigation pane check box if you want a category to display in the Navigation pane on the left side of the Mail view window.

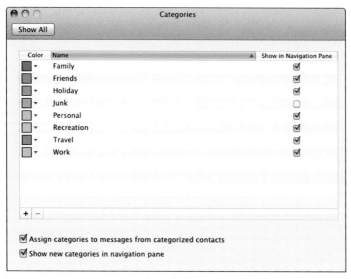

12.3 Create and delete categories to help sort your e-mails.

- **Fonts.** Select default fonts for creating HTML e-mail and for plain text e-mails.

- **AutoCorrect.** Tell Outlook to automatically correct your spelling, and to apply and replace items in your e-mails as you type using the AutoFormat tab.

Genius

Oops! You accidentally made Outlook your default e-mail client, but didn't mean to just yet (at least not until you're a little more familiar with it). That's easy enough to fix, so don't fret. Simply open Apple's Mail application, choose Mail ⇨ Preferences, click the General button, and change the pop-up menu for Default e-mail reader to the e-mail application you want to use (until you are won over by Outlook's clear superiority, that is).

The E-mail section lets you control the way Outlook behaves when you are reading and composing e-mails, such as marking items as read, using HTML by default when composing an e-mail, and applying signatures and rules to e-mail as you send and receive them.

- **Reading.** These options are available.

  - Decide whether to mark e-mails as read after they've been previewed for a specific amount of time, when you change to another e-mail, or when they are opened.

- Dictate how Outlook handles e-mail conversations (e-mails that are part of the same thread), and also hide e-mails that you've marked for deletion (IMAP accounts only).

- The final option in this pane is Security, where you can tell Outlook whether to download pictures in your e-mails.

Genius

If you want to receive pictures in your e-mail, which most of us are happy to do, I highly suggest selecting In all messages in the Security section of the Reading pane. This way you avoid a massive headache in the future when wondering where all the images in your HTML e-mails are (most e-mails are HTML these days).

- **Composing.** There are two tabs in the Composing pane: HTML and Plain Text. The options in both are pretty much identical, but one tells Outlook how to handle composition of HTML e-mails and the other details plain text messages.

  - Determine how original e-mails appear in your reply to the sender and whether to include an attribution for the original message in said reply. I suggest using the default, Include From, Date, To, and Subject lines from original message; this way you can keep up with who sent you an e-mail and when.

  - Make HTML your default format for composing e-mail. I would suggest so because e-mail looks so much better, and most e-mail applications are adept at HTML nowadays.

  - Decide whether to use the format of the original e-mail when replying or forwarding. I suggest you do so.

  - Determine whether to use the default e-mail account (if you have multiple accounts) whenever you reply or forward an e-mail. This one is better left deselected or you risk accidentally sending e-mail to people from an unintended account (you probably don't want to send work-related e-mail from your home account, or vice versa).

  - Choose to close the original e-mail window when you reply to or forward it.

  - You can also automatically Bcc yourself every time you send an e-mail, if you so choose.

- **Signatures.** Add, delete, enable, or disable signatures for your e-mail accounts.

  - Click the + or − buttons to add or delete signatures from the list.

  - Select a signature in the list to edit it, as shown in Figure 12.4. After you select it, make your additions or corrections in the Signature pane. Standard keyboard shortcuts apply here, such as ⌘+B for bold text or ⌘+I for italics.

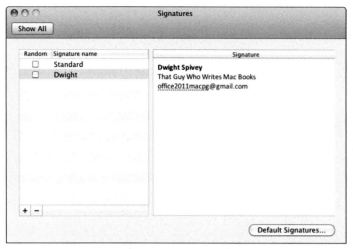

12.4 Signatures give your e-mails that polished and professional look (but you can also add silly quotes if you like).

- You can specify a default signature for each e-mail account by clicking Default Signatures and using the drop-down menus to match an account to a signature.

- **Rules.** Set rules to apply to your incoming and outgoing e-mails. This is covered in detail in Chapter 13.

- **Schedules.** Schedules tell Outlook when to perform automatic functions, such as sending and receiving e-mails at specific time intervals. To create a schedule, follow these steps:

  1. **Click the + button at the bottom left of the Schedules pane.**

  2. **Give the new schedule a title (something descriptive is best).**

  3. **Schedule a time for the task to take place in the When section.** Click the Add Occurrence button to create more instances for the task to run.

  4. **Choose an action from the Action section, choose an account for the action to affect, and click the Click here for account options button to specify the folders for this account that will be affected by the action.**

  5. **Select the Enabled check box to put this schedule into effect.**

  6. **Click OK to add the new schedule to your schedules list.**

The Other section of the preferences window helps specify how Outlook should display Calendar workdays, format information for contacts, synchronize address books, and more.

◉ **Calendar.** The Work Schedule section lets you tell Outlook what time of day your work-day begins and ends, which days of the week are considered workdays, and which day you consider to be the first in your week (see Figure 12.5). You can also enable a default reminder and set the time before the reminder alerts you to an appointment, and choose the time zone for your events.

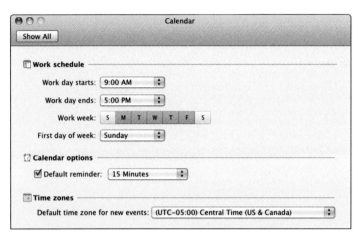

12.5 Set up your Calendar workdays, reminders, and time zone.

◉ **Contacts.** The Contacts pane is where you determine the default formats for contacts' addresses and phone numbers, as well as Contacts search sorting options and whether to check addresses of recipients before you send your e-mails.

◉ **Sync Services.** This great service allows you to merge your contacts from your Outlook Address Book, Apple Address Book, and your MobileMe account. The obvious huge benefits are cutting down on duplication and preventing you from having to manually add all the contents from one address book to the other.

◉ **Feedback.** This preference pane allows you to enable or disable the Customer Experience Improvement Program. If you enable this program Microsoft will be able to anonymously collect information about your Mac's hardware and how you use your software. As stated for the other applications, please read the information in this pane carefully before enabling or disabling this program.

Creating a New E-mail Account

Finally, let's get down to the nitty-gritty: adding an e-mail account. Needless to say, without an e-mail account you won't be sending or receiving much e-mail. As a matter of fact, while Outlook encompasses many functions other than e-mail, e-mail is its primary mover. This section looks at the various e-mail account types supported by Outlook 2011, as well as how to add new accounts and back them up.

Supported e-mail account types

Outlook 2011 supports many types of e-mail accounts:

- Microsoft Exchange accounts managed by Update Rollup 4 for Exchange Server 2007 Service Pack 1 and later versions.
- E-mail accounts from major providers such as Gmail, MobileMe, and Yahoo!
- Any POP or IMAP e-mail account.
- Directory service accounts that use the LDAP protocol. These types of accounts help you find address books that are stored on servers (for example, if you work for a large company).

Note

Outlook synchronizes your e-mails, contacts, calendar events, tasks, and notes with the Exchange server, ensuring everything is there when you need it, whether accessing your Exchange account from this Mac, another computer, or a handheld device such as an iPhone. However, the only things synced with POP and IMAP accounts are your e-mails; contacts, notes, and the like aren't synced.

Adding an account

New accounts are added from the Accounts preferences pane. Follow these steps:

1. **Choose Tools ⇨ Accounts to open the Accounts preference pane.**

2. **Click the + button in the lower-left corner of the window to add an account:**

   - Select Exchange to add an Exchange account.
   - Select E-mail to add a POP or IMAP e-mail account.
   - Select Directory Service to add an LDAP server account.

To add an Exchange account (see Figure 12.6), follow these steps:

12.6 Type the information for your Exchange account.

1. **Type the e-mail address of the account.**

2. **Select an authentication method.** If you don't know which method to use just ask your IT administrator.

3. **Type the username and password for the account in the appropriate fields.**

4. **Select the Configure automatically check box to have Outlook find the Exchange server on your network and gather all the other relevant information it needs to add your account.** If you don't select this check box you need to type the name or IP address of the server.

5. **Click Add Account.**

To add a POP or IMAP account, follow these steps:

1. **Type the e-mail address of the account.**

2. **Type the password of the account.**

3. **Select the Configure automatically check box to have Outlook contact the server of your e-mail provider and gather the information it needs to complete the account addition.** If Outlook isn't able to contact the e-mail provider or if there are any other issues, deselect this check box and proceed to the next step; if Outlook is successful in contacting the e-mail provider skip to step 5.

4. **Type the username of the account, the type of account (IMAP or POP), and the incoming and outgoing server details as provided to you by your e-mail provider, as shown in Figure 12.7.**

5. **Click Add Account to complete the process.**

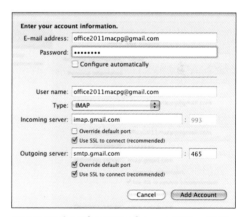

12.7 Type the information for your POP or IMAP account.

To add a Directory Service account, follow these steps:

1. **Type the address of your LDAP (Lightweight Directory Access Protocol) server in the appropriate field.** If you don't know this address, contact your company's IT department (you aren't likely to be using LDAP if you're not part of a company or other large organization).

Adding an Account from the Welcome Screen

When opening Outlook for the first time after installing it you may be honored with the Welcome screen. If so, there are a couple of ways you can create an account:

- **Click Add Account to be whisked away to the Accounts preference pane.**
- **Click Import to import accounts from other e-mail applications.** Follow the instructions in the prompts to import settings and accounts from several applications.

2. **Determine whether to override the default LDAP server port (typically 636).** If you do, type the desired port number in the field to the right of the server address.

3. **Use Secure Socket Layer to connect to the LDAP server by selecting the Use SSL to connect check box.**

4. **Click Add Account.**

Backing up e-mail accounts

I cannot stress enough how important it is to keep a backup of your e-mail accounts. Think about it: You've got thousands of e-mails in several different accounts, many containing information of a very confidential nature. Some of these e-mails contain important instructions that you simply must have; for example, Mom's tried-and-true recipe for broccoli cornbread (don't get me started!). What happens if that information is lost, whether due to some hiccup on a normally trusty Mac, or some catastrophic meltdown of your e-mail provider's servers (this has actually happened to me)?

Outlook is looking out for you by offering the ability to back up your e-mail accounts in Outlook for Mac Data Files. You can copy all of your information to an Outlook for Mac Data File, including your e-mails, notes, tasks, calendar events, and contacts. You can then use these files as backups or transfer them to another Mac that you need to use Outlook on.

To back up an e-mail account, follow these steps:

1. **Choose File ⇨ Export.**

2. **In the Export window, select Outlook for Mac Data File, as shown in Figure 12.8.**

3. **Decide whether to export items in a particular category or to export items according to their type.**

   - If you choose to export by category, select a category from the pop-up menu.

   - If you choose to export by type, be sure to select the check box next to the item(s) you want to export.

4. **Click the right arrow in the lower-right corner of the Export window to continue.**

5. **Let Outlook know whether you want to delete items from it after they are exported or not.** I would highly suggest that you not do so because if the sky was to fall during or after your export you may lose everything. If you want to delete items, do so manually after you've made sure the export was successful.

6. **Click the right arrow again to continue.**

7. **Type a name for the Outlook for Mac Data File in the Save As field, select a location to save the file, and click Save.**

8. **Click Done when Outlook finishes the export.**

12.8 Export your e-mails, notes, tasks, calendar events, and contacts to an Outlook for Mac Data File to back them up.

 Caution Outlook for Mac Data Files do not back up your account settings or your preferences. You may want to write these down or take screen shots of them in case you need the settings in the future (don't kid yourself; you probably will need them at some point).

To import an Outlook for Mac Data File, follow these steps:

1. **Choose File ⇨ Import.**

2. **Select the Outlook Data File radio button and click the right arrow in the lower-right corner of the window to continue.**

221

3. **Select the Outlook for Mac Data File option and click the right arrow again to continue.**

4. **Browse your Mac for the Outlook for Mac Data File (uses a .olm extension) you want to import, select it, and click Import.**

5. **Click Done once the import in complete.**

Genius

If you are switching from Outlook for Windows you can export your information from it and import it into Outlook for Mac using a PST (personal storage table) file. Import the PST file the same way you import an Outlook for Mac Data file (.olm).

Managing Identities

Outlook is a great e-mail application, so you might want to use it as your default e-mail application for all of your e-mail needs. For example, you may want to use it for work and for personal e-mail, but you may not want to mingle the two. You can set up Outlook to use different identities for each capacity. These identities store all your Outlook information and settings.

When you open Outlook for the first time, a new identity, called Main Identity, is created for you. Outlook doesn't manage identities: That distinction goes to Microsoft Database Utility, which is part of the Office 2011 for Mac suite. Microsoft Database Utility is found in the Office folder, which is located in your Microsoft Office 2011 folder.

To create an identity, follow these steps:

1. **Double-click the Microsoft Database Utility icon to launch it.**

2. **Click the + button in the lower-left corner of the Microsoft Database Utility window, seen in Figure 12.9.**

3. **Give a name to the identity you want to create.** I suggest making it a descriptive name, such as Work or Family, so you'll better associate it with its capacity.

You can create as many identities as you need. These identities are stored in the /Users/username/Documents/Microsoft User Data/Office 2011 Identities directory on your Mac. You can switch between identities, but it's not as simple as it was with Entourage, the e-mail application offered by Microsoft in the Office X, 2004, and 2008 for Mac versions.

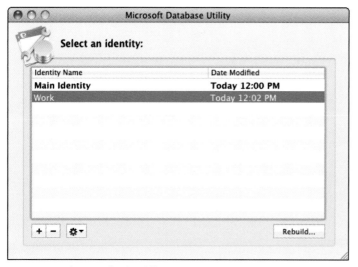

12.9 Create identities for the different capacities in which you use Outlook 2011.

To switch identities, follow these steps:

1. **Quit Outlook if it's open.**

2. **Open Microsoft Database Utility.**

3. **Select the identity you want to use in Outlook.**

4. **Click the Action button (looks like a gear) and select Set as Default.**

5. **Quit Microsoft Database Utility and open Outlook.** Your e-mails, notes, and so on, for the identity you selected in Microsoft Database Utility are now available within Outlook.

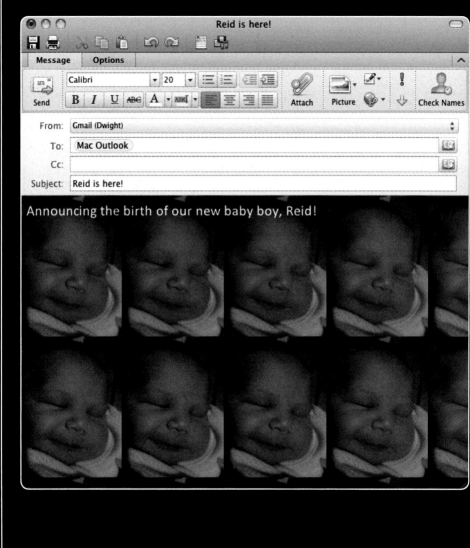

Outlook is adept at many things, but e-mail is its bread and butter. Sending, receiving, and forwarding e-mails are a daily part of most of our lives, and Outlook is a most capable assistant with those small tasks. However, Outlook can do so much more than the bare basics. It can handle junk e-mail with the ease and grace of a pro and help you organize your e-mails so that you know exactly where one is when you need it. And if organizing your unruly Inbox doesn't help you find that elusive e-mail, Outlook's powerful search features will do the trick nicely. I also look at using attachments, as well as printing your e-mails.

Sending and Receiving E-mails

Let's start with first things first. Even though this may seem like old hat to some, sending and receiving e-mails is a subject that still needs covered as this may be the first sojourn into Outlook for many a reader. If you were a user of Entourage in previous versions of Office for Mac you'll be slightly familiar with Outlook, but if not, Outlook may be a totally foreign environment to you. Fear not; once you get the feel for it you might not want to use another e-mail application.

Creating new e-mail

Creating new e-mail just can't get any easier than with Outlook (see Figure 13.1).

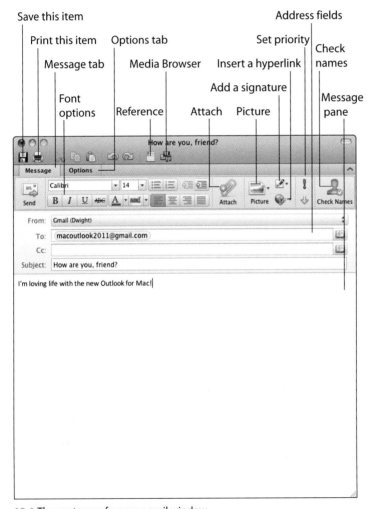

13.1 The anatomy of a new e-mail window.

Here are a few ways to get started:

- Press ⌘+N to open a new e-mail window.
- Choose File ⇨ New ⇨ E-mail Message.
- Click the E-mail button under the ribbon's Home tab.

Table 13.1 provides a helpful overview of the slightly less-obvious items.

Table 13.1 Functions Available in a New E-mail Window

Item	Function
Save this item	Click to save your new e-mail in the Drafts folder.
Print this item	Click to send your e-mail to your Mac's default printer.
Reference	Select to open the Reference Tools window, which offers a thesaurus, dictionary, bilingual dictionary, translation, and Web search tool.
Media Browser	Click this button to open Media Browser, which you can use to add pictures and other items to your e-mails.
Message tab	Offers items to help you format the content of your e-mail message.
Options tab	Gives fast access to items such as the Scrapbook and the spell checker, as well as letting you add a Bcc address field and toggle the format of your e-mail (HTML or Plain Text). You can also add a color or picture to the background of your message.
Send	Click to send your e-mail to its destination, the recipients you identify in the address fields.
Font options	Modify the look of your text by changing fonts, adding colors, and using other formatting options.
Attach	Click to add attachments to your messages.
Picture	Click to add pictures to your e-mails.
Add a signature	Select this option to add a signature to your message.
Insert a hyperlink	Add a link for a Web site to your e-mail messages.
Set priority	Marks your e-mail with a high or low priority, which may help the recipient to organize his or her time a bit better.
Check Names	Click to verify the names or addresses of recipients you typed in the address fields.
Address fields	Type the names of contacts or their e-mail addresses in the To or Cc fields.
Message pane	Type the content of your e-mail message in the Message pane.

Now that we have a new e-mail window open, let's get busy building your message. The major items are tackled first. To build and send an e-mail message, follow these steps:

1. **Choose an e-mail account in the From field.** If you have only one account this one's a no-brainer, but if you use several accounts you'll want to pay attention to the From field. Click the pop-up menu to select the account you want to use as your launching pad.

Caution Be careful here! You don't want to send an incredibly important work-related e-mail from an account your co-workers won't recognize. The e-mail may simply be placed in their junk folders if their e-mail application's filters don't recognize the address of the account you mistakenly sent the e-mail from.

2. **Type the names of contacts in your Address Book or manually type e-mail addresses in the To and Cc fields.** You can also search your contents by clicking the small phone book icon to the immediate right of both fields.

3. **Type the subject of your e-mail in the Subject field (no duh, right?).**

4. **Compose your e-mail in the Message pane.** Don't forget to use the font options in the ribbon to make your message even more interesting by jazzing up your fonts.

5. **When you finish composing your message, click Send.**

That's about as basic as composing and sending e-mail can be, but there are several items in the Options tab of the new e-mail window that haven't been covered yet. Click the Options tab in your new e-mail window to do a little exploring.

⦿ **Format.** Click the slider to change your e-mail format from HTML to Plain Text.

Caution Once you change an e-mail's format from HTML to Plain Text there's no going back. You have to start over with a brand-new e-mail if you don't want to go with plain text after realizing that it's so, well, *plain*.

⦿ **Bcc.** The Bcc field is another field for adding recipients to your e-mail. Unlike the To and Cc fields, though, any recipient added to the Bcc field won't be visible to other recipients.

⦿ **Background Color.** Give your e-mail a little pop by adding a color background to it. For example, if you're sending an e-mail announcing the birth of a new child you might add a light blue or light pink background to brighten up the message, as shown in Figure 13.2 using the RGB color sliders. To change the background color, follow these steps:

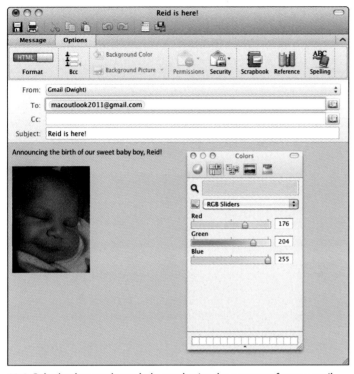

13.2 Color backgrounds can help emphasize the content of your e-mail.

1. **Click the Background Color button to open the Colors window.**

2. **Use the Color Wheel, Color Sliders, Color Palettes, Image Palettes, or Crayons to select a color.**

3. **As soon as you select a color it is applied to the background of your e-mail.**

- **Background Picture.** A background picture adds even more oomph! to an e-mail. However, one thing to remember: The busier the picture, the readability of your e-mail's text may wane.

- **Permissions.** Grant access or restrict access to the message using IRM (Information Rights Management).

Note You must acquire a digital certificate from a third-party certification authority and add it to your Mac's keychain in order to use the Security features. Consult Mac OS X's Help system for more information on certificates and using them in keychain.

- **Security.** Digitally sign or encrypt your e-mail message to keep its contents private.

- **Scrapbook.** Add an item from your Scrapbook, such as a clip from a Word document, into your e-mail.

  1. **Click the Scrapbook button to open the Scrapbook window.**

  2. **Choose a clip from your Scrapbook that you want to add.**

  3. **Click the Paste button under the clip list to add it to the e-mail.**

- **Reference.** You've used the same word in your e-mail to describe an activity more than twice. You want to convey the same idea, but you need another word to express the same meaning; however, it's not coming to you. That's just one example of how the Reference button can come to your rescue. You can also find the meaning of words, translate words from one language to another, and more.

  1. **Click the Reference button to open the Reference Tools window.**

  2. **Type a word into the search field at the top of the window and press Return (or Enter).**

  3. **Click the Thesaurus, Dictionary, Bilingual Dictionary, Translation, or Web Search tabs to get Outlook's help with the word you typed (see Figure 13.3).**

- **Spelling.** Even English professors misspell a word from time to time. If you find that you're running into spelling mishaps on a regular basis, follow these steps:

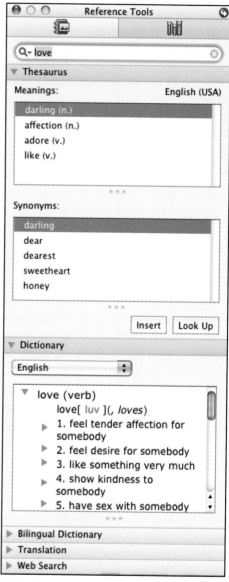

13.3 Reference tools help you get the scoop on words and their meanings.

1. **Click the Spelling button to have Outlook peruse the contents of your e-mail for any misspelled words.**

2. **If it finds one, it will display the incorrect spelling in the field at the top of the window and show you a list of potentially correct spellings in the box below.**

3. **Select the correct spelling you want to use and click Change.**

4. **If you're happy with the spelling of your word click Ignore, or if it's a word that you use regularly you can click Learn to add the word to Outlook's memory.**

Reading e-mail

To read e-mail, you first have to receive some. If your e-mail account has been set up correctly in Outlook and you've let your biggest fans know your e-mail address, you should have a bevy of e-mails to read in your Inbox. Here's a quick primer on reading e-mail within Outlook.

1. **Click the Send/Receive button in the upper-left corner of the Outlook window to query your e-mail provider's servers for new messages.**

2. **When a new e-mail arrives in your Inbox it appears in the Item list with an envelope icon to its immediate left.** The Inbox for the account that received the new e-mail reflects the new message by adding to the number of unread e-mails displayed in the Navigation pane.

Genius The Outlook icon in the Dock also reflects the number of unread e-mail messages. It shows the total of unread messages for all the e-mail accounts you are set up for in Outlook.

3. **Select the Inbox that contains the new e-mail from within the Navigation pane.**

4. **Click the new e-mail within the Item list and it appears in the Reading pane.** Outlook also marks it as having been read.

Genius If the Reading pane isn't your cup of tea, you can double-click the e-mail within the Item list. This causes the e-mail to open its own window, which you can then resize to suit your needs.

Outlook groups e-mails that contain the same subject into what Microsoft calls *conversations*. This helps you to organize your messages and keeps your Inbox from getting too cluttered. It also makes finding an e-mail much easier. Here are a few things to help you work with conversations.

● **When a new message arrives that pertains to a conversation, that conversation gets moved to the top of the Item list.**

● **Conversations may be collapsed by clicking the small gray arrow found to the left of the subject in the Item list.** Of course, you can expand it by clicking the same arrow. See an example of an expanded conversation in Figure 13.4.

● **You can change how conversations are displayed in the Outlook window.** Follow these steps:

　1. **Choose Outlook ⇨ Preferences.**

　2. **Click the Reading button within the E-mail section.** The Conversations area of the Reading pane gives you options to only expand one conversation at a time, automatically expand a conversation when you select it, and highlight messages that are part of the same conversation.

● **You can turn off conversation mode fairly easily:**

　1. **Click the Mail icon in the lower left of the Outlook window if you're not already in Mail view.**

　2. **Click the Organize tab in the ribbon.**

　3. **Click the Conversations button to toggle back and forth between on and off.**

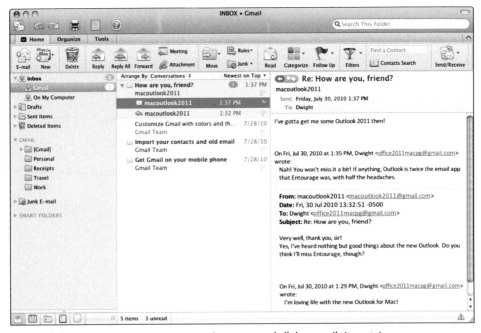

13.4 Click the gray arrow next to a conversation to expand all the e-mails it contains.

There's something else I need to quickly cover regarding reading e-mails. If there's one thing that I could even mildly complain about in Outlook, it would be the fact that Outlook does not download images in e-mails by default. If you receive an e-mail containing pictures, you will see a yellow bar under the subject and recipient area (like the one in Figure 13.5) explaining that said pictures have not been downloaded. Click the Download pictures button on the right side of the yellow bar to populate the message with the intended images.

If you're like me and abhor having to do this for every e-mail (most e-mails contain images of some kind nowadays anyway, don't they?), you can set Outlook to download images for you. Follow these steps:

1. **Choose Outlook ⇨ Preferences.**

2. **Click the Reading button in the E-mail section of the Outlook Preferences window.**

3. **In the Security section of the Reading window there are three choices for the Automatically download pictures from the Internet option:**

   - **In all messages.** Select this option to download all images in all e-mails, regardless of where they came from.

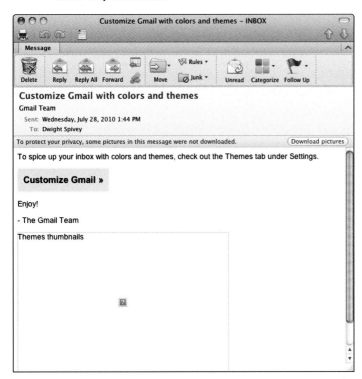

13.5 Click the Download pictures button to download images contained within your e-mail.

Caution The In all messages option opens you up to the possibility of seeing an image in an e-mail you may not expect, especially when it concerns spam messages. You may want to rethink using this option if you have small children in the home.

- **In messages from my contacts.** This option prevents pictures from downloading in e-mails that come from folks you don't have in your Address Book.

- **Never.** I think this one explains itself pretty well.

Customize the Outlook window

I love being able to make applications work the way I want them to, and Outlook affords me that opportunity in multiple ways. You can change a great deal of the way elements in the Outlook window display, if you choose to display them at all. For example, in my opinion the Navigation pane is given a bit too much real estate, so I make it slimmer and thereby expand the Reading pane. Enough of my preferences; let me show you how to effect some of your own ideas on Outlook's interface.

- **Does the Navigation pane get on your nerves?** Get rid of it then! Choose View and deselect Navigation Pane check box. Should you begin to miss it, simply perform the same steps to restore it.

- **Could you do without the ribbon?** Choose View menu, but this time deselect Ribbon. Select it again to restore the ribbon to its rightful place.

- **Outlook groups similar items from different e-mail accounts in the folder list of the Navigation pane.** For example, Outlook combines the inboxes from all your accounts into one Inbox. If you prefer to keep your accounts totally separate from one another you can disable this feature. Follow these steps:

  1. **Choose Outlook ⇨ Preferences.**

  2. **Click General in the Personal Settings section of the Outlook Preferences window.**

  3. **In the Folder list section, deselect the Group similar folders, such as Inboxes, from different accounts check box.**

Some folks don't care for the Reading pane on the right side of the Outlook window. If that's the case for you, you can change it:

1. **Click the Organize tab in the ribbon.**

2. **Click the Reading Pane button and select an option for displaying the reading pane: on the right side of the window (default), on the bottom of the window (my favorite, as shown in Figure 13.6), or don't show it at all.**

If you have chosen to move the Reading pane to the bottom of the Outlook window, or to remove it altogether, you now have the option of choosing which columns appear in the Item list. Follow these steps:

1. **Click the Organize tab in the ribbon.**

2. **Click the Reading pane button and make sure that Below or Hidden is selected.**

3. **Choose View ⇨ Columns.** Within the resulting submenu, select check boxes for the items that you want to appear in the item list, and deselect items you prefer to not be present in the item list.

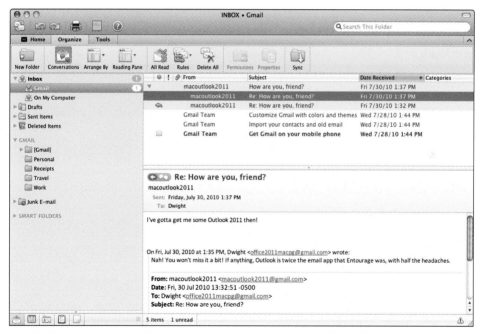

13.6 My favorite place for the Reading pane to reside is the bottom of Outlook's window.

Dealing with Junk E-mail

We've all received junk e-mail. Whether it's just an innocent advertisement or something more tasteless, junk e-mail is junk. If you don't filter it, you're going to be annoyed by it on a daily basis. Even if your company has invested in some of the best e-mail filters in the world, occasionally one nefarious e-mail may squeak in under the radar. Outlook is outfitted with its very own junk e-mail filters, and you'll want to know how to implement them ASAP.

 Note If you are using an Exchange account, Outlook won't filter junk e-mail for you. Exchange servers handle their own junk e-mail filtering, theoretically keeping the junk from ever reaching you in the first place.

To set up junk e-mail protection in Outlook, follow these steps:

1. **Click the Home tab in the ribbon.**

2. **Click the Junk button and choose Junk E-mail Protection to open the Junk E-mail Protection dialog, as shown in Figure 13.7.**

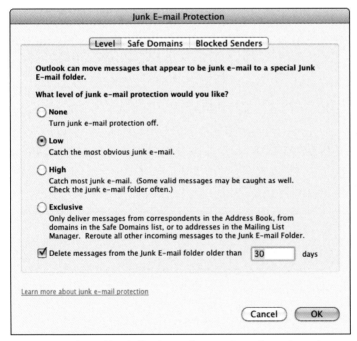

13.7 Set your desired level of junk e-mail protection to keep the garbage out of your Inbox.

3. **Click the Level tab to select the level of junk e-mail protection you need.** Your choices are None, Low, High, and Exclusive.

4. **The Junk E-mail folder may get full pretty quick if you're not careful, so Outlook gives you the option to automatically delete e-mails that are in the Junk E-mail folder for a set amount of days.** This feature, represented by a check box entitled Delete messages from the Junk E-mail folder older than X days, is enabled by default and the time limit is set at 30 days.

5. **Click the Safe Domains tab.** You can specify *domains* (domains are the part of an e-mail address that comes after the @) that you deem to be safe. Every e-mail that comes from that domain is allowed to come through to your Inbox unfettered.

6. **Click the Blocked Senders tab.** Add e-mail addresses and domains to this window that you absolutely don't want to receive any e-mail from.

7. **If e-mail comes into your Inbox that you feel is junk mail, you can manually specify it as such.** Click the e-mail in the item list, click the Junk button, and choose Mark as Junk or Block Sender.

Caution Using None for your junk e-mail protection level is the only way to ensure that a legitimate e-mail doesn't accidentally get marked as junk by Outlook. If you use any of the other settings it's a good idea to check your Junk E-mail folder periodically just to make sure no messages that you need have been mistakenly flagged as junk.

Working with E-mail Attachments

One of the great conventions of e-mail is not only the ability to communicate instantly with someone around the world, but through attachments you can actually send items such as pictures or documents along with the message. This is just a quick overview of how Outlook helps you send and receive attachments in your e-mails.

Sending attachments

Your boss is in Japan, and he wants to see the latest plans that you've been working on at home in the U.S. Because these plans are PDF files you can send them to your boss in an e-mail by attaching the plans to your message. Follow these steps:

1. **Create a new e-mail using one of the methods discussed previously (I'm testing you now).**

2. **Click the Message tab in the ribbon.**

3. **Click the Attach button.**

4. **Browse your Mac for the file you want to attach to the e-mail, select it, and click Choose.**

You can add multiple attachments to a single e-mail. One thing to consider when sending one or several is the size limit that most e-mail providers give you. For example, if your e-mail provider gives you a 10MB limit, you won't be able to send attachments that are larger than that, whether it's a single file or several files combined.

Viewing and saving attachments

When folks send you attachments you can save them, preview them, or remove them altogether (especially if you think it may be something malicious). To open an attachment in an e-mail, follow these steps:

1. **Select the e-mail in the Item list.**

2. **Find the attachment(s) listed underneath the To field in your e-mail.**

3. **Double-click the attachment in the attachment list to open it.**

4. **If you want to save the attachment to your Mac, right-click the attachment and select Save As or Save All, as shown in Figure 13.8.** You can also remove attachments in the same manner. Click Remove or Remove All in the contextual menu.

13.8 Save your attachments by right-clicking them and selecting Save or Save All.

If you are running Mac OS X 10.6 (Snow Leopard) or later and want to see what an attachment is before saving or removing it, you can see a preview of it. Follow these steps:

1. **Click the Preview or Preview All button next to the list of attachments.** A preview of the first attachment opens.

2. **Use the controls at the bottom of the Preview window to perform a variety of tasks.** Each file type has a different set of tasks that can be performed on it. For example, a picture preview may offer you the option of saving the picture directly into your iPhoto library.

3. **When you finish viewing the preview, press the spacebar to close the Preview window.** Your attachments are still in the e-mail.

A Clean House Is a Happy House: Organizing E-mail

Imagine the calm of a neat house versus the stress of a chaotic one. The same situation applies to your e-mail accounts. If they are unruly and willy-nilly, the chances of finding (in a timely manner) that e-mail Grandma sent you two years ago with a list of all her favorite gift ideas decrease dramatically. Outlook can help you avoid such a mess through the use of folders and rules.

Creating folders

Folders help you keep e-mails in their proper places. You can create folders to house messages from your family, your best friend, the PTA for your kids' school, particular work projects, and any other reason you can think of. The possibilities are endless, but the payoff is a much easier time finding your e-mails when you need them. To create a new folder, follow these steps:

1. **Select the account to which you want to add the folder.**

2. **Press ⌘+Shift+N or click the New button in the ribbon and select Folder.**

3. **Give the folder a descriptive name.**

4. **Go to the Inbox of your account and find e-mails that you want to add to a folder, and then drag them to the new folder.** The e-mail will still remain in your Inbox, but it's also associated with the folder you just created.

You can add subfolders to folders, as shown in Figure 13.9. This way you can streamline your organization by having a main folder act as a central category, like Family or Writing, and adding subfolders of individual subjects, like Mom & Dad or Mac Outlook.

13.9 Subfolders within main folders help keep individual items organized under central categories.

IMAP folder settings

When you have an IMAP account you can set the preferences to keep your folders synchronized both in Outlook and on the e-mail server. This is helpful to make sure that no matter where you access your e-mail you will have the same information handy.

To set the IMAP folder settings, follow these steps:

1. **Choose Tools ➪ Accounts.**

2. **In the Accounts window, select the IMAP account you want to set folder settings for.**

3. **Click Advanced in the lower-right corner of the Accounts dialog.**

4. **Click the Folders tab to set up default folders for Sent, Drafts, Junk, and Trash using their respective pop-up menus, as seen in Figure 13.10.**

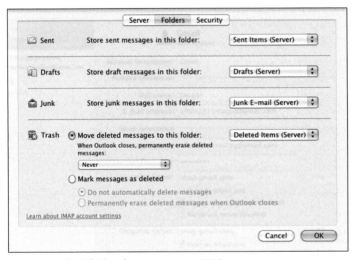

13.10 Set default folders for items in your IMAP accounts.

Table 13.2 briefly explains the options available in the Folders tab of the IMAP Advanced preferences.

Table 13.2 Outlook's Main Interface Elements

Option	Function
Store sent messages in this folder	Choose a folder on the server or on your computer to store e-mails that you send to others. Your options are the Sent Items folder on the server, the Sent Items folder on your Mac, or you can choose a different folder entirely by clicking Choose in the pop-up menu and selecting another folder.
Store draft messages in this folder	Select a folder on the server or on your Mac to store messages that you haven't completed yet.
Store junk messages in this folder	You can choose to keep junk e-mails in a folder on the server for your e-mail provider or on your computer.

Option	Function
Move deleted messages to this folder	Selecting this option moves deleted e-mails from their current folder to the folder that you choose in the pop-up menu. Click the pop-up menu under this option to choose a time in which these messages are permanently deleted.
Mark messages as deleted	Choose this option to mark messages as deleted. They remain in their current folder and aren't moved to a different folder.
Do not automatically delete messages	This option pertains to the Mark messages as deleted option. Select it if you want to erase all deleted items manually.
Permanently erase deleted messages when Outlook closes	This option also pertains only to the Mark messages as deleted option. Select this if you want Outlook to erase all deleted messages when it closes.

Note

Selecting folders on your computer for the options in Table 13.1 will save space on your e-mail server, but keep in mind that you won't be able to see or use these folders when using other computers to access e-mail.

Laying down the law: Using rules

Outlook can also be your e-mail traffic cop, directing incoming e-mails to new and exciting locations based on the rules you set for it. Rules are yours to make, and they can take almost any form you can come up with. To set up a simple rule, follow these steps:

1. **Click the Home tab in the ribbon.**

2. **Click the Rules button and choose Edit Rules to open the Rules preference pane.**

3. **Choose an account to apply the new rule to.**

4. **Click the + at the bottom of the window to create your new rule.**

5. **Give the rule a name; something descriptive is wise.**

6. **In the If section of the Edit Rule dialog, type your criteria for Outlook to look for in incoming e-mails, such as a folder the e-mail resides in, a name or e-mail address, and so on; the options in the pop-up menus are exhaustive.** Use as many criteria as necessary.

7. **In the Then section of the Edit Rule dialog, dictate what actions should take place if the criteria in the If section are met.** You can add as many actions as you need.

8. Select the Enabled check box in the lower left of the Edit Rule dialog to let Outlook know that the rule is in effect, as shown in Figure 13.11.

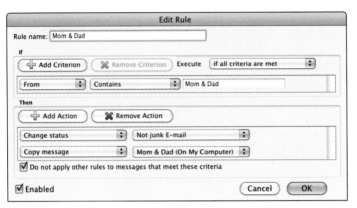

Edit Rule

Rule name: Mom & Dad

If

[＋ Add Criterion] (✖ Remove Criterion) Execute [if all criteria are met ↕]

[From ↕] [Contains ↕] [Mom & Dad]

Then

[＋ Add Action] (✖ Remove Action)

[Change status ↕] [Not junk E-mail ↕]

[Copy message ↕] [Mom & Dad (On My Computer) ↕]

☑ Do not apply other rules to messages that meet these criteria

☑ Enabled   (Cancel) (OK)

13.11 Enforce the law in your unruly Inbox to clean up its act.

9. Click OK to add the new rule to the list in the Rules preference pane. The new rule is applied the next time an e-mail meeting its criteria comes wandering into your Inbox.

Searching for Long-lost E-mails

If you're someone who has an Inbox that could stretch from here to Albuquerque, searching for one tiny e-mail can be a bit like the needle-and-haystack routine. Fortunately, Outlook is able to delve deep into your Inbox, or any other e-mail folder, to find just what you're looking for. To perform a basic search, follow these steps:

1. Select a folder from the Navigation pane in which to perform the search.

2. Type a search term into the Search field in the upper-right corner of the Outlook window and press Return (or Enter). Outlook zips through the e-mails in the specified folder and will display its findings for you under a new purple tab that appears in your ribbon, called appropriately enough, Search.

3. When you finish looking at the search results click Close in the Search tab.

That was easy enough, but what if you want to tweak your search a bit? Here's how to use the options in the ribbon's Search tab, shown in Figure 13.12:

13.12 The ribbon's Search tab is chock full of searching goodness to help you find just what you are looking for in Outlook.

1. **Narrow or expand your search by clicking a scope button.** Options are Folder, Subfolders, All Mail, or All Items.

2. **Click Advanced and a criterion appears beneath the Search tab.**

3. **Click the pop-up menus in the criterion to modify it to meet your needs and type any text in the text field if necessary.**

4. **Add additional criteria by clicking the + button to the right of the first criterion.** Remove criterion by clicking the − button.

5. **Outlook sifts through your e-mail to find matches for your criteria and displays them under the Search tab.**

6. **When you finish viewing the findings of your search, click the Close button in the Search tab.**

Printing E-mail

Ah, yes, the paperless office still hasn't materialized. Until it does, I'm afraid we'll have to make do with our printers. Printing e-mails is a good idea if you have an item you want to share with a colleague or friend and whipping out your laptop wouldn't be appropriate or practical. Not to mention that good old-fashioned hard copies of important documents are always good to have around if your Mac decides to go belly up for some reason.

Caution

I'm sure there's at least one reader who's saying to me: "The e-mail's stored on the server, right? They could just get it from there; they don't have to print it." That's true, as long as you're assuming they didn't elect to store all their e-mails on their Mac and delete them from the server.

Here's how to print your e-mails within Outlook:

1. **Select an e-mail that you need to print.**

2. **Press ⌘+P or choose File ⇨ Print to open the Print dialog, as shown in Figure 13.13.**

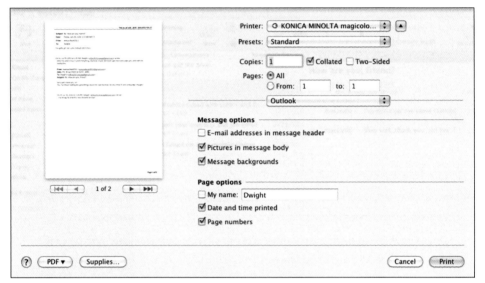

13.13 Outlook provides several options in the print dialog for printing your e-mails.

3. **Choose a printer from the Printer pop-up menu.**

4. **Type the number of copies you need, as well as which pages you intend to print.**

5. **In the Message options section of the Print dialog, elect to print one or all of the following:**

   - The e-mail addresses that appear in the header of the e-mail

   - Any pictures that are part of the e-mail (not attachments)

   - Background colors and images

6. **In the Page options section, you can include your name, the date and time the e-mail is being printed, and page numbers on the output.**

Note

If you don't see all of the options just described you need to expand your Print dialog. Click the blue box containing the black arrow that is located just to the right of the Print pop-up menu to expand the dialog.

How Can I Organize Contacts and Tasks?

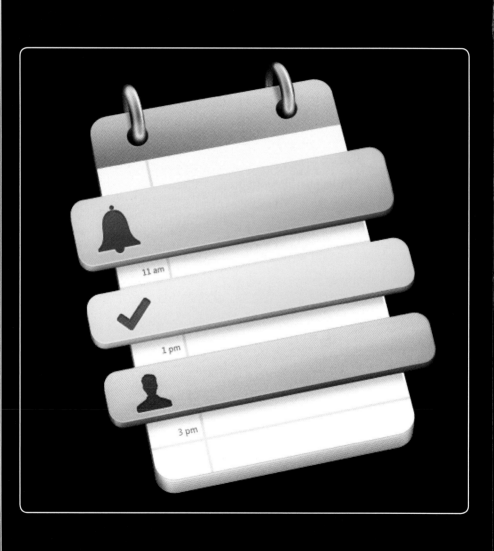

Outlook can do much more than e-mail; it can also help you get and stay organized. Staying organized can be difficult, but getting organized is another matter altogether. Once you have your ducks in a row it's much easier to keep them that way, but it's the process of getting to that point that can be difficult. Outlook is a pro at helping you organize your meetings, appointments, tasks, notes, and contacts. It's up to you to get the ball rolling, but life will be so much easier with Outlook's tools at your disposal.

Getting Around in Calendar

Your oldest child has a science class project due in two weeks, you have a meeting with your son's homeroom teacher tomorrow afternoon, your boss is asking you to have your latest project turned in by next Thursday, and your anniversary is coming up (or was it yesterday?).

We all have busy and seemingly unwieldy schedules that demand our attention. When your attention is pulled in so many directions you are bound to forget something unless you have a tool to help you keep your appointments tidy and to remind you of impending appointments or deadlines. Outlook Calendar is a great way to keep track of your busy life, and it won't let you down as long as you use it dutifully (see Figure 14.1).

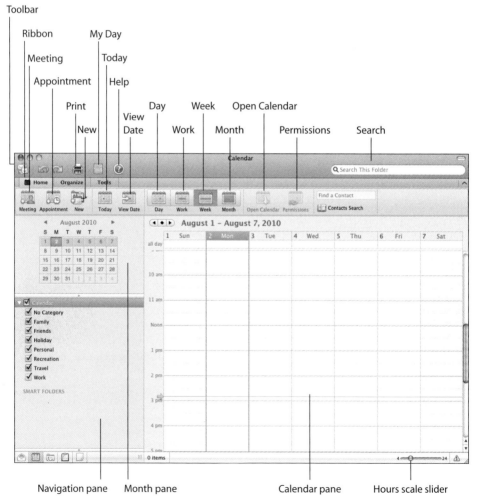

14.1 Calendar is ready to handle all the scheduling action you can hurl at it.

Table 14.1 briefly explains how each item can help you.

Table 14.1 Calendar View and the Home Tab's Main Options

Option	Function
Search	Type a search item to have Outlook comb your calendars for it.
Ribbon	Contains tabs for creating and modifying items with your calendars.
Meeting	Click to create a meeting and send invitations to possible attendees.
Appointment	Click to create an appointment in your calendar.
Today	Select to view only today's events.
View Date	Select to choose a particular date's events to view.
Day, Work, Week, and Month	Click one to determine the Calendar view.
Open Calendar	Open the calendar of another user on this Mac.
Permissions	View and set the permissions of a calendar.
Hours scale slider	Determine the number of hours that are shown at one time by dragging the slider.
Month pane	Use the right and left arrows to scroll through the months, or select a date to view its events.
Navigation pane	Choose a category to see its calendar events.
Calendar pane	View and edit the events of a particular time period.

Figure 14.2 shows features of the ribbon's Organize tab, and Table 14.2 offers a quick breakdown of what each can do for you.

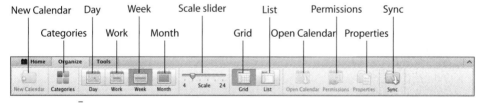

14.2 The Organize tab of the ribbon within Calendar view.

Table 14.2 The Organize Tab's Main Options

Option	Function
New Calendar	Click to add a new calendar to Outlook.
Categories	Select which categories to show in the Navigation pane.
Day, Work, Week, Month	Click one to determine the Calendar view.

continued

Table 14.2 continued

Option	Function
Scale slider	Determine the number of hours that are shown at one time by dragging the slider.
Grid	Display the calendar in Grid format.
List	Display the calendar as a list.
Open Calendar	Open the calendar of another user on this Mac.
Permissions	View and set the permissions of a folder.
Properties	View and set the properties of a folder.
Sync	Click to sync your calendar with the Exchange server.

Creating a meeting

When you create a meeting you are creating an event that includes other people. Outlook can help you create a meeting invitation that you can send to your attendees giving the time, location, and other pertinent information regarding the meeting, and they can respond to your invitation as their individual schedule dictates. Here's how to set up a meeting invitation:

1. **You must be in Calendar view, so click the Calendar view button in the bottom-left corner of the Outlook window (if you're not in Calendar view already).**

2. **Click the Meeting button found in the Home tab of the ribbon to open the Meeting window, as shown in Figure 14.3.**

3. **If you want to send the invitation from an account other than your default, click the From pop-up menu and select the desired account.**

4. **Type the names of your attendees into the To field.**

5. **Type the subject of the meeting and its location into the corresponding fields.**

6. **Select a starting and ending time for your meeting.** If this is event will take up the entire day, select the All day event check box.

7. **Type any information you deem pertinent for your attendees to know in the Message field.**

8. **Click Send to send the invitation to your meeting hopefuls.**

Note
Typing the name of attendees will only work if they are already in your contacts list. Otherwise you will need to manually enter their e-mail address.

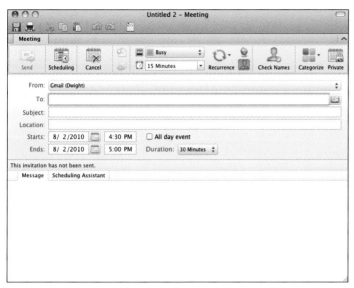

14.3 Set up your meeting parameters so that potential attendees know its what, when, where, and why.

You may have noticed a few more options that were available in the ribbon's Meeting tab, and these definitively need to be covered because if you are prone to send meeting invitations, some or all of those options may apply to you at some point. Figure 14.4 shows the Meeting tab and Table 14.3 explains the options in it.

Table 14.3 The Meeting Tab's Main Options

Option	Function
Send	Click to send the invitation to all those in the To field.
Scheduling	Select this to see what your schedule looks like and help you determine a good time slot for this meeting.
Cancel	Cancel this meeting and notify all attendees.
New e-mail message	Click to send a new e-mail to the attendees, perhaps informing them of any changes that may take place regarding the meeting, or any other information you need to share with them.
Reply to all	Send a reply message to all those attending the meeting.
Recurrence	If this is a meeting that will be occurring on a regular basis, click this button and select a time interval. Click the Custom button to get really detailed.
Time zone	Click this button to place a Time zone pop-up menu beneath the Starting and Ending times.

continued

Table 14.3 continued

Option	Function
Plan to attend	Click this button if you want people you've invited to the meeting to respond with their intention to come to the meeting or not.
Check Names	Click this button to verify that the names and addresses of contacts are correct.
Categorize	Select a category to add this meeting to.
Private	Click to hide the content of this invitation from others.

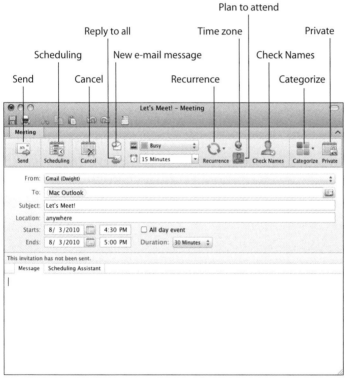

14.4 The Meeting tab in the ribbon offers several options for customizing your invite.

Update or cancel meetings

Even the best-laid plans can run into a barrier, so sometimes it's necessary to let your attendees know that there's new information regarding the meeting or that the meeting itself has been canceled altogether.

To update a meeting, follow these steps:

1. **Double-click the meeting in your calendar to open it.**

2. **If this is a recurring meeting and all subsequent meetings will be affected, the first thing you should do is click the Edit Series button to make sure this change applies to all future meetings.**

3. **Make the necessary changes to your meeting.**

4. **Click the Send Update button to send the updates to all those you invited to attend.**

To cancel a meeting, follow these steps:

1. **Double-click the meeting in your calendar to open it.**

2. **Click Cancel in the ribbon's Meeting tab.** If this is a recurring meeting, click the arrow next to the Cancel button and select Occurrence only if this occurrence of the meeting is being canceled, or select Series if all occurrences of the meeting are being canceled.

3. **Type a note explaining why the meeting is being canceled, if you want.**

4. **Click the Send Cancellation button to inform all former attendees that the meeting is no more.**

Creating an appointment

One of the 10,000-plus reasons for using Outlook is for scheduling and reminding you of appointments. To avoid forgotten appointments in the future, here is how to quickly create an appointment:

1. **Make certain you are in Calendar view.** Click the Calendar button in the lower left if you're not.

2. **Click the Appointment button in the ribbon's Home tab to open the new appointment window.**

3. **Type a subject and location for your appointment in the appropriate fields.**

4. **Select starting and ending times for the appointment.**

5. **If there's any information you need to remember about the appointment type it into the notes field at the bottom of the window, as shown in Figure 14.5.**

6. **Click the Invite button to add others to the appointment.** Click the Cancel button if you change your mind about the invitation.

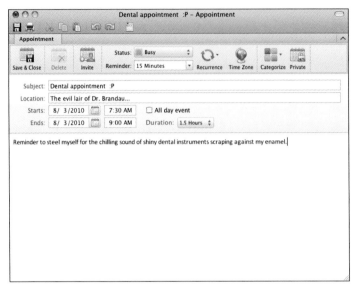

14.5 Make appointments to remind of you of important events that you need to attend.

7. **Use the Status pop-up menu to tell Outlook how to represent the time of the appointment in your calendar.**

8. **Click the Reminder pop-up menu to have Outlook give you a reminder well in advance of the appointment time.**

9. **If this appointment is something that takes place at regular intervals, click the Recurrence button.**

10. **Click the Time Zone button to add a Time zone pop-up menu.**

11. **Click the Categorize button to choose a category for the appointment**

12. **Click the Private button if you want to keep prying eyes from seeing your appointment information.**

Add or remove holidays

I don't know about you, but I can never have enough holidays. The idea of adding holidays to Outlook sounds fantastic, but unfortunately, sometimes you have to remove them too. No matter, both adding and removing holidays is a function of Outlook with which you'll want to be familiar. Here's how to add holidays to your calendar:

1. **Choose File ⇨ Import.**

2. **In the Import window, select the Holidays radio button.**

3. **Click the right arrow in the bottom right of the window to continue.**

4. **After Outlook builds the country and region list, scroll through the list and select the check boxes next to those countries, regions, or religious holiday categories that you want to add to your calendar, as shown in Figure 14.6.**

14.6 Select which holidays you want to import into your Outlook calendars.

5. **Click the right arrow again to continue.** Outlook pauses for a moment and then informs you that it is importing your holidays.

6. **Click OK when the import is complete.**

7. **Click Finish to complete the process.** The selected holidays now appear in your calendar.

When you import holidays, Outlook creates a new category for them using their name as the title of the new category. You will have to perform a search for items in that category in order to remove them from your calendar. Follow these steps to remove holidays from your calendar:

1. **Make sure you are in Calendar view.**

2. **Click the Search field in the upper-right corner of Outlook's window to make the purple Search tab appear in the ribbon next to the Tools tab.**

3. **Click the Advanced button within the ribbon's Search tab.**

4. **Click the Item Contains pop-up menu and select Category.**

5. **Click the None pop-up menu and choose the category named after your set of holidays, as shown in Figure 14.7.**

6. **When all the results for your holidays are displayed, select one.**

7. **Choose Edit ⇨ Select All.**

255

14.7 Select the holidays you want to remove from your Outlook calendar.

8. **Choose Edit ➪ Delete.** A confirmation appears to make sure that you absolutely beyond any shadow of any doubt really, really, really want to delete these items: Click Delete again. All holidays for the category are summarily removed.

9. **Click the Close button in the Search tab to finish the deed.**

You may have noticed when deleting holidays from a category that the category still remains in the Navigation pane. Here's how to remove the category from Outlook altogether:

1. **While in Calendar view, select the Organize tab.**

2. **Click the Categories button to open the Categories preference pane.**

3. **Click the category you want to delete from Outlook to highlight it.**

4. **Click the – button under the left side of the category list.**

5. **When Outlook asks if you are certain you want to remove the category, click the Delete button.**

Printing calendars

I am one of those people who need the occasional visual aid, especially when it comes to appoint-ments. It's nice to have my Mac squawk at me a couple of hours before a big meeting, but I like even better to have a printed calendar on my desk (I guess I'm old-fashioned that way). Digital calendars rock, but paper is sometimes still king. To print a paper calendar, follow these steps:

1. **Choose File ➪ Print to open the Print dialog.**

2. **Outlook gives you a slew of options to pick from when printing your calendar, as shown in Figure 14.8.** Your options include

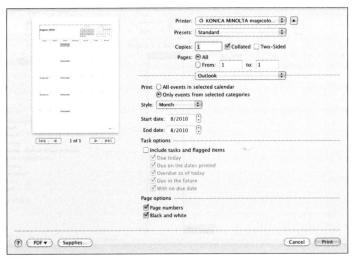

14.8 Outlook gives you plenty of options when it comes to printing calendars.

- Choose to print all the events in a calendar or only events in certain categories.

- Decide the style for your calendar from Day, Work Week, Week, or Month.

- Determine a starting and ending date for your printed calendar.

- Under Task options, select check boxes next to specific tasks or flagged items that you want to print from your calendar.

- In Page options, decide to print page numbers for your calendar or to print in black and white in order to save your color toner (assuming you have a color printer).

3. **Click Print to have your printer jettison hard copies of your calendar.** Printed pages fit much more neatly into your pocket than your iMac does, don't you think?

Getting Around in Contacts

Sometimes it's who you know that determines your course in life. Whether it be family, friends, co-workers, or an acquaintance you just met, people you converse with in one form or another are too important to forget. Adding someone to your contacts in Outlook is a great way to keep in touch and build a relationship.

Let's take a quick dip into the Contacts window and see what your options are. Figure 14.9 shows the Contacts window while Table 14.4 gives you a leg up on what each option can do.

Contact Group Delete Meeting Forward Categorize

Contact New E-mail IM Map Details List Contacts Search

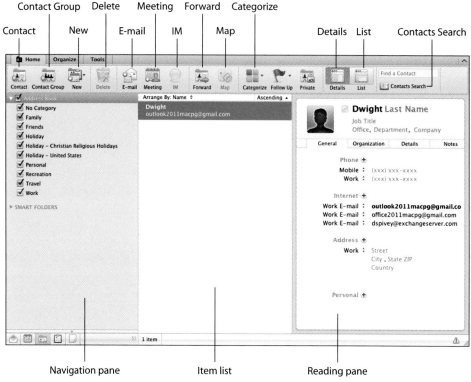

Navigation pane Item list Reading pane

14.9 The lay of the Contacts land.

Table 14.4 Options in the Contacts Window

Option	Function
Contact	Click to create a new contact.
Contact Group	Click to create a new contact group.
Delete	Click to delete a contact you've selected in the Item list.
E-mail	Select a contact in the Item list, and click this button to send an e-mail.
IM	Select a contact in the Item list, and click this button to send an instant message.
Forward	Select a contact in the Item list, and click this button to forward the contact information as a vCard attachment in an e-mail.
Map	Select a contact in the Item list, and click this button to open a map of his or her address.
Categorize	Assign a category to a contact you've selected in the Item list.
Details	Click to show the Reading pane on the right side of the window (default).

Option	Function
List	Click to show the Reading pane on the bottom of the window.
Contacts Search	Type the name of a contact you're looking for in this field.
Navigation pane	Browse categories for contacts assigned to them.
Item list	View your entire list of contacts or only those assigned to a particular category.
Reading pane	View and edit a contact's information.

Adding and removing contacts

A contacts list is pretty useless without actual contacts, right? You can create a contact for every soul you know and include all the information you can remember about them in the contact file. Imagine how happy life will be if you add a contact for your spouse so that you can then remember your anniversary.

To add a contact, follow these steps:

1. **Click the Contact button in the ribbon's Home tab.**

2. **Type your new contact's information into the appropriate fields.**

3. **Add a photo of a contact by dragging a picture onto the photo icon to the left of the contact's name field.**

4. **Edit fields under the General tab if needed:**

   - You can add fields as you need them by clicking the + next to the category name for the type of field you want to add. For example, click the + next to Internet and select an option from the pop-up menu that results, as shown in Figure 14.10.

   - Delete a field from a category by clicking the – to its left.

   - Change a label for a field by clicking on the label and choosing another option from the pop-up menu.

5. **Once you finish editing the contacts information, click the Save & Close button and the contact is added to your list.**

Note

Whenever you edit a contact from within any of the other applications in the Office 2011 suite, those changes are reflected in the contact's information within Outlook.

14.10 Editing information in a contact is very straightforward.

You can easily edit information for a contact you've created by double-clicking the contact to open its window. Make any changes necessary to the fields in the General tab and click Save & Close.

Should you need to streamline your list to people you actually do have some contact with, it's simple enough to do so:

1. **Find and highlight the contact you want to remove from your list.**

2. **Click the Delete button in the ribbon's Home tab.**

3. **Confirm that you really want to delete the contact by clicking Delete, or give your contact a second chance by clicking the Cancel button.**

Add the sender of a message to Contacts

No need to create a contact totally from scratch if the person you want to add as a contact is already corresponding with you via e-mail. Here's how to add them from inside an e-mail:

1. **Open the e-mail containing the e-mail address of the person you want to add as a contact.**

2. **Hold your mouse pointer over the e-mail address or name of the person in the From field of the e-mail, and wait a couple of seconds until a window pops up.**

3. **Inside the pop-up window, click the Contact button, as shown in Figure 14.11.**

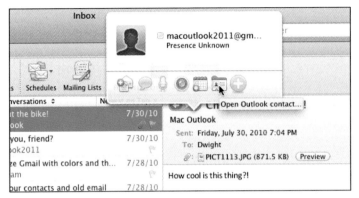

14.11 Cick the Contact button to add a contact to Outlook from within a message.

4. **A new contact window opens within Outlook.** Edit the contact's information as needed.

5. **Click the Save & Close button to add the new contact to Outlook.**

Importing contacts

You may already have a full slate of contacts in Mac OS X's Address Book or some other e-mail application. If that's the case, there are a couple of ways you can import your contacts into Outlook, avoiding the need to retype all that information in the process: Import the contacts from a text file (a CSV file, to be exact) that has been exported from another e-mail application, or by importing vCard files exported from Apple's Address Book.

To import using an exported CSV (comma-separated values) file, follow these steps:

1. **Open the application that you want to export your contacts from and export your contacts to a CSV file.** You will need to consult the help system for the application if you aren't sure how to do this.

2. **Open Outlook and choose File ⇨ Import.**

3. **Select the radio button next to Contacts or message from a text file, and click the right arrow in the lower-right corner of the window to continue.**

4. **Choose Import contacts from a tab- or comma-delimited text file and click the right arrow again to continue.**

5. **Browse your Mac for the CSV file you want to import, select the file, and click the Import button.**

6. **If the fields in the Import Contacts screen don't match you can drag fields from the Unmapped fields pane to the right side of the Mapped fields pane to force a match.**

7. **Click Next or Previous to check the information for each contact that is being imported.**

8. **Click the Import button to finish the interaction and import the contacts into Outlook.**

To import a vCard (Virtual Business Card) exported from Apple's Address Book, follow these steps:

1. **Open Address Book and export a contact as a vCard.** A simple way to do so is to click and drag a contact to the desktop, which will instantly create a vCard (the original contact in Address Book is unharmed).

2. **Open Outlook and go to Contacts view.**

3. **Drag and drop the vCard from the desktop into the Item list, as shown in Figure 14.12.**

14.12 Drag a vCard directly into Outlook's Item list to import it.

Synchronizing with Apple's Address Book and MobileMe

There is yet another way to get contacts from Apple's Address Book into Outlook: Outlook's Sync Services. Sync Services keeps contacts you add in Address Book synchronized with Contacts in Outlook, and vice versa. Sync Services also works with your MobileMe account, if you have one. To move contacts with Sync Services, follow these steps:

1. **Open Contacts in Outlook.**

2. **Click the Tools tab in the ribbon, and click the Sync Services button.**

3. **In the Sync Services window, select the Turn on Sync Services for contacts check box.**

4. **Select the check box next to the name of the account you want to synchronize.**

Exporting contacts

Outlook can export your contacts, too, should you want to use them in another e-mail application or on a different PC or Mac. Outlook exports contacts in a tab-delimited text file using a .txt extension, which most e-mail applications can import with no problem. To export contacts as tab-delimited text files, follow these steps:

1. **Choose File ➪ Export.**

2. **In the Export window (see Figure 14.13), select the Contacts to a list radio button.**

3. **Click the right arrow in the lower-right corner of the Export window to continue.**

4. **In the Save dialog, give the TXT file a name, select a location to store the file, and click Save.**

5. **Click Done in the Export window once the export process is complete.** You're done!

14.13 Export your contacts so they can be imported into other e-mail applications or shared with others.

Creating groups

You may find yourself routinely sending e-mails to the same set of contacts. For example, let's say that every time you want to send an e-mail to your family you have to hammer out the e-mail addresses of all 150 of them. Instead, simply create a group for your relatives and just address future e-mails to the group, typing only one item in the To field as opposed to 150. To set up a group, follow these steps:

1. **Go to Contacts within Outlook.**

2. **Click the Contact Group button within the ribbon's Home tab.**

3. **Give a name to your new contact group; something descriptive is a good idea.**

4. **Add contacts in a couple of ways:**

   - To add a contact that's not presently in Outlook, click the + button in the Group tab and manually type information for your contact under the Name and E-mail columns.

   - To add contacts that already reside in Outlook to your group, click the + button in the Group tab, begin typing the name of the contact, and select the intended contact from the resulting pop-up menu, as shown in Figure 14.14.

14.14 Select a contact from the pop-up menu to add them to the new contact group.

5. **To delete contacts from the group, select the contact in the list and click the – button in the Group tab.**

6. **If you want to keep members of the group from seeing one another's contact information, select the Use Bcc check box to hide member information.**

7. **Click the E-mail button in the Group tab to send an e-mail to all the members of the group.**

8. **Click the Meeting button in the Group tab to set up a meeting with all the members of the group.**

9. **Click the Save & Close button to save the group.**

From now on when you need to send an e-mail to the group, create the new e-mail and simply type the group name in the To field. All members of the group will be sent the e-mail.

To delete a group, follow these steps:

1. **Go to Contacts within Outlook.**

2. **Find the group in the Item list and double-click to open it.**

3. **Click the Delete button in the Group tab.**

4. **Confirm deletion of the group by clicking the Delete button.**

Printing your Address Book

As you can probably figure out by this point in the book, I love computers and all things digital, but still have a special affinity for the printed word, even when it comes to things like address books. You can print single contacts, a group of contacts that you have selected, or if you really want to punish your printer you can print your entire Contacts list. To print your Address Book, follow these steps:

1. **Go to Contacts within Outlook.**

2. **Select the contacts you want to print:**
   - Simply click a contact in the Item list to print a single contact.
   - Hold down ⌘ while clicking contacts to select and print multiple contacts.
   - To select all of your contacts, click the first contact in the item list and press ⌘+A.

3. **Press ⌘+P to open the Print dialog, as shown in Figure 14.15.**

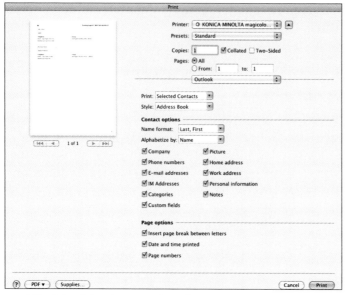

14.15 The Print dialog shows a variety of printing options.

4. **Choose your print settings in the Outlook section of the Print dialog:**

   - **Select an option from the Print pop-up menu.** Selected Contacts is the default, but if you change your mind you can choose All Contacts of Flagged Contacts.

   - **Decide on the layout of your contacts using the Style pop-up menu.** You can see a preview of what the printed page will look like on the left side of the Print dialog.

   - **In the Contact options section, choose the format for listing the contacts and decide to alphabetize them by name or company.** Also, select the check boxes next to items you want to print for the contacts, such as phone numbers, street addresses, personal information, notes, and more.

   - **In the Page options section, choose to insert page breaks, the date and time the contacts were printed, and page numbers.**

5. **Click Print to print the contact list.**

Getting Around in Tasks

Tasks help you keep a handle on the things you need to do, and who among us doesn't have things to do? Outlook can remind you of tasks and when they are due to be completed. This section looks at the Outlook window in Tasks view; Figure 14.16 points out the major landmarks, while Table 14.5 helps you understand their functions.

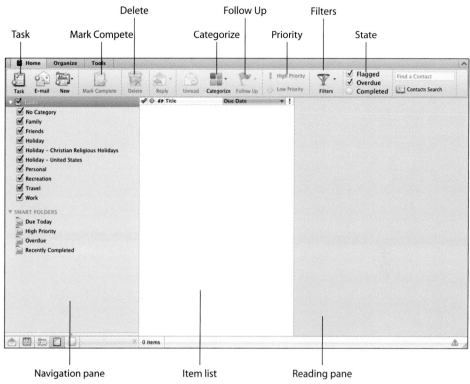

14.16 Tasks view within the Outlook window.

Table 14.5 Options in the Tasks Window

Option	Function
Task	Click to create a new task.
Mark Complete	Click to mark the task you've selected in the Item list as complete.
Delete	Click to permanently delete the task you've selected in the Item list.
Categorize	Assign a category to a task you've selected.
Follow Up	Click the arrow next to the button to determine when Outlook should remind you to follow up on this task.
Priority	Assign a priority to a task.
Filters	Sort tasks in the item list according to criteria such as due date and priority.
State	Sort tasks by their current state, such as whether they are flagged, overdue, or completed.
Navigation pane	Click categories to see what tasks are assigned to them.
Item list	View a list of all tasks or according to their categories.
Reading pane	View and edit the task within this pane.

Adding and removing tasks

As you are presented with new things to do every day you'll want to add them as new items in Tasks. You will also want to remove tasks that you mistakenly created or that are no longer necessary.

Note Removing a task is not the same as marking the task as completed. When you remove a task you delete it from the Tasks list altogether, but when you mark a task as completed you keep the task in your Tasks list but have a record of having finished it.

To add a new task to Outlook, follow these steps:

1. **Click the Tasks view button in the bottom left of the Outlook window.**

2. **Click the Task button in the ribbon's Home tab to open a new Task window.**

3. **Type a name for your task, and if necessary type more information pertinent to the task in the box at the bottom half of the window.**

4. **If necessary, set a Due date, Start date, and a Reminder date, as shown in Figure 14.17.** Click on No date next to the date you want to add, and browse the calendar to find the date you want. If you want to remove or change the date, click the X next to the date you established.

5. **If this is a task that you will be working on regularly click the Recurrence button and select a time interval from the pop-up menu.**

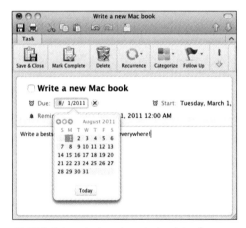

14.17 Set due, start, and reminder dates for your tasks to help you stay on top of them.

6. **Select a category for the task if needed by clicking the Categorize button.**

7. **Click the High or Low priority button in the Task tab to establish how important this task is.**

8. **Click the Save & Close button to complete the task creation and add it to your Tasks list.**

To remove a task from the list, follow these steps:

1. **Go to Tasks in Outlook.**

2. **Find the task you want to remove in the Item list and select it.**

3. **Click the Delete button in the ribbon's Home tab.**

4. **Confirm the deletion of the task by clicking the Delete button.** Poof! The task is gone from your life.

Editing, managing, and completing tasks

When the world throws you a curveball and you have to change the parameters of a task, editing the task in Outlook is no big deal. Follow these steps:

1. **Go to Tasks within Outlook.**

2. **Select the task you want to edit in the Item list.**

3. **You can edit the task in the Reading pane by clicking the title or the message box.** You can also edit the due, start, and reminder dates and use the items in the ribbon's Home tab to attach a category, set the task's priority, and more.

You can manage tasks in the Item list using the Filters button in the ribbon's Home tab. Follow these steps:

1. **Go to Tasks view in Outlook's window.**

2. **Click the Filters button in the Home tab.**

3. **Choose the filters you want to use to sort tasks in the item list by due and start dates, whether they are overdue or completed, by their priority, and whether they are unread.** Use as many or as few of the filters as you want. Outlook sorts your tasks on the fly as you select and deselect filters.

4. **When finished sorting your tasks, click the Filters button and select Clear All Filters to return to Normal view.**

Because you are a conscientious person and always tackle your responsibilities head-on, you'll no doubt be completing tasks hand over fist. In order to make Outlook reflect your accomplishments, you need to know how to mark a task as complete. It's a simple thing. Follow these steps:

1. **Go to Tasks in Outlook.**

2. **Find and double-click the task you want to mark as complete from within the Item list to open it.**

3. **Click the Mark Complete button in the Task tab or select the check box next to the task's title to mark the task as being completed, as shown in Figure 14.18.** If you accidentally mark a task as complete, simply deselect the check box next to the task's title.

4. **Click the Save & Close button to save the task.**

Printing your Tasks list

You can keep your list of tasks with you even when your Mac is not. How, you ask? Why, by printing them, of course!

1. **Go to Tasks in the Outlook window.**

2. **If you want to print only tasks you select within the Item list, hold down ⌘ while you select each individual task, and then press ⌘+P to open the Print dialog.** If you don't need to select individual tasks just press ⌘+P.

3. **Use the Print pop-up menu to print tasks that meet one of the criterion listed, such as All Tasks, Tasks Due Today, All Incomplete Tasks, and so on.**

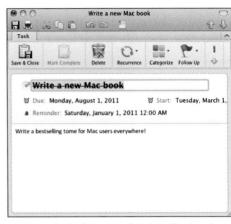

14.18 Mark a task as complete by selecting the check box next to its title.

4. **Choose Table or Memo from the Style pop-up menu.** I suggest Table if you have a really large task list; it can save you quite a bit of paper.

5. **In the Task options section, select the check boxes next to items you want to print as part of the task, such as its Priority, Category, Notes, and more.**

6. **Select the check boxes in the Page options section to add the date and time the tasks were printed, as well as page numbers to each page.**

7. **Click Print to send the Tasks list to your printer.**

Create and Manage Notes

This morning, the most amazing idea in the history of civilization came to mind. Because you have Office for Mac 2011, you whipped up Outlook, clicked the Notes view button, and quickly added this idea to a new note before the thought could flutter away. The idea is now preserved for the betterment of all mankind. Or. . .

You didn't know about Outlook's Notes, freaked out trying to find pen and paper, and by the time you put said pen to said paper the once-world-changing idea was lost to the shifting winds of your mind. Speaking for all the rest of us on this planet, thanks a lot.

You can make certain this scenario never takes place again by learning how to add notes to Outlook. These notes can be anything you want to jot down. Here's how to take a quick note:

1. **Open Outlook and click the Notes button in the bottom left of the window.**

2. **Click the Note button in the ribbon's Home tab.**

3. **Type a title for your note in the yellow bar, and any other information you need in the message body (white box).**

4. **Click the X next to the title of the note and click the Save button to add the note to your Notes Item list.**

5. **Edit the note within the Reading pane by selecting the note from within the Item list.** Click the title or the message body to make any changes.

A few other things you can do with your notes

- **You can add a picture to your note pretty easily.** Click within the message body, click the Picture button from the ribbon's Home tab, and choose a picture from the Photo Browser or by browsing your Mac for it.

- **Send a note as an e-mail.** Select the note in the Item list and click the E-mail button in the ribbon's Home tab.

- **Forward a note as an attachment to an e-mail.** Select the note in the Item list and click the Forward button in the Home tab.

- **Delete a note.** Select it in the Item list and click the Delete button in the Home tab.

- **Assign a note to a category.** Select it in the Item list and then choose a category from the Categorize button in the Home tab.

You can print your notes, too. Follow these steps:

1. **Select the notes you want to print from within the Item list, and then press ⌘+P to open the Print dialog.**

2. **Use the Print pop-up menu to determine whether to print all notes or just those you selected in Step 1.**

3. **Determine whether to print pictures that reside in your notes, and whether to print dates, times, and page numbers.**

4. **Click Print to print your notes.**

Keeping On Schedule with My Day

My Day is a nifty little tool that helps you see your schedule, contacts, and tasks right on your Mac's desktop. You can also add tasks to Outlook, without even needing Outlook to be open. This section explains how My Day can help keep your day running smoothly.

Open Outlook and click the My Day icon in the toolbar. The My Day window opens, displaying your schedule for the day. Figure 14.19 shows the My Day window, and Table 14.6 explains the main features.

Because you are already familiar with using Outlook, using the features in My Day won't be anything new, but you can customize the way you work with My Day using its preferences. Click the Preferences button at the bottom of the My Day window (looks like a gear) to open the Preferences window, as shown in Figure 14.20.

Here is a brief description of the choices available to you in each tab of the preferences window:

- **General tab options:**

  - **Show My Day in menu bar and Show My Day in Dock.** Selecting one or both of these options means that you don't have to open Outlook just to open My Day; you can click its icon from the menu bar or Dock.

  - **Keyboard shortcut to show or hide My Day.** Select this check box and either use the default shortcut (Control+M) or make your own.

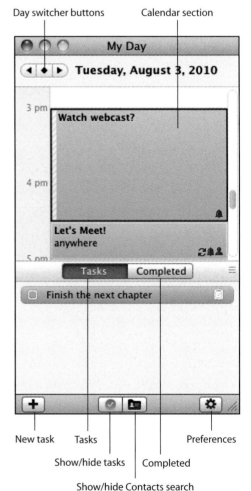

Day switcher buttons   Calendar section

New task   Tasks   Preferences
Show/hide tasks   Completed
Show/hide Contacts search

14.19 My Day puts the power of Outlook on your desktop, even when Outlook isn't running.

- **Open My Day when computer starts.** If you want My Day to launch when you first turn on your Mac, select this check box.

- **Always display My Day on top.** You can keep My Day on top of every other window on your screen by selecting this check box.

Calendar options:

- If you have multiple calendars in Outlook you can specify which calendars are displayed in My Day by selecting their check boxes in the Show these calendars in My Day section.

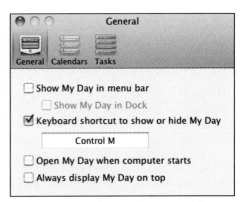

14.20 My Day's preferences let you modify it to work the way you want it to.

- Select the Show events with "Free" status to have your so-called free time appear in the calendar along with your scheduled events.

Tasks options:

- Determine whether to show flagged messages, contacts, overdue items, and items with no due date by selecting or deselecting the check boxes next to each one.

- Assign a default start date and default folder to new tasks you create using the Default start date and Default folder pop-up menus.

- Assign and use a keyboard shortcut to help you quickly create a task.

Table 14.6 Features of the My Day Window

Option	Function
Day switcher buttons	Click the buttons to move from day to day within your calendar.
Calendar section	View the day's events.
Show/hide tasks	Toggle to show or hide today's tasks.
Show/hide Contacts search	Toggle to show or hide the Contacts search section.
Tasks	Click to see the tasks you have yet to complete today.
Completed	Click to view tasks that you've already completed today.
New task	Click to add a new task to Outlook.
Preferences	Click to open the preferences window for My Day.

How Can I Work More Efficiently?

After you get to know a product, learning how to better use it is the next step. There are many ways to streamline your work in Office, such as viewing multiple worksheets in Excel and dragging and dropping information from one Office application to another, just to name a couple. While there are still many things about the Office suite that I simply won't be able to cover, I am happy to offer you a few ideas to help you work more efficiently within the Office applications.

Drag and Drop Information from App to App

Do you have an item in a Word document that you really want to get into Excel? You really don't want to spend all day re-creating the same information in Excel when you already have it in Word. What to do? Well, you can just drag the information from Word and drop it directly into Excel. Here's how:

1. **Open Excel and Word.**

2. **Within each application, open the documents you need to use.**

3. **In Word, open the document that contains the information you want to add to Excel.**

4. **In Excel, open the workbook into which you want to copy Word's information.**

5. **Position the Word document window and the Excel worksheet window so that you can see both.**

6. **In the Word document, select the item(s) that you want to copy to Excel by clicking it.**

7. **Click and drag the information from the Word document window into the Excel worksheet, position it where you want, and then let go of the mouse button to drop the information into Excel, as shown in Figure 15.1.**

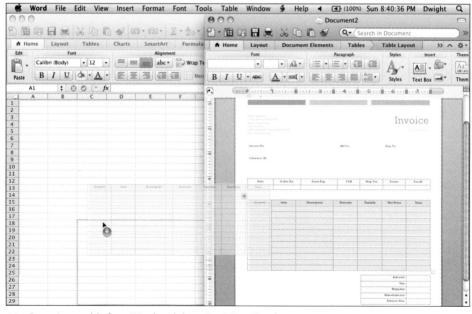

15.1 Dragging a table from Word and dropping it into Excel.

How cool was that? You can also do the same with other items in other applications. A few examples would be

- Drag an e-mail address out of Outlook into a Word document.
- Place an image from a PowerPoint presentation into a Word document.
- Copying a chart from an Excel worksheet directly into a Word document.

There are many more possibilities, too, so experiment when you get the chance. This is interaction at its finest, and it makes it that much easier to enjoy working with Office applications.

Genius

You don't have to just copy one item over at a time. Hold down the ⌘ key when selecting objects to choose multiple items.

View Multiple Worksheets in Excel

I like the sheet tabs at the bottom left of every Excel window. They make it simple to switch to a particular worksheet in a workbook without breaking a sweat. Sometimes, however, viewing every worksheet in a workbook one at a time can be counterproductive, to put it mildly.

There's an easy way to avoid having to switch from worksheet to worksheet, and that's to view them all at once, side by side. Follow these steps:

1. **Open the workbook containing the worksheets you need to view.**

2. **Note the number of sheet tabs that are in the lower-left corner, and decide how many of them you want to view (just some or do you want to see the whole enchilada?).**

3. **Choose Window ➪ New Window.** Do this for every worksheet you want to view (don't forget, you already have one open; it contains the first instance of opening the workbook from Step 1).

4. **In each window, click the sheet tab that you want to view within that window.**

5. **Click Window ➪ Arrange.**

6. **Select an option from the Arrange Windows box.** Experiment with each view until you find the one that suits you best. There are four views:

   - Tiled (shown in Figure 15.2)
   - Horizontal

- Vertical
- Cascade

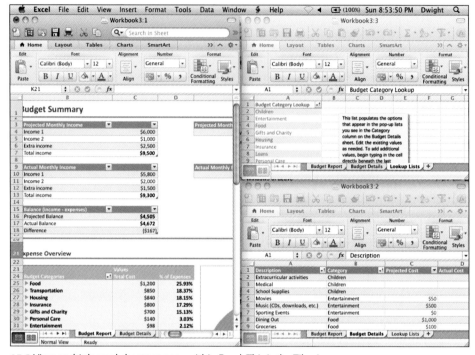

15.2 View multiple worksheets at once within Excel. This is the Tile view.

Using AutoComplete in Excel

Have you ever noticed when working in Excel that when you begin to type information into a cell a list suddenly jumps up suggesting possibilities that you might want to use for the cell? This handy-dandy feature is called AutoComplete. You saw how to change preferences for AutoComplete in Chapter 6, but you never saw it in action.

AutoComplete can save you time when you are typing a slew of similar information in a column. Basically, Excel is taking an educated guess at what you want to type into the active cell based on what you've previously entered in the same column so far.

For example, say you have information in cells A1 through A5 and you are just beginning to type information into cell A6. Excel checks what you're typing, and if the first few characters match something in any of the cells above it in the column, then Excel offers you the list of matches it thinks you might like to choose from for the cell in A6.

Watch out for blank cells in your column; they will stop Excel in its tracks. Say you have information in cells A1 through A10 and A15 through A25, and you want to add more information to A26. When you begin to enter your new information into A26, Excel will only list matches it finds within cells A15 through A25. The information in cells A1 through A10 is ignored.

Another caveat to remember is that Excel only matches cells that contain text or a combination of text and numbers. Cells with only numbers are highly discriminated against by AutoComplete because the wrong number may accidentally be placed in a cell simply because it may start with characters that are contained in other numbers.

To see AutoComplete in action, follow these steps (I use the famous-author table from Chapter 7):

1. **Open a worksheet you need to work in.**

2. **Type information into several rows of a column.** As you type, Excel tries to AutoComplete some cells because the cells above them contain similar information, as shown in Figure 15.3.

3. **Highlight the match you want to use and click Return or just click the mouse button to enter the match into the cell.**

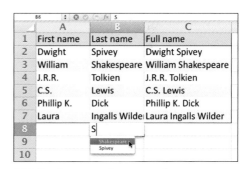

15.3 Excel suggests the names of two great authors simply because an S is typed into the cell.

Now some Excel users just can't seem to stand AutoComplete. They hate the list that plagues them as they type information into cells, and they would just as soon be rid of it. Simple enough. Follow these steps:

1. **From within Excel, press ⌘+, (comma) to open the Excel Preferences window.** You can also choose Excel ⇨ Preferences to open it.

2. **Click AutoComplete in the Formulas and Lists section.**

3. **Deselect Enable AutoComplete for cell values.**

4. **Click OK.** No more pesky AutoComplete.

Linking Excel Objects in Word

So, you've got this table in an Excel spreadsheet, and you want to place it into your Word document. However, you want it to do more than just sit there. You want the table to be updated in the Word document just as you've updated it in the original spreadsheet. In other words, you want to be able to edit your table in Excel and have those changes immediately reflected in your Word document.

Do you just drag and drop the table into your Word document? Nope, that won't allow the information to be automatically updated. You need to link the table back to the original Excel spreadsheet. Linking to the original spreadsheet will cause any updates in it to appear instantly in the linked Word document.

Let's give this one a go. Follow these steps:

1. **In Excel, open the spreadsheet that contains the information you want to place into Word.**

2. **In Word, open the document you want to link the Excel data into.**

3. **Back in Excel, select the information you want to copy, and then click the Copy button in the toolbar.**

4. **Go back to Word and click the insertion point into which you want to place the Excel information.**

5. **Click the Paste button in the toolbar and the information displays in the Word document.** But you're not finished. Notice that down and just to the right of the information you just pasted into Word there is a little clipboard. This is called the Paste Options button.

6. **Click the Paste Options button and choose one of two options, as shown in Figure 15.4 (ignore the rest for this exercise):**

   - **Keep Source Formatting and Link to Excel.** This option tells Word to retain the formatting the information enjoyed while residing in Excel.

   - **Match Destination Table Style and Link to Excel.** This option tells Word to apply the formatting it's using in the current document to the information just copied from Excel.

7. **Save the Word document to make it retain the link to the Excel spreadsheet.**

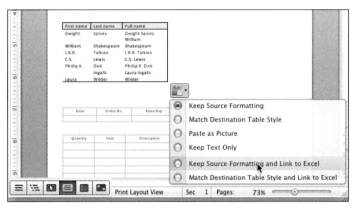

15.4 Select a formatting and linking option from the Paste Options button.

From now on, every time the information in the Excel spreadsheet is changed or updated, the Word document reflects the changes.

Save Documents as PDFs

You've got these really great documents for which you spent days getting the formatting just right. Now you're about to send those gorgeous documents off to all your customers in an e-mail blitz. Do you keep the document in its original format? Here are some questions to ask yourself before you make a decision:

- **What if it's a PowerPoint presentation?** Some folks don't have PowerPoint, so they wouldn't be able to view it.

- **What if it's a Word document?** Everyone's got Word, right? Nope, not everyone.

- **Well, they can open the Word document in another application, right?** Not if the application they use is unable to read the format you saved your Word file to.

- **You don't want your customers to be able to edit the documents you sent them, do you?**

- **It's an Excel file, but how many folks really know how to use Excel?** Remember, you're sending this out to customers, and your customers cover a broad spectrum of the population; not everyone on the planet uses Excel or has a need to.

After pondering those questions, it's clear that you don't always want to send your documents in their original formats. So, what to do?

Send your document as a PDF (*Portable Document Format*). You can save your Word, Excel, and PowerPoint files as PDF files. A PDF not only retains the layout, fonts, images, and colors as you intended the document to be viewed, but it also prevents the customer from mucking up the layout. Another bonus is that PDFs look the same no matter what kind of computer or operating system they are viewed on. Most people have a PDF reader, like Adobe Reader, installed, whether they use Windows, Linux, or Mac OS X.

Here's how to make your Excel, Word, or PowerPoint presentation into a PDF:

1. **Open the document you want to transform into a PDF.**

2. **Press ⌘+P to open the Print dialog.**

3. **Click PDF in the lower-left side of the Print dialog and select Save as PDF from the menu that appears, as shown in Figure 15.5.**

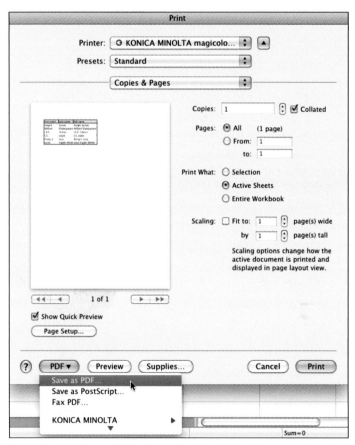

15.5 Select the Save as PDF option in the Print dialog to save any document as a PDF file.

Genius

There's no need for a third-party PDF reader if you own a Mac. Preview is an application built right in to Mac OS X, and it opens PDF files with ease.

4. **In the Save dialog, give the document a name in the Save As field.**

5. **Select a destination for your new PDF file.**

6. **Click Save and your PDF file is created in exactly the location you specified in the previous step.**

Open your PDF using any PDF reader, but because you're on a Mac, trusty Preview does just fine, thank you. Notice the formatting has been retained, and now you can pass your document along to others with extreme confidence that they are able to view it as you intended.

Turbo-Paste: How to Use Paste Special in Excel

Paste Special is the Paste function on steroids. While Paste simply drops into a document whatever you may have copied previously, regardless of its format or content, Paste Special does something, well, special: It gives you the opportunity to paste contents in certain formats or to paste only certain elements of what you copied.

Take the example of a table in an Excel spreadsheet. I'll use my famous-authors list from Chapter 7 again. What if you want to copy a range of cells in the spreadsheet, but don't necessarily want to copy the formulas contained within those cells? Or what if you do want the formulas, but not the returns those formulas gave in the cells you're copying? To do that, follow these steps:

1. **Open the spreadsheet you need to work with.**

2. **Select the range of cells you want to copy, and click the Copy button in the toolbar.**

3. **Move to the location on the spreadsheet you want to paste the copied cells.** Don't do a traditional paste. Click the arrow next to the Paste button in the ribbon's Home tab and select Paste Special.

4. **As you can see in Figure 15.6, the Paste Special dialog has opened and offers all sorts of ways to paste the information into the new cells.** For example, if you only want to copy the formulas and not their results, select the radio button next to Formulas.

5. **Click OK and the very special pasting commences.**

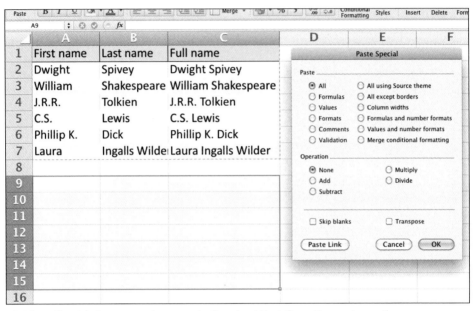

15.6 Paste Special allows you to be very selective about the information you're pasting.

What Other Applications Are Part of Office 2011?

You already know that Microsoft Office for Mac 2011 comes loaded for bear with four of the most well-known and oft-used applications on the face of the earth. But did you know there was still more beyond Excel, Outlook, PowerPoint, and Word? Office 2011 comes with several more utilities that help you communicate with colleagues, family, and friends, and even use another computer remotely. Will the good folks in Microsoft's Macintosh Business Unit ever let up? Let's hope not!

Collaborating with Communicator

Microsoft has a really cool tool that allows workers in an office environment to communicate with one another via e-mail, instant message, conference call, video call, and even the tried-and-true phone. What makes Communicator unique to other instant-messaging clients is that these communications take place within the confines and safety of your network. Even if you sign in to Communicator remotely through an Internet connection you are still working within the parameters of your corporate network, which should provide for safe communications with colleagues.

Note Communicator for Mac requires that your company's network runs Office Communication Server 2007, and typically it may be required that someone within your company's IT department will have to configure Communicator for you to make sure you can sign in and sign out correctly.

The Office 2011 installer application doesn't load Communicator for Mac within the Microsoft Office 2011 folder, but instead just sticks it right in the Applications folder (/Applications/Microsoft Communicator). Find Communicator on your Mac and learn how to get started with it.

Caution When you launch Communicator for the first time it prompts you to find out if you want to set it to be your default application for telephone calls and for conference calls. I can't help you with those answers; that's something for your IT department to answer for you. Don't set either one if you don't know the answer. You can always come back and make those settings at a later time.

You must sign in to Communicator to begin using it. Follow these steps:

1. **Open Communicator for Mac by double-clicking its icon.**

2. **Click Sign In, as shown in Figure 16.1.** You may have a few options depending on what you want to do or what you've done before:

   - **If you see your account name or e-mail address above the Sign In button:** This means that you have signed in to Communicator before. Communicator will use your account information, which it saved from your previous session, to automatically connect to your network when you click Sign In. This assumes that you told Communicator to remember your password the last time you signed in.

- **If you want to sign in to Communicator with a different user account:** Click the Sign in with a different account or change your online status link.

- **If this is the first time you've signed in to Communicator:** Clicking Sign In opens the User ID and password window.

3. **Use your network ID and password to sign in, or skip to Step 4 to use your e-mail and password.** If you use your network ID and password, Check the box at the top of the window called Use my network ID and password. Type your network ID and password in the appropriate fields and Communicator attempts to find your user ID and password for the Office Communications Server.

4. **If you use your e-mail address to sign in, as shown in Figure 16.2, type your e-mail address in the E-mail address field.** Type your Office Communications Server user ID and password in the appropriate fields, and select the Remember my password check box to make signing in faster the next time. You can leave it deselected to keep some security for your account.

5. **Select an option from the Status pop-up menu to use as the default status every time you sign in to Communicator.**

6. **Click Sign In to begin using Communicator.**

16.1 Click Sign In to begin working within Communicator for Mac.

Signing out of Communicator is even more complicated: Click the Network menu and select Sign Out. Exhausting, isn't it?

Caution

You may only sign in to one account on your corporate network at one time, but you may sign in to the same account on several different computers.

16.2 Using the method to authenticate your account with the Office Communications Server.

Here are just some of the cool things you can do with Communicator:

- Chat with others in your office or company, local or worldwide, via instant messaging (IM).

- Make computer-to-computer phone calls, whether the person you are contacting is on a Windows-based PC or a Mac.

- Manage your availability status so that others can know if you are available.

- View the status of other users so that you better determine who to contact if you have a quick question.

- Conduct video conferences with others in your company to anywhere in the world from anywhere in the world (assuming you have access to the Internet, of course).

- Share your documents.

- Thanks to Communicator's close ties to Outlook, you can schedule meetings, reply to e-mails (using e-mail, video conference, or IM), and more from within Communicator.

Check out Communicator's Help (click the Help menu and select Communicator Help) for more information on getting the most of corporate communication with Communicator for Mac.

Chatting Using Messenger

Messenger has been Microsoft's go-to application for instant messaging for a very long time, and it just gets better with each iteration. This version of Messenger, 8 to be exact, allows you to do much more than simple instant messaging with your friends, family, and otherwise, and it's much closer to the Windows version in terms of features. Following are a few of the tasks it's capable of:

- Chat via instant messages with anyone in your contact list, assuming they are online, of course. You can easily see a contact's status to see if they are available or not.
- Make computer-to-computer audio or video calls. The audio calls are cool, but the video just simply rocks.
- Invite up to 15 contacts to take part in the same conversation.

Note
You must have a Windows Live ID account to use Messenger. You can sign up for a free account as *https://signup.live.com/*.

Here's how to get rolling with Messenger for Mac:

1. **Find the Microsoft Messenger application icon in the Applications folder (like, Communicator, the Office installer application doesn't place it in the Microsoft Office 2011 folder), and double-click to launch it.**
2. **Click Sign In.**
3. **In the Microsoft Messenger window (see Figure 16.3), do the following:**

16.3 Type your Windows Live ID account information to sign in.

1. **Type the e-mail address you use to log in to your Windows Live account.**
2. **Type the password for the account.**

3. **Select a default presence status from the Status pop-up menu.** This is what your contacts see as your status when you first sign in.

4. **Click Sign In and you're ready for instant messaging the Messenger way.**

Now you are signed in and ready to chat. You can see your list of contacts in the Contact List window that opens by default. If you don't have any contacts, click the Add button in the upper right to add some. Their status will give you a heads up on whether you can contact them now or not.

Chatting is simple enough:

1. **Double-click a contact in the Contacts List and a conversation window opens, much like the one in Figure 16.4.**

16.4 Starting a chat with a good friend.

2. **Type your message at the bottom of the conversation window to get the party started.** Press Return when you're ready to send your message. When your friend replies to your message you will see it in the conversation window and will hear an alert sound.

3. **Use the buttons in the toolbar to perform other functions during your connection.** Your options include the following:

  ● If you decide that your conversation would be better spoken, click the Call button in the toolbar at the top of the conversation window.

  ● Maybe video is more your speed. If so, click the Video button in the toolbar to place the video call to your buddy.

  ● Are you getting fed up with the jerk on the other end of the line? Simply click Block in the toolbar and you can consider that person as good as gone.

  ● Click the Send File button to send a document or a photo to your friend.

  ● Click Save to keep this conversation for posterity.

  ● Click the History button to make your conversation history.

  ● If you aren't afraid to look at your friend's mug, click the Display Pictures button in the toolbar to see who you're speaking with.

4. **When you finish with your conversation, click the red button in the upper-left corner of the conversation window, or press ⌘+W.**

5. **If this is the first time you've struck up a conversation in Messenger, it will prompt you to see how you want to handle the saving of conversations in the future (see Figure 16.5).** Read each choice and make the call.

16.5 How do you want to handle saving conversations in the future?

6. **If prompted to save your conversation, choose either Don't Save or Save.**

Messenger doesn't get much more complicated than that, but it's been a worthy addition to the Office suite for quite some time.

Connect with Other Computers Using Remote Desktop Connection

Do you work in a home or office environment where there are multiple computers you must work with, and sure enough, they are in different locations? I'm pleased to say that Microsoft just may have a solution for you: Remote Desktop Connection.

Remote Desktop Connection allows you to sit squarely and comfortably in front of your Mac, and true to its name, allows to remotely work with another computer. You can call up a computer, log on to it, and use it as if you were sitting down in front of it instead of your Mac.

Note

There is one major caveat I must mention. Remote Desktop Connection only allows you to connect to PCs running Windows. You cannot connect to another Mac or to a Linux box using Remote Desktop Connection; however, there are plenty of ways to do so. Look in Mac OS X help for more information, or do a search on the Web.

To get started, follow these steps:

1. **Make sure that the PC you want to access remotely is set up to allow a remote desktop connection.** Consult the Help for your version of Windows to find out how to do this (I'd show you, but this is a Mac book).

2. **Open the Remote Desktop Connection application on your Mac.** You can find it in the Microsoft Office 2011 folder.

3. **When Remote Desktop Connection asks for the address of the PC you want to connect to, you can type the address for the PC in a variety of ways, but I prefer to enter its IP address.**

4. **Click Connect.**

5. **Remote Desktop Connection now asks for your credentials.** These are the username and password you normally use to log in to the PC you're trying to remotely connect to. Ask your IT department if you think a domain is needed.

6. **Click OK to connect to the remote PC.** A new window opens where you can work happily away on the remote PC from the comfort of your Mac's keyboard and mouse (or trackpad).

Figure 16.6 shows a sight that some to this day still find too disturbing to look at for very long: Windows running on a Mac.

You can work within this window as if you were sitting right in front of the remote PC and work to your heart's content. However, you may run into a stumbling block or two along the way. If things aren't working quite the way you expect them to (say a keyboard shortcut doesn't quite behave the way it should, or the desktop of the remote PC just doesn't look right), Remote Desktop Connection provides many preferences you can customize to make things work the way you need.

Click the RDC menu and select Preferences to see what you can do:

- The Login pane lets you type your credentials for the PC you want to connect to.

- The Display tab, shown in Figure 16.7, helps you set the defaults for viewing the PC's desktop on your Mac. If you have a slow connection, disabling some of the items in the While connected section might help.

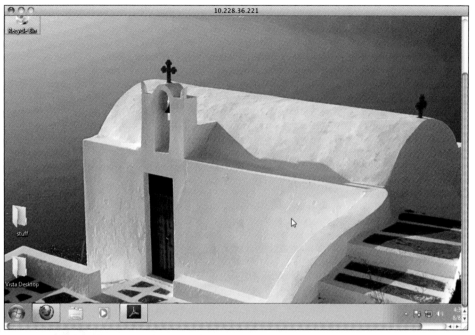

16.6 Notice the Windows 7 start button in the lower left of the Remote Desktop Connection window: Windows on a Mac!

- Select a resolution size from the Remote desktop size pop-up menu if something other than the default 1024x768 is desired.

- The Colors pop-up menu can help render the screen a bit faster if there are connection problems. Just set Colors to something less than what it is currently set to (default is Thousands).

- If your Mac uses two monitors you can have the remote connection open on one of them using the Open remote desktop window on pop-up menu.

- The Keyboard tab allows you to set Mac keyboard shortcuts to use while working within Windows. Deselect a command in the list to disable it, or double-click a command to edit it.

- The Sound tab offers three options for playing the sound that emanates from the remote PC.

- The Drives tab is pretty cool, as it allows you to make the drives and folders on your Mac available to the remote PC. Now you can easily exchange files with the two machines.

- Using the Printers tab, you can use the printer your Mac has installed to print documents from the PC you're remotely connected to. That rocks.

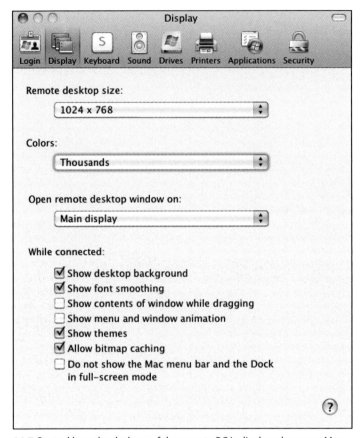

16.7 Control how the desktop of the remote PC is displayed on your Mac.

● The Applications tab lets you specify an application that will open automatically when you log in to the PC remotely.

● The Security tab gives you three choices for setting authentication options to make sure you connect to the correct Windows-based PC:

   ○ **Always connect, even if authentication fails.** If you're connecting to Windows XP or earlier, this would be a good choice because they can't provide their identities anyway.

   ○ **Warn me if authentication fails (default).** I recommend this setting so that you at least have the opportunity to continue even if there is a failure.

   ○ **Do not connect if authentication fails.**

One last thing I'd like to mention is *full-screen mode*. Some people just can't stand to work on a remote computer within the confines of a window, and I don't blame them. You can view your remotely connected PC in all its full-screen glory by pressing ⌘+2. Now your remote PC appears on your screen as if you were sitting in front of it, as shown in Figure 16.8.

16.8 A remotely connected PC running in full-screen mode on a Mac.

Notice the Dock on the right side of the window? If you move your mouse pointer to the top of the screen, the RDC menu pops down and you can make any adjustments you need there, or select any other items you need, say System Preferences from the Apple menu. You can also hold your mouse pointer to the portion of the screen where your Dock resides when you are viewing the Mac OS X interface and the Dock pops out, affording you access to any applications within it.

To return to the windowed mode, simply press ⌘+2 again.

How Can I Get Help with Office 2011?

Even the best and brightest of us need a helping hand from time to time, while others like myself need all the help they can get. The most Office-savvy individual will run into a stumbling block in the midst of creating the document to end all documents, the presentation of all presentations, or the spreadsheet that will change the direction of mankind forever. Fortunately the folks in Microsoft's Mac Business Unit are aware of the need for a little guidance once in a while, and they have provided ample assistance to the Office-needy.

simply can't cover the entire gamut of your Office inquiries (certain issues may not be discovered until well after the product has been released), but it sure tries to. The index is a compilation of all known issues up to the time of the product's release as well as instructions necessary for basic usage of the particular application.

Opening the Help index

The Help index can be opened in one of two very simple ways:

17.1 Choose the Help for the application you are using from the menu bar.

● **Click the Help menu in the menu bar and select the appropriate Help for your application, as shown in Figure 17.1.** For example, when you click the Help menu, choose Word Help if you are using Word, Excel Help if you are using Excel, and so on.

● **Almost hidden in the Standard toolbar of your application's windows is a little Help button that looks like a purple circle containing a white question mark, as shown in Figure 17.2.** Simply click that button to zip right into the application's Help index (you will save one whole click using this method, which over the next year can add up to quite a lot of saved time and wear and tear on your mouse; no kidding).

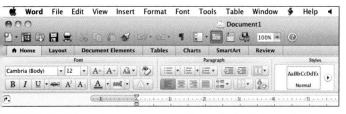

17.2 Click the Help button to save yourself one whole click over the menu method.

Genius

You can quickly locate hard-to-find items in Office's surplus of menus by performing a quick search. Click the Help menu and simply type your search query in the Search field. A list of matching items will appear under the Search field automatically as you type.

Genius Get even more (and updated) information from the Help index by enabling Online mode, which allows the Help index to access new or updated Help articles from Microsoft. To enable Online mode, click the Go Online button in the upper-right corner of the Help window.

Once you've used one of the prescribed methods mentioned, you should be awarded with a Help index window that looks remarkably like the one in Figure 17.3.

Perusing the Help index

Getting around in the Help index is a breeze once you get the hang of it.

The quick-and-easy way to search for a topic is to simply type it into the search field in the upper right of the Help window. Once you type your topic, just press Return to see your search results in the Help window, as shown in Figure 17.4.

Cull through the list of relevant items to see if one applies to your query. If you find one, click it to display information about it.

Lightning-fast Answers: Online Support

The Internet is for more than just ordering movie tickets and surfing the latest headlines. That's right, you can get the most up-to-date help available for your Office applications using the handy-dandy World Wide Web!

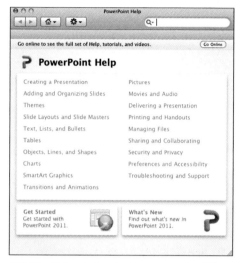

17.3 The Help window is your gateway to Office information, tips, and troubleshooting.

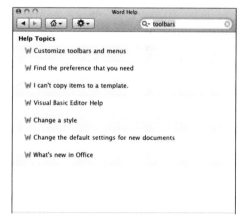

17.4 Search results display in the Help window.

Specifically, you can get help from one really helpful Web site: Mactopia. Mactopia is Microsoft's official Web site for Apple-related products (oh yes, it makes more than just Office applications for the Mac). You can bask in the glory of Mactopia, shown in Figure 17.5, by visiting www.mactopia.com or www.officeformac.com.

Certainly you can take the time to check out all the neat things the site has to offer, but the purpose here is to show you how to get great help from Mactopia. There are four links at the top of the page that can point you in the direction of information you may need: Downloads, Help and How-To, Forums, and Blog.

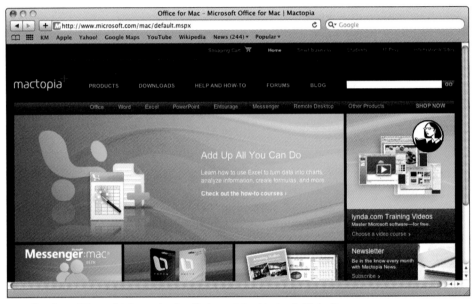

17.5 Check out Microsoft's latest Apple offerings at the Mactopia Web site.

Downloads

The Downloads section of Mactopia works as advertised: You can download individual updates for your Office or other Microsoft applications, templates for Word, PowerPoint, and Excel, Windows Media Player for Mac, and more.

The real meat and potatoes are at the bottom of the Downloads page, where you can quickly and easily browse for the latest downloads by product, as shown in Figure 17.6.

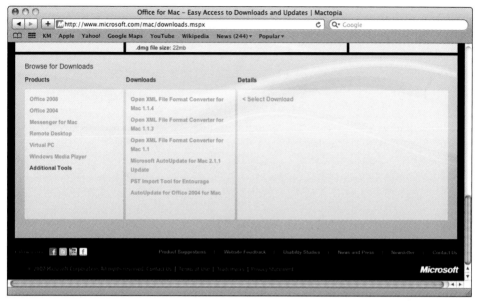

17.6 Browse Mactopia's Downloads section for updates to your Office applications or other Microsoft products for Apple.

Help and How-To

The Help and How-To section of Mactopia is a great place to learn even more about how to use your Office applications as well as find the latest troubleshooting tips.

Simply type a question into the Search Help and How-To box in the upper left of the page, as shown in Figure 17.7, and click Go to retrieve documents and articles that can hopefully answer it.

Mactopia offers training courses that will help you go even deeper into your understanding of the Office suite of applications. You can find these courses by clicking the Courses link on the left side of the Help and How-To page.

Note

If you are more of a visual learner, there are also video courses offered by Lynda.com that offer online instructor-led training for a modest fee.

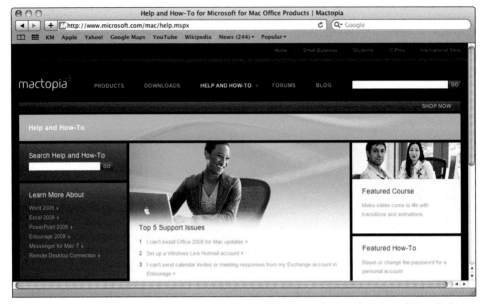

17.7 The fastest way to get an answer is to type your question into the Search Help and How-To box and click Go.

Forums

When you experience problems with your Office applications, or you simply don't know how to accomplish a certain task, you can get that lonely feeling, as if no one else in the world can feel your pain. Well, take heart, Office for Mac users, the Mactopia forums, as shown in Figure 17.8, will quell that loneliness with one click of the mouse on the Forums link at the top of the Mactopia Web page.

The forums are brimming with folks just like you, who at one time or another had a question or problem they just didn't know how to tackle. Thankfully, many of them have found the answers to their questions and they are on the forums waiting to share their wealth of information with you.

You can type a question into the Search Forums box and click Go, or browse the forums by application and topic. Don't forget to pay it forward, though: If you discover the answer to a problem you've been having, be a good neighbor and share that information by helping others on the forums in the same manner that you were helped.

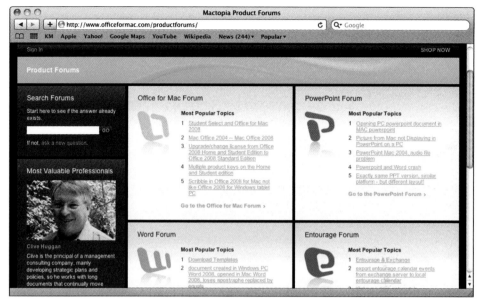

17.8 The Mactopia forums may contain the answers to your most elusive Office-related problems.

Blog

If you're an Office newshound who likes to keep up with the latest comings and goings of the Office for Mac team at Microsoft, the Mactopia blog page will quickly find its way into your browser's favorites list.

The blog is where you will find all the latest news and tips from the Office for Mac team, as well as some of the team members' own individual blogs and Web sites. There are tons of posts on the blog, so the good folks at Mactopia also give you the ability to browse the posts by topic and author.

Updating Your Office Applications

Keeping your Office applications updated to their latest-and-greatest versions is a very wise thing to do. Some people are wary of installing updates early and often, especially if they've been snake-bitten before by bugs still hiding in early updates, but thankfully these instances are mercifully rare.

Note Unexpected results from updating your Office suite will be even more rare if you are certain to read the notes given for the updates to make sure that they don't mention any loss of services you typically use with your Office apps.

You can go to the Downloads section of the Mactopia Web site to manually download updates for each application, but the preferred method is to let your Mac do all the legwork automatically. When you install the Office suite on your Mac, you install a utility called Microsoft AutoUpdate, which you should be able to find in the same directory where your Office applications are installed.

AutoUpdate will run according to the timetable you set for it. To set up AutoUpdate to run at specified times, follow these steps:

1. **Choose Help ➪ Check for Updates from within any of the Office applications.** The Microsoft AutoUpdate dialog appears.

2. **Select the Automatically option and choose a timeframe from the Check for Updates pop-up menu, as shown in Figure 17.9.**

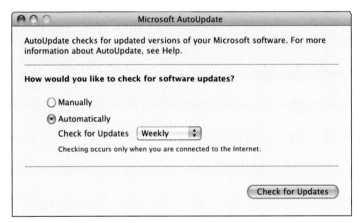

17.9 Determine how often to have AutoUpdate check for the newest updates for Office.

3. **Click Check for Updates to search Microsoft's servers for the latest updates to your applications.**

4. **If AutoUpdate finds updates for your application(s), it displays information about the update, as shown in Figure 17.10.** Be sure to read this information before proceeding, and then click Install to begin the update process.

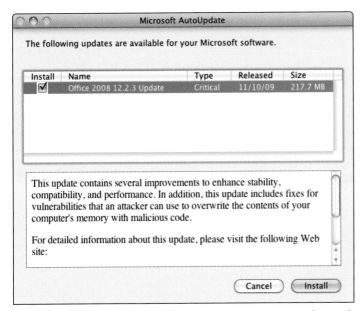

17.10 AutoUpdate gives you info about available updates so you know what issues are resolved by installing them.

Index

The Genius is in.

Macs
PORTABLE GENIUS

978-0-470-29052-1

Mac OS X Leopard
PORTABLE GENIUS

978-0-470-29050-7

iPhone 3G S
PORTABLE GENIUS

Also covers iPhone 3G!

978-0-470-52422-0

Final Cut Pro
PORTABLE GENIUS

978-0-470-38760-3

iMac
PORTABLE GENIUS

978-0-470-29061-3

MacBook Air
PORTABLE GENIUS

978-0-470-38108-3

MacBook
PORTABLE GENIUS

978-0-470-29169-6

MacBook Pro
PORTABLE GENIUS

978-0-470-29170-2

Switching to a Mac
PORTABLE GENIUS

978-0-470-43677-6

iPod & iTunes
PORTABLE GENIUS

978-0-470-38259-2

iLife '09
PORTABLE GENIUS

978-0-470-41732-4

iPhoto '09
PORTABLE GENIUS

978-0-470-47569-0

The essentials for every forward-thinking Apple user are now available on the go. Designed for easy access to tools and shortcuts, the *Portable Genius* series has all the information you need to maximize your digital lifestyle. With a full-color interior and easy-to-navigate content, the *Portable Genius* series offers innovative tips and tricks as well as savvy advice that will save you time and increase your productivity.

Available wherever books are sold.

WILEY
Now you know.